DR. CHARLIE BURRY, JR.

Light Bulb Moments from the Life of a High School Teacher, Counselor, Coach, and Principal

BookBaby
7905 North Cresent Boulevard
Pennsauken, NJ 08110
www.BookBaby.com

Print ISBN: 978-1-09839-3-021

Printed in the United States of America on SFI
Certified paper.

First Edition

CONTENTS

Acknowledgements

"I saw that wisdom is better than folly, just as light is better than darkness."

Ecclesiastes 2:13

"How much better to get wisdom than gold, to choose understanding rather than silver."

Proverbs 16:16

"If any of you lacks wisdom, let him ask God, who gives generously to all without reproach, and it will be given him."

James 1:5

Foreword

In 1978, I met Coach Charlie Burry for the first time. It was my junior year in high school and he had been named as our new basketball coach. Since I had been a starting guard for the Hartsville Red Foxes during my sophomore year, I was excited to play for my new coach and filled with anticipation. Except for one thing: Coach Burry wanted our team to wear black Converse high-tops for our game shoes!

I remember the disheartened look on the faces of my teammates when he first introduced this idea. We were stunned, underwhelmed by the thought of having to wear those ugly shoes, and down-right embarrassed at the prospect of showing up in antiquated relics from Bob Cousy and the Boston Celtics era! However, this was the first significant lesson of many that I learned from Coach Burry. He had a better idea.

Instead of looking all fancy and showing off at game time, he thought a better idea would be to focus on what's important. Those shoes were a way of keeping our eyes on the priority of playing at our highest level. The shoes were a strategic way of translating meaning into our game, and actually into our lives. Soon I found that's what Coach Burry is all about. He translates meaning into everything . . . experiences, relationships with people, and words . . . yes, especially words.

So, it was no surprise to me that *I Got a Better Idea* is a compilation of stories that bring meaning to life and underline what matters most. It is full of laughter, faith, holy moments, family, memories, friends, and truth. Page after page, the light bulb moments reminded me of all the wonderful people and countless blessings we have been given. It leaves you a better human being than you were before you started reading it. It leaves you with a brighter, better idea of what life is all about!

Years later, I was at a garage sale and saw a small pair of children's black Converse high-top shoes that were used and tattered. They immediately reminded me of our experience so I bought them and sent them to Coach Burry. It was a nostalgic connection that I thought he would value and appreciate. A few weeks later, I received a letter back from him with a picture of his daughter, Beth, sitting in his lap. She was proudly wearing the black high-top shoes! I still have that photo and I smile when I look at it today.

Thanks, Coach, for writing this book, but more important, for giving meaning to my life and many, many others through your words and example. Some ideas really are better . . . and last forever.

Dr. Danny Nicholson
President
Connie Maxwell Children's Ministries
Greenwood, South Carolina

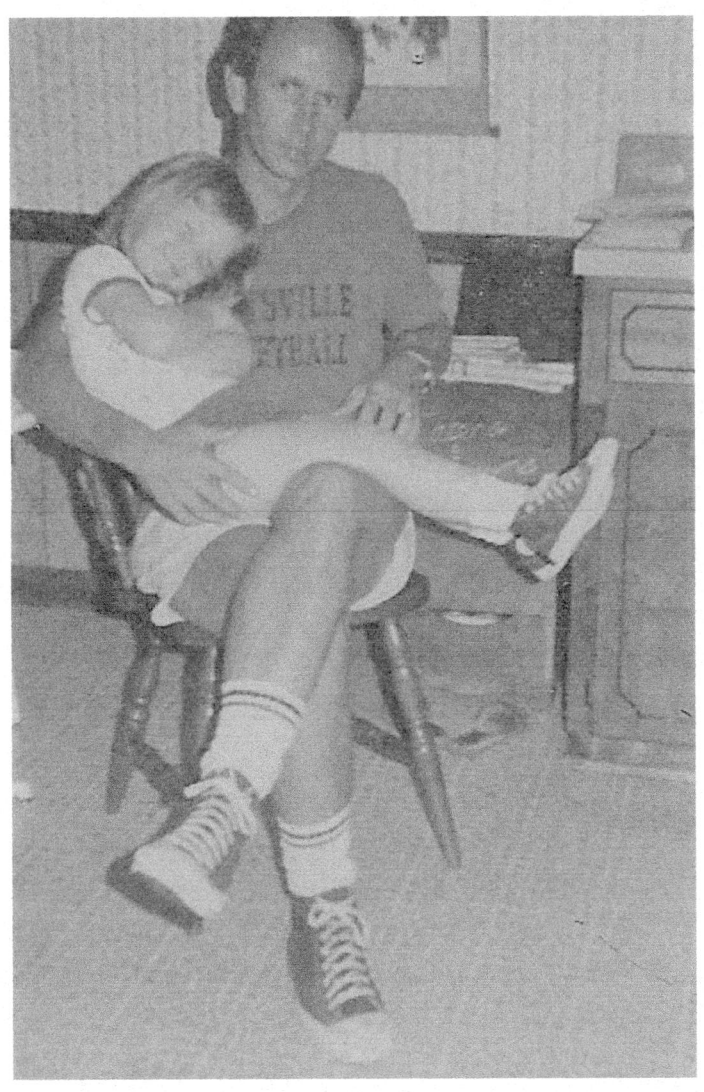

Beth and Dad

A Second Time Around

Here we have it, Dr. Charlie Burry's second book—*I Got a Better Idea*—and true to form it entails more of Dr. Burry's life and legacy. He gives his readers insight into how he came to be the man he is today—a person filled with faith, kindness, and laughter. If you're looking for stories about small-town southern life and big opportunities to live life to its fullest, you won't be disappointed.

This book is a must-read for those who grew up in Hartsville, as well as for those who want to experience genuine life in a small, close-knit community. As Dr. Burry mentions people and situations that aided in the development of his character over the years, it is easy to see how he became a person filled with the "hope and possibility" that he continues to pass on to future generations. He honors the individuals who impacted his life so that they, too, can know the value of their influence on the lives of those they encountered in their own life journeys. Through this book, the reader gets to know these inspirational icons of the Hartsville community as well.

I Got a Better Idea will also entertain and educate readers through more "light bulb moments" revealed in Dr. Burry's experiences, from his interactions with young people at the SC School for Boys to the antics and practical jokes of himself and his friends. Dr. Burry's eloquent prose and carefully organized sections offer a little something for everyone.

Mrs. Ashley Burchfield

English Teacher

International Baccalaureate CAS and EE Coordinator

Hartsville High School

Prologue

In April 2020, I accomplished one of my life goals by writing a book and having it published (even though I had to go the self-publishing route). The responses which I received from those who read *Life Lessons . . . Principally Speaking* were all positive and encouraging and if there were folks who didn't like it, I appreciate them not bursting my bubble. Do I wish that my parents—who owned an iconic independent bookstore in our adopted hometown—had been alive to share the accomplishment with me? Absolutely, but I hope that my own children will be proud of their author dad. The icing on the cake was hearing from so many friends and former colleagues who said they enjoyed reading what I wrote and that they'd been moved emotionally by some of the stories. It's nice to know that maybe some folks learned from reading about my life lessons just a little bit of what I did by living them.

I learned some things in that process, too, made enough seed money to fund a scholarship program at Hartsville High School, and—I think—became a better writer. Maybe the jury is still out on that. Along the way, I recalled other stories of "light bulb moments" in my life, people who influenced me, and more life lessons learned that I believed might be fun to write about and enjoyable for others to read. The overall experience was rewarding enough to whet my appetite for another crack at it, and I also wanted to prove to myself that I could do it again . . . and maybe even do it better. So, that's one of the things I've been doing for the last year or so while we've all been holed up trying to stay safe and well, and now here we are with a second book—*I Got a Better Idea*. I worked regularly and sometimes even diligently at it, but I also tried to take time to appreciate the journey and be patient with the process. It's important to recognize when you get to the point where, as Mark Twain said, "the ink well in your mind has run dry, and you just need to quit and let it fill up again." When the words wouldn't come, I usually took his advice and just quit for a while. All of the chapters are newly written—none were pulled from my old principal's file as was the case with parts of *LLPS*, and they've never been read or heard by anyone before—so that aspect of the project has been enjoyable as well.

I never expected to be, or wanted to be, the next national best-selling author. I just wanted to write and publish a book, hold the finished product in my hands, and be able to be proud of it. It's rewarding to think that, even in retirement, my career in education might be continuing in a different manner. I'm glad that I've been able to pay it forward some, just as my parents, teachers, and coaches did for me. While one never makes much money by self-publishing a book, in terms of personal satisfaction, I believe that I hit the jackpot the first time. It would be nice to be able to do it again with another book. So, I hope you'll settle in for a few more stories because . . . I got some better ideas!

About the Author

Dr. Charlie Burry, Jr., is a native of Nevada, Missouri, born in 1951 to Charles and Wilma Burry. The Burry family also lived in Grand Junction, Colorado, and Biloxi, Mississippi, before moving to Hartsville, South Carolina, in 1959. As a child of avid readers, young Charlie also developed a love for books which was nourished further when his father opened Burry Bookstore in 1972. The Burry family has been influential in the growth and development of the Hartsville community for 60 years. As a self-professed wordsmith, Burry enjoys the process of sharing his thoughts through the written word.

Dr. Burry is a 1969 graduate of Hartsville High School. He received his B.A. degree in History in 1973 from Furman University, a Master of Education (M.Ed.) degree from Francis Marion University (College) in 1976, and in 1993 completed his Doctor of Education (Ed.D.) degree in Curriculum and Instruction from the University of South Carolina. Burry began his teaching and coaching career in 1973 with the Department of Juvenile Justice at the South Carolina School for Boys in Florence, South Carolina, as a physical education teacher and at Francis Marion College as a graduate assistant basketball coach. He taught social studies and coached basketball and football at Gilbert High School in Lexington County, South Carolina, for two years before returning to Hartsville in 1978. Burry taught US History and Sociology for nine years at Hartsville High School, was a guidance counselor for 17 years, and became principal of Hartsville High School in July 2004. He coached in the Red Fox football program for 26 years, working as a varsity assistant from 1987 through 2003, and coached basketball and tennis at other times during a 31-year coaching career prior to becoming principal. Burry served as the AAAA Representative on the Executive Committee of the South Carolina High School League from 2014 until 2018 and was recognized by the South Carolina Athletic Administrators Association as the 2018 AAAA Principal of the Year. He was also honored with the 2014-15 Distinguished Principal Award by the Darlington County School District. Burry retired in June 2018 after 45 years in public education—40 of which were at Hartsville High School—and completed the last 14 years of his career as principal of the school.

Dr. Burry is a member of First Baptist Church in Hartsville where he taught Sunday school for a number of years and chaired the Board of Deacons on three occasions. He enjoys watching sports, listening to music, reading, writing, kayaking on Black Creek near Hartsville, South Carolina, and spending time in the Blue Ridge Mountains near Saluda, North Carolina. Burry is married to the former Debby Sturgeon of Columbia, South Carolina, who is a retired registered nurse. They have two daughters, Beth and Caye—both graduates of Hartsville High School and Furman University—who are highly successful in their own personal and professional lives.

Dr. Charlie Burry, Jr.

Section 1—
Some Better Ideas

It's often said that experience is the best teacher. I've also discovered in my lifetime that the best way to get experience is, well, to get experience. That life truth makes learning from experience almost always interesting, usually productive, sometimes difficult, and—once in a while—downright painful. During my time as a high school principal, I sometimes counseled students and parents that the hardest lessons are the best ones. If you're smart, you don't have to repeat the same lessons, especially the painful ones. And, if you're really smart—when faced with similar circumstances in the future—you come up with a better idea.

This section holds some stories about times in my life when I learned to come up with better ideas. Some of these lessons I managed to learn on my own. Others I learned from teachers and coaches, some from people I love, and a couple from total strangers. Sometimes the situations were humorous, a few of them were dangerous, and a couple of them were tragic. When I tell these stories, some still bring tears to my eyes. I just shake my head about a couple of them. I can—thankfully—laugh at myself a little, and I can also—with even more gratitude—thank God for looking after me on other days.

In most of these situations you'll see that, with the benefit of hindsight, I've been able to learn a few lessons. I hope that you'll enjoy reading about them, and maybe remember an event or two in your own life when you could have benefited from some better ideas, too.

Where Is Your High School Class Ring?

During the 14 years that I was a high school principal, the most enjoyable part of every year for me was graduation. There was some stress involved in assuring that the ceremony went smoothly, but the pure joy of the occasion was far and away the most prevalent emotion of the evening. Being able to stand on the stage, watching the graduates proudly stride toward me with smiles on their faces, and handing them a diploma while shaking their hands was one of the truly great privileges of my career. I did that approximately 3,500 times, and each one was special. The second-most enjoyable evening of the school year for me was the Junior Class Ring Ceremony in which the rising seniors would receive their high school class rings. That was also an emotional time as the students and their parents would come forward to meet me at the podium and receive their rings, realizing that in only four months, they'd be start-ing their last year of high school. As I would hand the rings to the parents to present to their sons and daughters, there was always evidence—even if the students tried to hide it—of the love and gratitude for the mutual effort that had gotten them to that point. At the conclusion of the ceremony, I would always take a couple of minutes to tell them a story about my high school class ring.

I am a 1969 graduate of Hartsville High School, and in the spring of my junior year, I also received my class ring. I didn't wear mine much, though, because I gave it to my girlfriend. It was customary back in the day, that if you were going steady with a girl, she symbolically wore your class ring. It was usually necessary for her to melt and form some candle wax into the inside of the ring so it would fit. My girlfriend was a year behind me in school, so I had to wait until the spring of her junior year to wear her class ring—on my pinky finger. We dated steadily for two years, mostly going to movies and ball games, and then heading back to her house to listen to music. She had about half a dozen albums by *The Tams*, and we wore them out. To this day, I still can't hear a song by that group—especially "Be Young, Be Foolish, Be Happy"—without thinking of her. We'd playfully talk about marriage from time to time, but her father was a Methodist minister, and she'd say, "My daddy would shoot me dead if I married a Baptist boy!" By the summer after I graduated, we'd both begun to realize that things would be different in the fall when I moved to Greenville to attend Furman. We mutually agreed that we'd no longer go steady, which would allow us some freedom in our social lives while still trying to maintain a long-distance relationship. I'll honestly have to admit that I may have been thinking more about being a big-shot college man and being able to play the field, but she just as well could have been thinking the same thing about her own dating prospects. She came to see me one weekend at Furman, but after that we just drifted apart, and although we're Facebook friends now, I haven't seen her in more than 50 years. At any rate, by mid-summer I was wearing my own high school class ring again.

At some point during that summer, I took a trip to the beach with a few of my high school buddies. We spent some time in the ocean while we were there, and one day I was in about chest-deep water throwing a red rubber ball back and forth with one of my friends. I was wearing my high school class ring on my right hand, and you might be able to guess what happened next. As I let go with a throw, my ring slipped off my wet finger and sailed out about ten feet in front of me into the ocean. My heart sank as quickly as my ring did, and even though we spent a long time feeling around in the sand with our feet and even diving from time to time to feel with our hands . . . we never found my ring. So, to answer my own question in the title to this chapter—I don't know where my high school class ring is. My best regrettable guess is that for the last 52 years, it's been somewhere in the Atlantic Ocean off Garden City Beach.

I have another ring, however, that has become even more important to me in the last 25 years. My dad passed away in 1996, and one of the things that I inherited with my mom's blessing was his Army Air Corps ring from his service in World War II. He wore it every day of his life for 50 years, and one of the best memories I have of him is of his hands—signing checks and invoices at his store, handling the tools in his workshop, or saying the blessing before a family meal—and he's wearing that ring. It seems wrong to me in a strange way that my dad's ring is too small to fit me, except on my little finger. How could it be that my hands are larger than my dad's . . . when he was a much bigger man than me, maybe not physically, but in every other way? You can see, I hope, that when I told those students and their parents the story about my high school class ring and my dad's Army Air Corps ring, it became personal. That ring is one of my most cherished possessions, and it draws the memory of my dad closer when I hold it in my hands. My point in telling that story was to help our students understand that the rings they received on that night could become cherished possessions in their own families, not only in their own memories of their high school days, but as heirlooms for their children, grandchildren, or even great-grandchildren.

Dr. Charlie Burry, Jr.

Maybe this story has some further meaning, though. It might be a metaphor for another life lesson. Maybe it will help us understand that when we're getting ready to do something—carelessly or even purposely—that might cause us to lose something precious, it might be good to step back and see if we can think of a better idea. Or, at least to be sure we're standing on dry land.

Charles E. Burry, Sr. Army Air Corps Ring

2

Knowing When Not to Laugh

Laughter can be good medicine. When I was young, I can remember looking forward to the arrival of my parents' subscription of the *Reader's Digest* magazine because of the "Laughter, The Best Medicine" feature. A funny story can alleviate, even if only for a brief moment, a bout with depression. Laughter can ease the tension of an awkward situation. It can balance the perspective of what might seem to be an issue of critical importance. As with any medicine, though, the prescription has to be right for the condition. If it's not, it doesn't do any good, and the patient doesn't improve. If the joke is inappropriate, it can fall flat. It's also important for the correct dosage of laughter to be administered at the proper times. An overdose could have the adverse effect of making a problem worse. A person can just get fed up with something until it's not funny anymore. Sometimes it might be best not to prescribe any humor at all and advise the patient to just take it easy. There can be somber situations in which there's no place for humor. In other words, when something crazy happens, you've got to know when sincere sympathy, caring concern, and a serious response is appropriate, or when you can just laugh out loud. In my lifetime, I haven't always possessed such a discerning level of insight.

During my childhood, our family almost always had a garden. Gardening became one of my dad's hobbies during his spare time, and a vegetable garden—especially during our

Dr. Charlie Burry, Jr.

first few years in Hartsville—also put some food on our table that we didn't have to buy at the grocery store. We had the typical things—corn, squash, tomatoes, peas, beans, and maybe even a couple of watermelon vines. A few chores related to tending the garden were assigned to me. There wasn't really anything hard about any of it—certainly nothing like cropping and hanging tobacco, or putting up hay like some of my other friends—but I didn't like working in the garden even a little bit. I'd rather have been playing baseball with the other kids in my neighborhood. Weeding the garden was on my chore list one summer day, and I wasn't looking forward to it. A group of my friends were getting up a ball game about the middle of the morning, and they'd gathered around the backdoor of our house. My mom came to the door as we were about to head out to a vacant lot and asked if I'd been in the garden yet. I hadn't, and I apparently conveyed that information in a manner that greatly displeased her. She had a paddleball paddle handy for such occasions and stepped out after me to apply some corrective measures. She whacked my backside with that paddle . . . and it broke. That flustered her a little bit, and with my audience watching, I made a crucial mistake. I laughed at my mother. She headed back inside the house and emerged about 20 seconds later brandishing the hairbrush that my dad used for the Grade A whippings that he sometimes administered. I knew there was no way that hairbrush was going to break. She grabbed me by the arm, and I was soon dancing in a circle around her as she applied a Grade A whipping of her own to my smart-aleck rear end and my misguided sense of humor. My friends were the ones laughing by then, and as they headed to the ballfield, I headed to the garden. Needless to say, I didn't play any baseball that day.

About ten years later, the memory of that childhood lesson having faded a bit, I made the same mistake again. This time it was with my high school basketball coach, Tim Watson.

Our team had finished practice one night, and we were in the locker room after showering, changing into our street clothes and getting ready to head home. Coach Watson was ready to go home, too, and he stepped into the locker room to hurry us up. The weather was cold, and he had on a hat—it was a kind of fedora that none of us had ever seen him wear before. The locker room got a little quieter as he looked around, and then I snorted out a laugh. He gave me the stink eye and said, "What's so funny, Burry?" I answered, "Your hat, Coach, it's the ugliest thing I've ever seen." I still can't imagine what got into me, and my teammates looked at me like I'd broken out speaking in tongues. Coach Watson did a quick about-face, and I knew where he was going. He kept a paddle in his office in the gym, similar to the one he had in his assistant principal's office, and I'm sure he was getting his arm loose as he was making the quick trip to get it. My teammates scattered from the locker room like they'd seen the devil himself, and I knew that the next worse thing was going to be back for me in about 30 seconds. You have to understand that this was back in the day when what we call corporal punishment in educational circles now was just known as getting a licking, and most parents didn't have the slightest problem with it. So, knowing what was coming and being the quick thinker that I was, I stuffed a towel down in the back of my blue jeans. Coach Watson came back in the locker room, I bent over, he swung that paddle, and it made contact with my padded backside with a big whomp sound instead of the expected report of a sharp smack. Realizing what I'd done, he jerked the towel out of my pants and laid into me again, this time getting the result he was after. As we walked out of the locker room together a couple of minutes later, looking straight ahead, he asked me, "Like my hat any better now, Burry?" My answer this time was more satisfactory, as I said without batting an eye, "Yes, sir, Coach. Where'd you get it? I'd like to have one just like it."

Dr. Charlie Burry, Jr.

There's only one thing more hazardous than laughing at your mama or your coach at the wrong time, and that's when the situation involves your girlfriend. On this occasion, it wasn't entirely my fault, but I still bore the brunt of the consequences. Debby and I were attending a summer-time pool party with a number of my fraternity brothers and their dates, and everyone was sitting around the water enjoying the sunshine when a couple of guys decided that they'd like to have a little more fun. They figured that throwing some of the girls in the pool would liven things up some, and one of them grabbed Debby. The problem with that—and I'm not sure I knew it at the time—was that Debby couldn't swim. The backstory there (which I soon learned) is that she'd had a traumatic experience as a child, thinking that she was about to drown, and had never been able to learn to swim. The prospect of being thrown into the pool terrified her, and even though she fought the guy like a wildcat, he was able to toss her in. She came up sputtering, gasping, and well . . . mad as a wet hen. Luckily, she was in the shallow end and made her way to the side of the pool pretty quickly. I met her there and helped her out, and while I don't think that I was actually laughing, I was apparently enjoying the scene way too much to suit her. Needless to say, the incident put a damper on the rest of the afternoon.

The life lesson learned from these stories, in hindsight, carries some humor. At the time those things occurred . . . not so much. So, while laughing when something funny happens or enjoying a practical joke can—under the right circumstances—be good medicine, it's also important to know when not to laugh. If it involves circumstances that could be embarrassing to someone who won't appreciate the humor of the situation, I got a better idea. Keep a straight face and a civil tongue in your head.

As a postscript to this chapter, I should add that I grew to love Coach Tim Watson like a second father. It was one of the great privileges of my life to give the eulogy at his funeral more than 38 years after he whacked me with that paddle for laughing at his hat. I've also been married for almost 47 years to the girl that got thrown in the swimming pool. Finally, I don't have a garden, and I don't have plans for one, either.

Coach Tim Watson

3

A Furman Thanksgiving

Despite my notably impressive claims about eating frogs in Chapter 36 of *Life Lessons . . . Principally Speaking*, I have been known to have a serious problem with procrastination. That was especially the case in my younger years. Even today, my lifetime membership in the Perpetual Procrastinators Club (PPC) remains active, although I haven't paid my dues in . . . well, I can't remember when. I did deviate successfully from PPC standards, at least most of the time, in my work as principal of Hartsville High School. My weekly superintendent's reports to Dr. Knight were always punctual, as failure to comply with that directive was something that no Darlington County School District principal was willing to risk. It was my policy to always return phone calls and emails within 24 hours of receiving them, and I can honestly say that any failure to do that was rare. I did learn, however, when there was something on my to-do list for which the importance of taking care of it was far out-weighed by the aggravation of actually doing it, to occasionally slip that item to the bottom of the pile. I sometimes found that by the time I got back down to it, the need to address the problem would have miraculously disappeared, or one of our assistant principals would have resolved the issue for me. The key to that strategy, as is pointed out in another chapter of *LLPS*, is being able to differentiate between the rabbits and the elephants. Unfortunately, I did not possess that degree of good judgment during my high school and college days as a student.

I was a history major at Furman University and while taking most of the courses required for that program, I managed to get by with average grades. During my senior year, however, it became considerably harder for me to fly under the radar of my professors. In the spring term, I had to take a seminar course in European history. The class met once a week, I sat in a circle with about 20 other students, and struggled to even understand the discussions, much less contribute anything meaningful—possibly because I didn't do much of the required reading between classes. I still refer to it as my "Weekly Hour of Intellectual Intimidation." I think I managed to make a C. The other significantly higher hurdle which I faced came earlier during the fall term with a course that required a senior thesis in American history. We were allowed to pick most any credible topic for a thesis and approval from the professor was not a problem. It got a little harder after that. Researching the topic was obviously of crucial importance before I could even begin writing. My problem with that issue was most of my time in the Furman library up to that point had been spent studying with a girl named Debby. Keep in mind, this was long before the Internet and the convenience of a Google search became available. The Dewey Decimal System was like a foreign language to me, and I had only a passing acquaintance with the card catalog. Researching my thesis topic was like a Rubik's Cube to me, which I've never been able to do, either. As a result, the required weekly meetings with my professor to update him on the progress of my research became progressively more problematic. He was a brilliant and demanding scholar who did not suffer fools easily. So, as procrastination began to enable my incompetence, I resorted to the only logical escape that I could see. I began skipping my weekly meetings with Dr. Newton Jones, which is where the sad tale of "A Furman Thanksgiving" begins.

On the Tuesday before Thanksgiving, I was sitting in my dorm room with my roommate, Rusty Harter, and a couple of other guys discussing the merits of a special lunchtime deal at Pizza Hut. We all had plans to leave campus the next day for a highly anticipated long holiday weekend in our hometowns. The buzzer in our room sounded, letting us know that either Rusty or I had a call on the hall telephone. Again, keep in mind—this was in 1972, so there were no cell phones, and we didn't even have a landline in our room. I ambled down the hall to the phone completely unaware of the fate awaiting me. I answered, and a voice that struck fear into my heart said, "Mr. Burry, this is Dr. Jones." I managed to get out a "Yes, sir," and Dr. Jones continued, "Mr. Burry, if you intend to graduate in June, you should be in my office at 10:00 on Monday morning to discuss the research you've been doing on your senior thesis." I croaked out another "Yes, sir," and walked on quaking legs back to my room as it slowly dawned on me that I was faced with doing ten weeks of thesis research in five days—during the Thanksgiving holidays. Rusty swears to this day that I was as white as a ghost when I walked back into the room, gradually morphing from complete shock into total panic mode. As I sat down at my desk and relayed the phone conversation to Rusty, he did what any loyal and compassionate friend would do. He headed out to lunch with the other guys for pizza and beer. I headed out to the James Buchanan Duke Library.

The Furman campus during the Thanksgiving holidays was deserted. There was no one left on my hall, and I don't think there was anyone even left in my dorm. It was spooky. The dining hall was kept open, and when I went there for meals, I would see some of the 15 or so other students who were spending their holidays at Furman. Students from China, Japan, and Australia—places a little more distant than the 180 miles to Hartsville, South Carolina. I have no recollection of how I justified to my parents spending Thanksgiving at school instead of coming home, but they must have accepted it without too much fuss. If only they'd known what a dedicated and conscientious student their oldest child was. Thankfully, the library remained open, too, and I powered through those five days on coffee and No-Doz. I managed to collect and organize enough research to be prepared for my meeting with Dr. Jones. I was punctual that Monday morning and somehow managed to convince him that I was on track to complete my thesis. About two weeks later, one of the administrative assistants at the law firm where Rusty was interning was kind enough to type my paper for me. I paid her $50 and a six-pack of Old Milwaukee. I think that I made a C.

So, what kind of lesson might we learn from "A Furman Thanksgiving" that could be applied to life in general? I think mainly that when we find ourselves regularly attending meetings of the Perpetual Procrastinators Club instead of keeping our appointments with Dr. Jones, it would probably be a good thing to think of a better idea—one that doesn't work out to be quite so lonely.

Dr. Charlie Burry, Jr.

4

Ma'am, I Don't Think That's Such a Good Idea

One of the great privileges of my professional career was to be able to work in the Hartsville High School Counseling Office for three years with Mr. Ray Petty before he retired. If you've read Chapter 5 of *Life Lessons . . . Principally Speaking*, you know that he was my guidance counselor when I was a high school student. Mr. Petty is one of two men—other than my father—who have had the most influence on my life. So, becoming a colleague with one of my heroes and mentors—his office was right beside mine—was another tremendous learning experience for me. We accumulated a lot of interesting stories—some funny, and some not so funny—during our time together. This is one of them.

All of the counselors were working in our offices on what had been a quiet day when I heard a disturbance in the reception area of the counseling office. Mr. Petty and I stepped out into the area at about the same time and observed two females rolling on the floor and fighting. Chairs were being knocked around, hair was flying (not mine and Mr. Petty's!), and their language was polluting the air. Mr. Petty grabbed one from behind, I grabbed the other one, and we were able to separate them and get them to their feet. When I put my arms around my fighter, I noticed that something just didn't feel quite right. Then, when Mr. Petty and I turned them around and

I Got a Better Idea   **25** got them seated, we were surprised to discover that the two individuals were not Hartsville High School students. They were adults and each appeared to be about 40 years of age. As the dust settled, and Paula Terry and Juanita McFarland were picking up gobs of hair off the floor, we discovered that the women were the mothers of two of our students. Their daughters had been in a fight earlier that morning, and they'd been called to the school by administrators. The women had been placed in the counseling area while their daughters were being calmed down in other offices. The mothers' discussion of the issue, each one defending her daughter's actions and accusing the other of starting the fight—had boiled over into the ruckus that Mr. Petty and I had just broken up. While I was questioning my offender, she began to sniffle and cry, and said, "May I please call my husband to come up here?" I gently replied in my most conciliatory manner, "Ma'am, I don't think that's such a good idea. We've already got enough to handle without him." By the middle of the day, both daughters had been suspended from school and sent home, and their mothers were explaining themselves to personnel from the Hartsville Police Department.

Fighting among our students was probably the issue with which I had the least amount of patience during the time I was principal. That part of our school culture was horrible when I took the job in 2004, and it seemed like we had at least one fight every day. I remember walking around campus one morning as our students were gathering to enter the buildings before the beginning of the school day. Cathy Hines, who was teaching in our Business Education Department, greeted me by saying, "Good morning, Dr. Burry, how are you today?" My terse reply to her was, "Just great, Mrs. Hines. Nothing better than walking around school in the morning waiting for another fight to start." That's the way things were. You don't change the culture of a place overnight, and it took several years for us to get our fighting problem under control. Was that any wonder when we had the parents of our students not giving us any better support on the issue? The story that I told you earlier about the fight that Mr. Petty and I broke up certainly was not commonplace, and in fact, that's the only time I can recall something like that happening. But, we had far too many parents who actually encouraged their children to fight. Unfortunately, what was not unusual was for me to be conducting a discipline hearing with a student and a parent, and for the adult to say to the child, "If that girl says one more word to you, you slap the hell out of her. You have my permission." Under those circumstances, I wondered how much good it did for me to offer what I thought might be a better idea.

One of the keys to changing a school culture is getting the students on your side. Right from the start, in 2004, we began to try to help our students understand that Hartsville High School was going to be the kind of school that they wanted it to be. We told ninth graders that by the time they graduated, they would have more to do with what kind of school culture we had than anyone else because they'd have been with us longer—four years—than any other class. We told our students that if they wanted to have a school with no bullying (even with all of our interventions) they would be the ones—with their choices and actions to discourage bullying—who would make it a comfortable and safe place for everyone. With the fighting issue, we told our students that if they were really someone's friend, they'd try to keep that person from fighting instead of pushing it up. We tried to get our students to understand that if they fought, they were going to be the ones who would be disciplined, not their bunch of so-called friends who stood around and watched them get into trouble for the entertainment. One of the big changes that we began to notice toward the end of my tenure was in the way that other students reacted to a fight. In the early years, I can remember watching video from the school security cameras as we tried to determine exactly what had happened in a fight, and we'd see students running to the melee. I watched students scramble over and run across the tables in the cafeteria to get a front-row vantage point. It was disgusting. In the last few years, though, we'd often see other students trying to prevent or break up a fight before teachers and administrators could get there. During the last year that I was principal, we had only two fights, and they occurred during the same week in May. We went nearly an entire school year without a single fight. We'd finally gotten our students to accept what was a better idea, and that didn't come without parental support. The culture of a school is the responsibility of every-one—students, faculty and staff, administration, parents, and the community. If you create a school that all of those folks can be proud of, they'll take more ownership in maintaining and improving that culture. They might even think that they were the ones who had a better idea. And that's fine because it doesn't matter who gets the credit, as long as there's no hair pulling.

Ray Petty and Charlie Burry

Dr. Charlie Burry, Jr.

5

The Fickle Finger of Fate

The word "fate" has a bit of a negative connotation in my mind. It's defined as "the development of events beyond a person's control, regarded as determined by a supernatural power." Some synonyms for fate are listed as being destiny, future, and outcome. Those words seem to me to be more positive, especially when you throw in the supernatural connection to fate. Whether you believe in that particularly troubling aspect of fate or not, we're talking about the future—at least to some degree—being out of our control. To Obsessive Compulsive Disorder folks like me, that's uncomfortable. I'm a cause-and-effect person, and I like to think that the choices that I make give me some control over both my current and future circumstances. That's why adults in particular are always advising children and young people to plan ahead, to anticipate the consequences of their actions, and to choose wisely. If you make good choices, theoretically, things turn out more positively for you. Except when The Fickle Finger of Fate steps into your life, taps you on the shoulder, and says, "You're it."

In addition to the choices one makes in life, the timing of those choices also has a great deal to do with the outcomes. When good choices coincide with good timing, there's a pretty strong likelihood that the results are going to be to one's liking. The unfortunate combination of a bad choice at a bad time almost always has a pretty predictable penalty. What happens, though, when a good choice is made at a bad time, or a bad choice is made at a good time? That's when The Fickle Finger of Fate sees its greatest opportunities. For example, there are some schools that are tough situations where an aspiring first-time principal might have been better off declining the job offer. Sometimes it's better not to follow a coaching legend, and instead be the coach who comes after the coach who followed the legend. There are times when you might take a position, and the internal conditions are not at all what they seemed to be from the outside looking in. You might call a terrible play, but the call was so audacious that the defense wasn't ready for it, and it resulted in a touchdown. Those are situations where you need some luck. And that's when you find out whether fate is on your side—or not.

The Curious Case of Benjamin Button is one of my favorite movies. It stars Brad Pitt (Benjamin) and Cate Blanchett (Daisy) in the story of a baby—Benjamin—who is born with the appearance of an old man and ages in reverse through adulthood, adolescence, childhood, and back into infancy. Benjamin and Daisy fall in love, and their romance, in addition to having them age in opposite directions, has many other twists and turns. One of those twists occurs when Daisy steps out into a street behind a theater after a dance rehearsal and is struck by a taxi. Her injuries result in a long, agonizing period of painful recovery and an equally painful separation from Benjamin. The movie presents Daisy's accident scene in a manner that perfectly illustrates our discussion about the fateful combination of choices and timing. A series of about ten different events and circumstances—one as minor as a broken shoelace—led to Daisy stepping out in front of the taxi at a precise moment in time and being hit . . . instead of narrowly missed. If any one of those ten events and circumstances had happened in even a slightly different manner or with slightly different timing, Daisy would never have been tapped on the shoulder by The Fickle

Finger of Fate. The movie script describes it this way: "Sometimes we're on a collision course, and we just don't know it. Whether it's by accident or design, there's nothing we can do about it."

On the afternoon of the third football game of the 1994 season, our team left Hartsville High School—unknowingly, also on a collision course—to travel to Camden. About 20 minutes later, at a crossroads on a remote part the Old Camden Highway, The Fickle Finger of Fate tapped us on the shoulder. A car, driven by a young woman who may have been confused by being on an unfamiliar road, ran a stop sign and entered an intersection at the exact same split-second as our team bus. Our bus, having no time to brake, hit the car on the driver's side at about 50 miles per hour. I was behind the accident in a smaller bus, and I watched our team bus, with about 45 players and coaches on board, roll over three times and come to rest on its side in a ditch, facing the opposite direction in which it had been traveling. I ran to the back emergency door of the bus, not knowing what I was going to find inside. By the time I got there, players were crawling out of the windows. Coach Lineberger and Coach Sanders, who had been driving, crawled out of the broken front windshield. Unbelievably, there were no critically serious injuries to anyone on the bus. Players had only cuts and bruises, no doubt due to the fact that they were wearing their padded uniform pants. Coach Sanders had a dislocated shoulder, and Coach Lineberger suffered a back injury that later required surgery. Tragically, the young woman who was driving the car was killed.

I can't count the number of times that I've seen that accident in my mind during the last 27 years. Each time, I've thought about the timing. If the car had entered the intersection a half-second sooner, it probably would have made it through. If it had been a half-second slower, it probably would have hit our bus broadside, and there would have been many more deaths. I've also thought about another circumstance because I could have easily been on the first bus instead of the smaller one behind it. For seven years as an assistant coach, I had always ridden on the big bus, sitting in the right front seat next to the window, beside Coach Lineberger. That season, we had a young coach on our staff who had just gotten his Commercial Driver's License (CDL) Permit, which meant he could drive a bus as long as he had someone who had a CDL on board with him. For the first two games of the season, that had been me. We hadn't played well in either game, and being somewhat superstitious, Coach Lineberger and I were anxious to get back to our normal travel arrangements. As we walked out of the gym that afternoon to board the buses, I asked Coach Lineberger which bus he wanted me on. He hesitated a moment and thought, weighing proper procedure against superstition, and then said, "I guess you'd better ride with Trey." So, on what probably was not much more than a flip-of-a-coin decision, I was a witness to the accident instead of a victim.

What lesson can we learn, then, from the tragic death of a young woman, a football trip to Camden cut short, and Daisy's accident? I think we should continue to have confidence in our own good judgment, make decisions to put ourselves in the best possible situations, and live life to the fullest, just like Benjamin and Daisy did. I think we should have hope for the future and confidently plan for what seems to be ahead of us. However, I think that we also have to understand that at any moment The Fickle Finger of Fate could tap us on the shoulder and say, "I got a different idea."

6

Me and Jesus, Got Our Own Thing Goin'

Do you believe in the power of prayer? Most people who I know do, and we've all probably spent some extra time in prayer, especially since March of 2020. It seems that it's human nature to resort more to prayer when we're going through troubling times, like a pandemic. When family members, friends, or others whom we love become ill, we ask God for healing and a return to good health for them, whatever the specific medical issue might be. If we're looking down the road a little more, our prayers might be along the lines of preventive maintenance, like praying for continuing good health. Sometimes those prayers aren't answered, though, and people die. When that happens, we pray for strength, comfort, and peace for those who are grieving. When the hard times involve other things like employment or personal problems, we pray about those things, too—that those difficulties might be resolved in the manner in which we're asking. Sometimes those prayers aren't answered, either, at least not in the way we had in mind when we were praying. And then other times, we should remember that some of God's greatest gifts are unanswered prayers (see Chapter 22 of *Life Lessons . . . Principally Speaking*). We often pray for understanding, although the Bible teaches us not to seek that but to rely on faith. So, then we pray for faith, and we pray for wisdom, good judgment, and guidance in making decisions. If we have a prayer life that's a little deeper than just asking for occasional emergency roadside assistance, we also offer prayers of thanksgiving for all the blessings we have in our lives—good health, family and friends, a good job, and a comfortable standard of living. We thank our Creator for the world we live in, and all its beauty and miracles. If our lives don't always measure up to the standards of good conduct, and we have a fairly active conscience, we ask for the forgiveness of our sins. Hopefully, at some point, we also get down to the most important issue in life, and we thank God for the gift and sacrifice of His son, Jesus Christ, and the promise of eternal salvation for those who believe in Him. Unfortunately, our prayer lives sometimes become mere rituals, with the habitual reciting of words that really don't have much meaning. However you might look at it, the power of prayer is a complicated issue and certainly can't be adequately covered in a paragraph. And, since my own prayer life is no doubt substandard, I'm assuredly not qualified to write a book on the topic. Let's narrow things down, then, with another question. Do school principals believe in the power of prayer? I know this one did.

I prayed over a number of issues while I was principal of Hartsville High School, despite the philosophical (and sometimes legal) challenges of separation of church and state. On the way to work, I most often just prayed for a good day. If there had been a mass shooting recently, I lifted those victims up in prayer, and then prayed with all my heart that my school would not be the next one on the national news. At the beginning of each school year, about 20 members of a local church would come to our school, and they'd have a prayer circle with me for about 20 minutes in the hallway of the administration building, asking that God's hand be on us during the year. At the beginning of each school day, we had a moment of silence during the morning announcements in which I hoped many in our Red Fox Family would spend in prayer. Violence or unrest in our community nearly always had a family or neighborhood connection to at least a few of our students, and I prayed that emotional peace and calm would prevail until time began to heal the wounds. We had fire drills, earthquake drills, tornado drills, and lockdown drills as parts of our emergency management plan, and my prayer was that we would never have to deal with the actual reality of any of those situations. We had a bomb threat from time to time, and I prayed for the safety of our administrative team and law enforcement while the search dogs cleared the buildings. I also prayed for the safety of our students, faculty, and staff at the evacuation site. One of the neatest things we did was to have our public address announcer leave a 25-second gap of silence after the National Anthem before football games so that the crowd, in unison, could voluntarily recite the Lord's Prayer. I had some difficult decisions to make with discipline situations on a regular basis, and I asked for wisdom in making those become teachable moments for the students and their parents. There were some troubling personnel issues occasionally, and I prayed for sound judgment, conviction, and compassion in making the best decisions for our school. Finally, we sometimes had to deal with the death of a student, which is by far the most painful ordeal that any school ever faces.

I attended more funerals of students than I can remember during my 40 years at Hartsville High School. I can tell you that there is absolutely nothing in this world more agonizing than watching a parent bury a child. Life just isn't supposed to work that way. It's impossible to understand, and at least for a while, to even comprehend. There are no words of sympathy that can begin to touch the pain for the family. It is difficult for the school family as well, as classmates and teachers see the empty desk, mourn their friend, and try to express their own loss and pain. One student death during my time as principal of Hartsville High School was particularly difficult. The student was well-known and popular and the circumstances of the death were in a very public setting. Part of my job was to prepare the school for dealing with the tragedy in the coming days. Our administrative team met, we arranged for additional counselors to be on campus, and I made plans for a general faculty meeting before students arrived on the next school day. I wanted to be sure that everyone had accurate information about the situation, and I wanted to be able to offer suggestions to our teachers about comforting their grieving students. I had prepared a few remarks, but I was extremely apprehensive about that meeting. Before I went to bed that Sunday night, I prayed for wisdom and the right words to say to our teachers the next morning.

An early morning workout with either an exercise regimen or 30 minutes on an elliptical machine was part of my daily routine while I was working as a principal. That Monday was an elliptical day, and I always listened to music on my iPod during that time. I probably had 500 songs from 50 different artists—from Patsy Cline to Maroon 5—on the iPod, and the songs were set to come up randomly. That morning, after praying to God the night before for guidance, a song by Tom T. Hall entitled "Me and Jesus" came up first. The song begins with the lines, "Me and Jesus, got our own thing goin', Me and Jesus, got it all worked out." This is the third stanza in that song:

> "Jesus brought me through all of my troubles,
>
> Jesus brought me through all of my trials,
>
> Jesus brought me through all of my heartaches,
>
> And I know that Jesus ain't gonna forsake me now."

I told that story to our faculty and staff later that morning, and I think we all took comfort throughout a difficult day in the knowledge that my prayer from the night before had been answered. Was it just a coincidence, against 500-to-1 odds, for that song to come up first on that particular day? I don't think so. I think God had a better idea.

7

I Almost Drowned My Daddy in Lynches River

My dad enjoyed fishing during his lifetime, although not on a regular basis. According to my mom, he and a friend once built a wooden fishing boat from a mail order kit and plan. I have a vague memory from my childhood of his taking me on a fishing trip to Biloxi Bay when we lived in Mississippi. I also have a few childhood memories of him fly fishing during family trips to the North Carolina mountains after we moved to Hartsville, and his fly-tying kit and supplies were in our attic for many years. My clearest memories of fishing with him are of pond fishing on a friend's farm in Chesterfield County where we caught a lot of jack fish. When we weren't fishing with cane poles, he used an open-face spinning reel instead of a bait-casting reel, so that's what I've fished with all my life. My interest in fishing could described best as mild until I moved to Lexington County to teach and coach at Gilbert High School (GHS). That's where I met Jack Cunningham, who was the Agriculture teacher at GHS, and we became great friends. Jack enjoyed bass fishing and bought a nice bass boat to take advantage of the fishing on Lake Murray, just a few miles north of Gilbert. I became Jack's first mate, and we fished together almost every Saturday during good weather. We had some great times, and we even caught some fish occasionally.

When I took a teaching and coaching job at Hartsville High School, I'd become hooked on fishing and was determined to continue. I thought that I needed a boat, so I talked my dad into going halves with me on buying a used v-bottom fiberglass boat, 9.8 Mercury engine, and trailer from a retired local doctor. I wanted more stability and a better fishing platform than the v-bottom boat, so we traded that for a 14-foot jon boat. My dad and I fished together a few times, but then his interest seemed to wane, and Hal Baldwin became my regular fishing partner. We fished for bass on Lake Ashwood between Bishopville and Sumter, went catfishing on the Big Pee Dee River, and caught redbreast and bream out of Lynches River. I've never had much luck fishing in Prestwood Lake. The fishing for redbreast was fun and pretty easy, as long as you kept an eye out for water moccasins in the low-hanging tree branches over the river. I thought my dad would enjoy that, so I started badgering him to go along with me sometime. He finally agreed, and we planned to go fishing on a Saturday morning. That's when I found out, at least on the day which The Fickle Finger of Fate picked for our trip, that there was more than water moccasins to worry about on Lynches River.

On Highway 15, about three miles northeast of Bishopville, a bridge crosses Lynches River, and there's a boat ramp under that bridge. That's where my dad and I put our boat in at about 7:00 on that fateful morning. In the past, I'd done most of my fishing upriver from the bridge, so that's where we headed. Shortly after we got on the water, a sudden thunderstorm came up, and—looking back on things—we should have taken that as a bad omen. After all, how many summer thunderstorms happen at 7:00 in the morning? We pulled over to the bank and got out of the boat to wait out the storm. The rain and wind blew through quickly, and we were soon back on the river and ready to fish. Within about 15 minutes, though, before we were even 100 yards from the bridge, we had cause for much greater alarm. We heard, coming from the boat ramp area, the sound of gunfire from automatic weapons accompanied by wild screaming and laughter. It was sporadic and lasted several minutes. I couldn't imagine what was happening, especially at that time of day. Was the gunfire from guys just having fun firing off the weapons, or was it a drug deal gone bad? Where we were located on the river, there was a footpath along the bank where people walked from the bridge to fish. We knew that whoever it was had seen my truck and boat trailer, and would know that someone was on the river. Would they come walking down the bank looking for us and shoot us like sitting ducks? I decided not to wait around to find out. I fired the motor quickly, and we headed upriver to get farther away from whatever mayhem was happening.

I began thinking at that point about what else to do after the initial escape plan. Cell phones hadn't been invented yet, so we didn't have a way to communicate with anyone else. Should we just wait a while and then go back to the bridge, hoping the gun-happy crowd would be gone? Would my truck be shot full of holes? I knew that there was another Lynches River bridge upriver on the Kelleybridge Road. As the crow flies, that bridge is about five or six miles north of the Highway 15 bridge. Of course, by river, it's probably twice that far. I also knew that Lynches River ran parallel to the road to Ashland for some distance, so I decided we'd keep going upriver until we saw some sign of civilization, or worst-case scenario, go all the way to the Kelleybridge Road bridge and flag someone down there. It wasn't long before the folly of that plan became apparent. We began to encounter blow-downs—trees that had been felled by storms and were at least partially blocking our way up the river. We were able to slip under a couple that had fallen completely across the river, but we soon came to one where we had to get out of the boat, lift and pull the boat across the tree trunk instead of going under, and climb back in the boat as it slid back down into the water on the other side. We accomplished that tricky maneuver, but soon came to another one where we'd have to do the same thing. I decided that once of that was enough, and maybe the upriver escape route wasn't such a good plan after all. It had been a couple of hours since we'd heard the gunfire, so we turned around.

When we got back to the tree that we'd have to go across, we didn't hesitate. After all, we'd done it once, right? As we got the front of the boat onto the tree again, I decided to have my dad go ahead and get back in, and just ride down the other side instead of trying to climb in the boat while it was moving. That would be less risky for him, right? Well, as the boat reached its tipping point, and the bow—with his extra weight—suddenly shifted downward, my dad was pitched out of the boat into the river. At the same time, a fish hook caught in my hand as I was trying to hold onto the boat. As the boat slid down into the water and the fishhook ripped out of my hand, I searched frantically for my dad, but all I could see was his hat floating down the river. And of course, the thought running through my mind in the next few seconds was "My daddy is going to drown in Lynches River, and it's all my fault." Thankfully, within just a few seconds—although it seemed like an eternity to me—he surfaced, sputtering and coughing. And, if he'd been a cussing man, I'm sure he would have been letting me have it with both barrels. He managed to grab a tree branch that was in the river and pulled himself to the bank. I got control of the boat and made my way over to him. We sat there for a while collecting our thoughts—him soaking wet, and my hand gashed and bleeding—and then he said, "Looks like I lost my hat."

An hour or so later, we slowly and quietly approached the bridge and the boat ramp . . . and found it deserted. My truck and the boat trailer were fine, so we loaded up and headed home. My mom and my wife were immensely relieved, as a planned three-hour fishing trip had taken twice that long. I don't think my dad was really angry with me, but I was mad at myself and felt terribly guilty about nearly losing him because of my poor judgment. We never did talk about that day much as over the years we retold stories of other less dramatic family adventures. And every time that I suggested another fishing trip, my dad would say, "I got a better idea. You go with Hal and just come back and tell me about it."

8

Ray, the Tree Man

I like all kinds of trees, and in 1980 when we built our house on Edgewood Drive in a grove of pine trees, it was a beautiful setting. I soon discovered, however, that if you have a lot of pine trees on your property, you're also going to have a lot of pine straw. And most of it is not going to fall in the shrubbery beds where you want it to be. So, in order to keep our yard looking respectable, I raked a lot of pine straw and picked up hundreds of pine cones while we were in that house. I cut a lot of the smaller trees down myself during the 28 years that we lived there and hired Buzz Shaw to take down some of the bigger ones that I couldn't handle. While my family was cowering in the hallway all night during Hurricane Hugo in 1989—fearing that one (or more) of the six or eight huge trees that we had left in the yard might fall on our house at any moment—I swore that we'd never go through that again. I had them removed as quickly as I could and planted some oak and maple trees in the yard, none of them close to the house. I figured that was a pretty good trade-off, as leaves from hardwood trees fall once a year, and it seemed that I raked pine straw year-round.

When we became interested in buying another house in back section of Club Colony, one of the first things that I noticed was about 20 huge pine trees on the property. Again, it was a beautiful setting, and the saving grace was that much of the yard remained as natural areas that didn't require much maintenance. In other words, you actually wanted the pine straw to fall there—a brilliant landscaping concept. The trade-off for not having to rake pine straw, though, was that we had to buy the stuff to put in the shrubbery beds. We have a dependable person who does that for us regularly now, but during the first few years that we lived there, it was a hit or miss proposition. So, whenever a truck and trailer pulled up in the driveway with a load of pine straw for sale, we were usually willing customers. That's how we met Ray, the Tree Man.

Ray rang our front doorbell one morning, and it looked like he had a load of fresh pine straw that we could use. We came to an agreement on a price for putting it out, and Ray and a couple of guys with him went to work. The crew seemed to be doing a good job, and as they were finishing, I was inspecting what they'd done. That's when Ray mentioned that he also did tree work. He'd probably noticed a dead pine tree in our back yard that had been hit by lightning. It was a fairly large tree, maybe 50 feet tall, near the back of our lot. It was also within about 15 feet of the Duke Power electrical service wires that ran along the property line, which I'm not sure that Ray had noticed at the time. I'd been wanting that tree taken down before it fell on my dog pen, so Ray and I walked over to look at it. He told me that he'd cut it down and haul it off for $100. I knew that one of the first things you do when hiring out that kind of work is to find out if the person has liability insurance. Ray talked like he knew what he was doing, however, and I thought that was a pretty good price, so—going against my wife's advice—I didn't ask. My first clue that failure to inquire about liability insurance would be regrettable was when Ray started up the tree.

Ray didn't have any climbing equipment. He just put a coil of rope over his shoulder, hooked a chainsaw to his belt, and—in a feat of raw strength and agility that amazed me—he climbed about 35 feet up that tree trunk. If you've ever watched Barney

Odom's dog, Flatnose, climb a tree on the *Johnny Carson Show*, well, that's how Ray did it. When he finally got to some branches that he could hang onto, he looped the rope around the tree and threw the rest of it down to his co-workers. He told them to pull on the rope, and it was then that I realized he was just going to top the tree instead of cutting branches off first, and he didn't want that part of the tree to fall on the electrical wires. Ray then managed to tie himself off with another piece of rope to free his hands so he could operate the chainsaw, and he fired that baby up. By that time, I was getting pretty nervous from my vantage point on the back deck of our house. You've guessed by now that the rope stretched, and the ground crew couldn't pull hard enough for the top of the tree to fall in the right direction. As it fell onto the electrical wires, sparks started flying, the tree caught fire, and smoke obscured Ray from view. But you could hear him hollering, "Call the fire department! Call the fire department!" One of my neighbors who was outside came running with a water hose but then made a hasty retreat when he realized that it was an electrical fire. Ray had somehow managed to finish the cut, though, and the top of the tree fell to the ground, the wires stopped sparking, and the fire went out. The next sound that I heard a few seconds later was a big whump. Ray had fallen out of the tree and landed flat on his back.

Ray miraculously survived the fall, and as a matter of fact—once he could breathe again and came to his senses—he stood up unassisted and dusted himself off. We began to assess the damage and realized that the power was out in our house. We called Duke Power instead of the fire department, and when their crew arrived, they advised us that the whole neighborhood in that part of Club Colony was out, too. Once they got started with their business of restoring power, Ray walked over to me and said, "OK, I guess we'll finish up now." The rest of our conversation went like this:

Me: "Look, Ray, you just nearly electrocuted yourself, started a fire, knocked out power to 30 damn houses, and could have killed yourself falling out of that tree. We've done enough damage for one day."

Ray: "What do you mean?"

Me: "You're fired, Ray."

Ray: "You owe me $100, then."

Me: "Ray, you cut down half a damn tree. Clean that up, I'll pay you $50, and you need to move on."

That tree trunk—35 feet high—stood for about six more months as a reminder of my stupidity and as a monument to Ray, the Tree Man. He never came around selling pine straw again, and Duke Power never billed me for their repair work that day. Considering what the consequences could have been, the whole episode turned out pretty well. However, the next time I had trees cut down, I had a better idea. I hired a professional.

9

Road Rage at Watford's Bar-B-Q

During the time that I was principal of Hartsville High School, I once read a website essay to our teachers about a hypothetical correlation between driving habits and other social behaviors. The author's proposal was, since millions of people in our country drive automobiles and other vehicles every day, that if we placed an increased emphasis on becoming more considerate and courteous drivers, those tendencies would transfer over to our other social behaviors, thereby resulting in a better society. It seemed logical to me since so many of our behaviors are habitual or reflexive, so I was interested to see what impact sharing the theory with our faculty, staff, and students might have on the social climate at our school. Perhaps testing the hypothesis on a population of mostly teenage drivers wasn't such a good idea, but I didn't see how it could hurt anything. When you throw stuff on the wall with high school students, you never know what's going to stick. And, even if all it did was to slow the traffic down some in our student parking lot, that would be a good thing. Of course, if you buy the author's theory about the correlation between more courteous driving and people's better emotional health and social behavior, you could also wonder if the opposite might be true. Why has road rage become so prevalent these days?

We see examples of road rage every day. We hear the impatient driver blowing the horn when someone is a little slow pulling away from a green light. We indignantly blow the horn when someone pulls out in front of us or changes lanes without looking (more on that later). We also see reports of road rage on television news reports or in the newspaper when the results of it have been particularly unfortunate. We seethe about people who ride for mile after mile in the passing lane of an interstate highway at 69 miles per hour, seemingly oblivious to the train of vehicles behind them and others passing them on the right. Is it an elderly person who gets stuck in the left lane and seems afraid to move over, or is it someone just daydreaming? If the car in front of us doesn't move quickly enough when the light turns green, did it unavoidably stall out, or was the driver just finishing a text? When someone pulls out in front of us, and we have to slam on brakes, was the driver simply careless, or was he blinded by the sun? When a car is tailgating us while we're going the speed limit, is the person just being a jerk, or is she late for work? And, why didn't that driver dim the headlights?!?! There are all kinds of variables and possibilities to consider and maybe be more understanding about while we're on the road. Those were some things that I didn't think about when I stopped at a restaurant in Bishopville on the first Saturday night in December, 2016, and ordered up a gigantic serving of road rage with extra hot sauce.

Watford's Bar-B-Q was one of my family's favorites for many years. The restaurant is closed now, but the building is still there. It's on the right as you're coming into Bishopville on Highway 15 from I-20. Just as you get there, Highway 15 narrows from four lanes to two, and if you're in the right-hand lane, you have to merge left. That's where all the trouble started. I was coming home from Hartsville's 2016 state championship football game in Columbia and had decided to stop at Watford's and pick up supper for my wife and myself. Just as I got to where the road narrows coming into Bishopville, a car beside me in the right-hand lane cut over in front of my truck so quickly that

I had to brake and swerve to the left to avoid a collision. My road rage meter went up a few degrees, and I saw the taillights of the car ahead of me as—believe it or not—it turned into the parking lot at Watford's Bar-B-Q. As I made my turn into the parking lot, I saw the driver get out of his car and go inside, and I decided that he and I would have a good opportunity to discuss the virtues of courteous driving.

I walked inside, and the guy was standing at the counter waiting to order with several other customers. There wasn't any real line, so when he and I approached the counter together, I motioned for him to go ahead of me and said, "Go right ahead, sir, you seem to be in a hurry." He shot me an irritated look, placed his order, and then turned around and said, "What the hell you talking about?" Sensing that I'd gone too far, I acted like I hadn't heard him, placed my own order, and sat down in one of the chairs by the door. He walked over to me and repeated his question, this time a little more loudly. That was my next chance to say something sensible, but I'd apparently left the ability to do that in the parking lot. Instead, I snapped, "Well, you pulled over on me back down the road, and you almost hit me." That triggered an eruption of profane indignation that drew the attention of everyone in the place. At that point, I raised my hands in a gesture of surrender and began to apologize for offending him. He continued to curse me for all I was worth, and the more I apologized, the louder and the worse it got. And the whole time, I was thinking two things—(1) Dr. Burry, you are the principal of Hartsville High School and you cannot call your superintendent from the Lee County Jail and tell him that you've been in a fight at a barbeque joint, and (2) Charlie, you have a wife and two daughters, and this fool is going to go get a gun out of his car and kill you. Thankfully, his order was ready just a minute later (no doubt due to the quick thinking of the ladies behind the counter); he picked it up and continued to dog cuss me on his way out the door. I asked one of the other customers to watch the parking lot to see if the man was leaving or coming back inside to murder me. Another lady who had heard everything came over to me and said, "Sir, don't you go out in that parking lot—he could be waiting for you. My brother works for the Bishopville Police Department. I've called him, and he's on the way." I kindly replied, "Ma'am, I think it's okay now," and after apologizing to all the Watford employees for starting a ruckus, I walked out into the parking lot with my head on a swivel. As I rode on through town with my eyes peeled for my new friend's vehicle, I met a police car headed to Watford's Bar-B-Q with its blue lights flashing, and I gave it a wave.

Every time I stopped at Watford's Bar-B-Q from then on, I'd step up to the counter and say to the lady who always waited on me, "Ain't had any troublemakers in here lately, have you?" She'd answer, "No, baby, don't you worry about that. That man was crazy." As I was truly afraid for my life that night, I've often wondered who was crazier: me or him. So, based on my informal research into the correlation between driving habits and other social behaviors, I'll offer this advice: the next time you might be inclined to flip somebody off for blowing a horn at you, I got a better idea. Chill out, and just drive on.

10

God, I Think She's Tough Enough Now

Having spent 31 years in athletics as a coach, toughness is a personal quality which I value highly. When I played sports, my coaches were great men whose memories I cherish, but they were tough. They coached us hard. We took a great deal of pride in being tougher than our opponents. I learned from them that sometimes the difference between winning and losing in a close game was just being more hard-nosed than the other team. I came to understand that persistence and toughness over the course of a contest sometimes tipped the scoreboard in the final minutes toward a lesser talented team. So, when I became a coach, I was determined that—if nothing else—my teams were going to be mentally and physically tough. We did things that were physically tough with our conditioning. We ran sprints until some of our players threw up. We did box jumps that took the skin off of many a shin. Some of our exercise routines required doing reps until physical failure. I designed some of our practice drills for players to compete against each other under very difficult circumstances in which no quarter was given or expected. I intentionally created practice situations that challenged the mental toughness of our players, too, because that's where physical toughness begins. A person can't be physically tough without being mentally tough. One of the mantras that I remember from my coaching days was when our players would think they'd reached the point of physical exhaustion, they'd say to each other, "Come on, let's go! It ain't nothing but a mind thing!" I coached for six years before

I became a father, and—for better or for worse—I took some of my coaching philosophy into the world of parenthood.

Debby and I have been blessed with two beautiful, intelligent, and personable daughters—Beth and Caye. Debby deserves most of the credit for the remarkable young women they've become because she raised them while I was off coaching other people's children. We were also blessed to live within a stone's throw of my parents' house, and they were wonderful influences on our girls as grandparents. Debby and I were in general agreement most of the time with our parenting philosophy although she claims that I sometimes sabotaged some of her discipline measures when I got home and one of them climbed up in my lap. I probably have to plead the Fifth Amendment on that charge. Having said that, though, I wanted my daughters to be tough. I wanted them to be able to defend themselves physically if the need arose and have the mental toughness and courage to stand up for themselves in the face of adversity or injustice. Tough love is a fine line to walk sometimes, however, and it's difficult for parents to always be on the same page with that issue. I can remember a few occasions when Beth and Caye were in high school and I worked in the counseling office that one of them would have a disagreement with a teacher. If Debby believed that the teacher was wrong, she'd sometimes pressure me to intervene. I didn't do that very often, making the argument that our girls needed to learn that life isn't always fair. Usually, I'd make my way out of the doghouse after a few days. The fact that children, even sisters, sometimes are a little different made those situations even more interesting. Beth was usually a little tougher in her earlier years, maybe because she got the first-born's dose of her dad, the coach. Caye was the more sensitive one, and I used to worry that she wasn't tough enough. That was on my mind, even when she graduated from Furman.

Caye spent a couple of months in Hartsville after graduation and then moved to Cleveland, Ohio, where Beth was living at the time. She'd been in Cleveland the summer before completing dual internships with *The Cleveland Free Times* and the Rock & Roll Hall of Fame and Museum, but still, I worried about her, and one of my prayers was that she'd get tougher. Even with her sister there, most of her close-knit circle of Furman friends had scattered all over the country, she'd broken up with a boyfriend, and it was a lonely time for her. I prayed that she'd find good friends, and that, in the meantime, she'd get tougher. She later went to work for Junior Achievement (JA) of Greater Cleveland, and that was not an easy job. She and her colleagues recruited volunteers and managed financial literacy programming for 45,000 students in northeast Ohio, a portion of whom attended schools in inner-city Cleveland. Witnessing the challenges faced by students and teachers in those neighborhoods fueled her motivation but was also emotionally and mentally draining. She made a couple of great friends with JA (Hi, Maria!) and generally enjoyed the work, but she also ended up in an urgent care facility in Milwaukee at 6:00 one morning with a severe case of food poisoning on her first work trip. When she talked on the phone with us about those things, especially when she was sick, I tried to be sympathetic and supportive. But I wanted her to get a little tougher, too, and I prayed about that. Before she'd been in Cleveland long, as if she didn't have enough to worry about, the front end of her brand-new car was smashed by another vehicle. While she was dealing with that, I prayed every night for God to make her tougher. She lived with Beth for a while and then found a place of her own in a six-unit apartment building in trendy Cleveland Heights. She was out on her own—which was a great step—but the building had a number of problems. Her landlord was not at all cooperative in fixing them, and she became very frustrated with that situation. I told her to be more assertive with the guy about it, and I asked God to make her tough enough to deal with him. What else could I do? Her difficulties continued, and we got a call from her with the news that someone had broken into her apartment and stolen jewelry and electronics belonging to her and her roommate.

Thankfully, they weren't home at the time, but it was a terrifying experience for her—and especially from 600 miles away—for her mom and dad, too. I prayed for her safety and for her to be emotionally tough enough to handle it. Her landlord, true to form, was uncooperative in getting an adequate alarm system installed, and—in what was the last straw with him—gypped her out of her security deposit when she finally moved out. I wrote the shyster a nasty letter, and then prayed for God to make her tougher. Are you seeing a pattern here? I finally did.

What I'd been too blind to see was that God had been answering my prayers all along. You see, a person doesn't just miraculously become tough one day. Toughness is developed through dealing with tough circumstances. It's not a character trait that is simply bestowed on people when they're born or when they wake up one morning. Toughness is a character trait that's built by surviving the tough things that happen in a person's life—like loneliness, workplace issues, illness, a wrecked car, a landlord who's a jerk, a home invasion, and a lease disagreement. All of those things had been making my baby girl tougher, and when I finally realized that, I decided to pray for something else. My next prayer for her was "God, I got a better idea. Let's back off some. I think she's tough enough now."

Caye Burry

Section 2—
Better Lessons from
the Boys School

After surviving the Thanksgiving Holidays at Furman during my senior year, I did my practice teaching in US History at Eastside High School in Greenville during the two-month winter term and then began looking forward to my graduation in June 1973. I also began searching for a teaching and coaching job, and I submitted applications to several school districts in the upstate, as well as those closer to home in the Pee Dee area. That spring, my high school basketball coach, Tim Watson, had been hired as the head men's basketball coach at Francis Marion College (FMC) in Florence. He'd been looking out for me and called one day to let me know about a job opportunity in that area. I applied, interviewed, and was hired. So, less than a month after graduating and leaving my social bubble and the pristine campus of Furman University behind, I was teaching Physical Education (PE) at an all-male juvenile corrections school.

The South Carolina School for Boys was a division of the South Carolina Department of Juvenile Justice (DJJ) and was located on National Cemetery Road in Florence. I soon found a place to live at Gregg Apartments, which was only about a quarter mile from the Boys School. As a bonus, I would be able to serve as a graduate assistant for Coach Watson in the FMC basketball program while I was working on a master's degree. My teaching certification at the time was in Social Studies, but the Boys School needed a PE teacher, and apparently my lack of certification in that subject area wasn't a problem. The annual salary for my first contract was $8,800, and it was a 12-month contract since our student population—having been sentenced to serve time there by the court system—didn't have a summer vacation. I worked at the Boys School for three years, and I'm not sure how much my students learned from me, but they sure taught me a few life lessons.

11

I Learned a Lot in a Hurry

It's been my experience in life that the first time around with anything is almost always the most difficult, and I think that's especially true with teaching. During the first year, the subject matter actually becomes a secondary concern, as things like figuring out school policy and procedure, complying with submission deadlines, meeting professional development requirements, and—most important—developing the people skills to effectively manage a classroom become higher priorities. While undergraduate courses are fine for establishing a philosophy based on both current and historical educational theory, there's only one way to learn to teach, and that's to teach. My practice teaching while I was at Furman gave me a taste of what it was like to actually be in charge of a classroom, but Eastside High School was a different world from the South Carolina School for Boys.

To say that I experienced culture shock during my first few months at the Boys School is to put it mildly. My experiences in life just hadn't given me much opportunity to be around people who came from the backgrounds of many of my students at the Boys School. What made this school population really interesting was that they'd all—in some form or fashion—been found guilty of violating the law. That's how they got there. Some had been found guilty of relatively minor offenses, such as truancy or incorrigibility. Others were shoplifters or had stolen cars. Some had committed robberies or burglaries. A few were violent offenders, and one of my students had killed a man. They were all 15 years old or younger: when students reached the age of 16, they were transferred to John G. Richards School in Columbia. They'd been sentenced to anywhere from a three-month evaluation period to an indefinite term, depending on the offense. Most were evaluated every six months for parole, mainly depending upon their behavior. One of the most discouraging things to me about the Boys School was that, while we might have been making at least some academic progress with them, we seemed to be doing very little to help them become better citizens. In fact—in my opinion—during their time with us, I think most of them probably got worse in that regard. Too many came in as pretty good kids who had just made mistakes or maybe were victims of difficult circumstances, but you could see them change as they learned the ropes from the more hardened ones. Therefore, I learned that trust was always a major issue, regardless of how well I thought that I'd gotten to know a student.

The Boys School campus had an administration building, some on-campus housing for a few employees, five dormitories (called cottages) for the students, a kitchen and cafeteria, a maintenance shop, a classroom building, a gym, a farm, and a jail. Each dormitory housed around 30 students, was supervised by a youth counselor, and had an assigned social worker. One of the dorms was reserved for students deemed to be more at-risk than the rest of the general population. They all wore jeans in cold weather and shorts when it was warmer, and a shirt (long or short sleeve) that was a specific color—red, blue, purple, green, or orange, as I recall—depending on their cottage assignment. The students counted off every time they left one location on campus and arrived at another—from the cottage to the school, from school to the cafeteria, from the cafeteria back to the school, and from the school back to the cottage. They walked in a line everywhere they went. Each class stayed together throughout the school day as the students moved from room to room for their different subjects. I met each of my PE classes outside the classroom building, took attendance, walked them to the gym, and took attendance again. When we walked into the gym, I had pieces of green plastic tape on the floor six feet apart, and each student was to stand on a piece of tape to prepare for calisthenics. We also played different sports during the period, and their favorite was basketball. At the end of the period, I took attendance, walked them back to the classroom building, and took attendance again. Everyone became familiar with the routines and complied almost automatically. Occasionally, though, the school atmosphere became a little tense when it was reported that something was missing that could be used as a weapon or when it was rumored that one of the students was thinking about taking an unauthorized vacation.

While there was a six-foot-high chain link fence along the back of campus, oddly enough, there was no fence along the front of campus on National Cemetery Road. Also, oddly enough, whenever a student would try to escape, or run, he usually went over the back fence. During the three years that I worked at the Boys School, I kept scars on the palms of my hands from hitting the top of that chain link fence. You see, whenever a student ran during the school day, it was expected that the male faculty members—especially the PE teacher— would try to catch him. Unless the student managed to get a good head start, that usually happened pretty quickly. I had to go over that fence about once a month, though. Other than that, an occasional fight was the most excitement that we had, and I developed an efficient method to break those up since a lot of them happened in PE class. I wore my college ring every day at that time, and it's a fairly large one. I discovered that if I turned my ring around with the stone on the underside of my finger and popped the students on the top of their heads with my open palm, that quickly distracted them from whatever they were fighting about. That tactic became so well-known that whenever a disturbance came up, and I'd start walking towards it, I could see the students' eyes shift to my right hand to see if I was turning my ring around. A lot of times, that's all it took to settle things down.

As compared with most first-year teachers' experiences, I'll humbly suggest that mine at the South Carolina School for Boys was a little different and might be better described as a baptism of fire. As with most experiences in life, however, it turned out to be beneficial. I learned quite a bit, and I learned in a hurry.

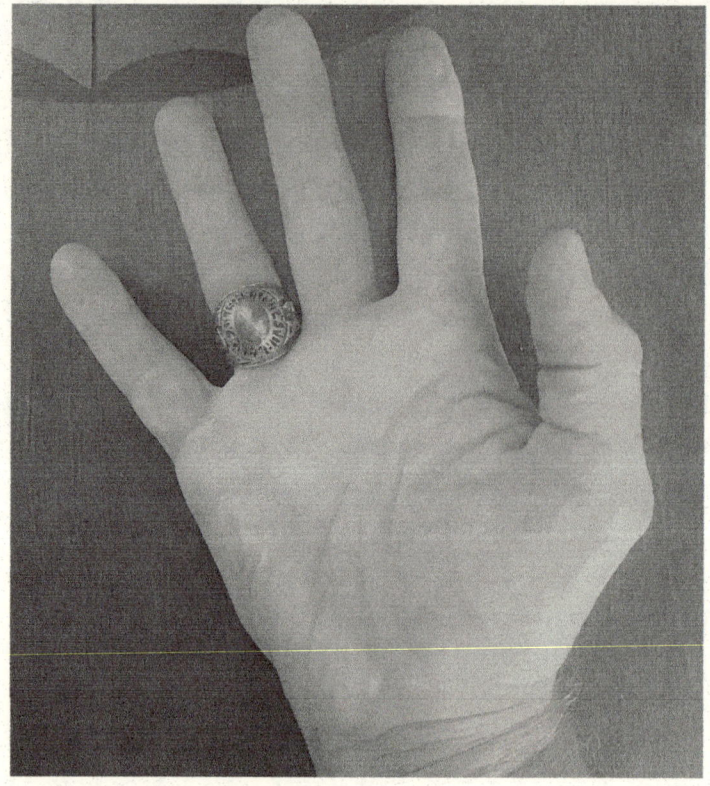

Charlie Burry College Ring

12

Make Them Think You're a Little Bit Crazy

The Industrial School for White Boys was established in Florence by the South Carolina General Assembly in 1907, at the same time that the Reformatory for Negro Boys was built in Columbia. Some years after that—I believe in 1966—the schools were desegregated, and the name of the Florence school was changed to the South Carolina School for Boys. When I went to work there in the summer of 1973, though, some people in the Pee Dee area still referred to it as the Industrial School. There was an older gentleman on the faculty, and he and his wife actually lived on campus. I'm not sure how long he had worked there, but I would guess he'd seen at least 40 years of the school's history. Still being wet behind the ears, I was open to any information I could get about how to do my job. I figured that he would be a good source of advice, so I sought him out. One of the first things he told me was, "You got to make them think you're a little bit crazy. Be sure you don't hit anybody, but throw a chair against the wall once in a while. Chase after one with a baseball bat, but be sure you don't catch him. Don't kill anybody, but make 'em think that you'll do anything. You got to remember where these boys come from."

"Don't kill anybody, but make 'em think you'll do anything." Old-school philosophy about respect, indeed, and no doubt an idea shaped by the main focus of correctional institutions of the time. My educational philosophy evolved quite a bit over the years, but in the 1970s, my thinking on respect between students and teachers agreed that it was pretty much a one-way street. I was absolutely certain that I was always a lot more concerned about keeping my teachers and coaches happy than they were about keeping me happy. I'd been paddled a time or two in high school, but I knew that even my coaches had their limits. But they weren't teaching at the Boys School, either, and my new mentor had survived for an entire career there. So, I took his advice. I threw chairs against the wall, carefully. I chased some students with a baseball bat, slowly. I threw softballs at them, aiming poorly (they thought). I continued to raise knots on their heads when I broke up fights. And I kept doing it until I was sure that my reputation as a crazy man was well-established, and there was only one-way traffic on Respect Avenue. All that time, though, I continued to mull over that advice. I had tremendous respect for my coaches and teachers, but I wasn't really and truly afraid of them. Despite the tough coaching I got and the strict teachers I had, I knew that they respected me and cared about me. There were a number of them that I grew to love. And I knew, deep down, that was the kind of relationship I wanted to have with my students and players. That's why I became a teacher and a coach. I just didn't know if I could do it that way at the Boys School.

I kept thinking. What kind of connection could I make that would assure the kind of respect from my students that I needed to survive without having them be afraid of me? What was it that most of them liked more than anything else, and what did they do in their spare time whenever they had the opportunity? The answer was right in front of me in the gym every day—basketball! They loved basketball! And, so did I! I'd played basketball in high school and on the freshman team at Furman. I'd stayed active in all intramural sports during my last three years in college, and was still in relatively good physical condition. I was coaching basketball at Francis Marion, and occasionally an honor roll group from the Boys School would come to one of our games and see me there. I started playing HORSE and pickup games with my students—one-on-one and three-on-three. And I won because I was the best player on campus. Now, before you think that I'm blowing my own horn too loud, obviously, I should have been better than anyone else. I was a 22-year-old man, 5'11" and 175 pounds, and I was playing against 15-year-old boys. Some of the students were close to my size physically and would be competitive at times, but on the rare occasions when I lost, we immediately played best two-out-of-three which reestablished order in the Boys School basketball universe. It also helped that, for some reason, one of the gym goals was only 9'6" high instead of the regulation ten feet, and—believe it or not—I could dunk a volleyball on that goal. In three years, nobody else at the Boys School could do that. So, I began to earn respect in a manner that was more acceptable to my own conscience, and one that—in the eyes of my students—was legitimate. Respect Avenue became open to two-way traffic.

"You got to remember where these boys come from." That second piece of advice continued to eat at me, too. I don't mean to make excuses for them, but most of our students were products of their environments. The circumstances of their lives had shaped them into who they were. Did it make any sense for a crazy man to reinforce those influences, or did they need something different? I gradually decided to take the high road, and while I still couldn't afford to show any weakness, I could at the same time show that I cared about them. I'd throw my arm around a student's shoulders after I beat him in a game of HORSE. When a 12-year-old boy got bad news from home, I'd try to help him deal with it. I'd sit down and listen to a student talk about the disappointment of having his parole denied.

When a little boy got beat up in the dorm the night before, I'd go to bat for him with his youth counselor. Most of them still needed to change habits of making excuses for bad choices and refusing to accept responsibility for their actions, and we talked about those things, too. And, I started to enjoy my job a little more.

It didn't always work. Some of the students had built up such walls and defense mechanisms that it was hard to get through to them. They found it hard to trust anybody and believe that anyone truly cared about them because that concept was so foreign to their lives. I kept working on those hard cases, too, however. After all, you got to make them think you're a little bit crazy.

13

You Don't Demand Anything Around Here

During my three years at the Boys School, in addition to learning about teaching and student-teacher relationships, I also learned a few things about relationships between teachers and school administrators. At the Boys School, there was a principal's office in the academic building, and that person was responsible for the educational piece of student life. At the top of the organizational chart for the entire facility was a superintendent whose office was in the administration building on the front part of campus. Our principal was directly responsible to that person, and every other department head—cottage life, kitchen and cafeteria, maintenance, farm, security, etc.—also reported to the superintendent. The principal who hired me was not very visible in the school building, had a hands-off management style, and seemed to prefer a "no news is good news" policy of communicating with the faculty. After a year, a new principal arrived whose administrative philosophy was more proactive, and who actually seemed interested in running a good school instead of just keeping a lid on things. He was an older gentleman on the back end of a long career in education, so his experience was a helpful source of learning for a young teacher like myself. I got along with him well and enjoyed our relationship. On the other hand, the school superintendent—because of his broader responsibilities—was more distant and more difficult to approach. He seemed to like being perceived as the big boss, and his appearances at the academic school always made everyone a little nervous. As PE teacher, my classroom was the gym, so I missed the privilege of seeing him on a lot of his visits.

My classroom was an old building probably constructed during the early years of the Industrial School. The wooden floor was barely large enough to accommodate a regulation size basketball court, and the wooden walls of storage areas that ran the length of the gym were about three feet from each sideline. Staircases hidden in each corner of the gym provided access to three or four rows of bleachers that were built on top of the storage rooms. The lighting was poor, at best. Restrooms, always locked, were located at one end of the building. There were four exterior doors, only two of which were ever used. Air conditioning, or any kind of air circulation for that matter, was only a dream. My office—or desk—was located inside one of the storage rooms, along with a collection of ancient athletic equipment and old uniforms. At the beginning of my first year, I was allowed to buy some new equipment for volleyball, badminton, and softball, new basketballs and footballs, jump ropes, and a tug-of-war rope. I also bought two new dust mops for sweeping the gym floor.

As a first-year teacher—excited, ambitious, and idealistic—I took a lot of pride in my new classroom. I even asked my parents to come over from Hartsville one Sunday afternoon to take a look at it, and I showed it off to my fiancé on one of her visits from Columbia. All of the PE equipment was always stored properly and in an orderly manner. Because there were no sidewalks around the building, a lot of sand got tracked inside (as my mother would say), and the new dust mops were used at the end of almost every class period. It had probably been years since the wooden floor had seen a coat of varnish, so it still had a dull finish even when it had just been swept. At the end of each school day, though, I left that place as clean as I could get it. The problem with that was that my gym wasn't all mine. During the afternoons and early evenings after supper, the youth counselors often brought their cottages inside the gym. Supervision was easier in the gym for them, and it beat sitting outside under the trees, especially in extreme weather. As a result, the gym got dirty again: they never swept or cleaned up when they left, and the clean classroom that I left each afternoon usually wasn't that way when I arrived the next morning. The straw that finally broke my camel's back was that while the cottages (anywhere from fifty to a hundred boys) were in the gym, the counselors never unlocked the restrooms. So, most mornings when I walked into the gym, the first thing that hit me was the stench of where the boys had relieved themselves in the corners of the gym. That led to my first lesson about dealing with school administrators.

On the day that the camel's back broke, later that night I wrote a flaming letter to the Boys School superintendent—the big boss—expressing my outrage at having to deal with such a nasty, filthy situation every day. I used the word "demand" a number of times in my letter to convey the level of improvement that I wanted to see. I was quite satisfied with myself and sent my letter to the administration building the next morning. About the middle of the day, my principal received a phone call requesting my presence in the administration building as soon as the school day ended. When informed of my appointment, I thought to myself, "Well, I certainly got some quick action on that," and spent the rest of the day eagerly anticipating my meeting. As soon as the last bell rang, I marched straight over to the administration building and announced my presence to the administrative assistant. Within a short time, I was sitting in my superintendent's office, and he was looking over my letter. He tossed the letter down on his desk, looked me dead in the eye, and said, "Mr. Burry, let's get this straight right now. You don't 'demand' anything around here." The tone of the meeting didn't improve even a little bit after that opening salvo, and I was very shortly on the way back to my gym with my tail between my legs.

So, one of my first lessons as a young teacher was, when communicating with supervisors, to choose my words carefully. And more specifically, to absolutely refrain from making any demands. My world wasn't always ideal during the remainder of my career as a classroom teacher and a school counselor, but I was fortunate—with one brief exception—to have good relationships with administrators who treated people well and for whom I had great respect. During my time as a principal, our school certainly wasn't perfect, but we tried to make the teaching and learning environments as good as they could possibly be for our teachers. I'd learned early in my career that few people are happy with situations in which they feel like they have to demand anything.

14

Know Who's in the Kitchen

In the time that I worked at the Boys School, especially during the first year when I was a bachelor, I spent a lot of time at Coach Watson's house. My schedule—teaching, coaching, and grad school—didn't leave much time for even quick trips to Hartsville, and Coach Watson and Mrs. Watson (Joanne) became like a second set of parents to me. I found it particularly convenient to be at their house around supper time, and Mrs. Watson—even though she was fully aware of the coincidence of that timing—often invited me to eat with them. I never hesitated to accept because she was an excellent cook and prepared wonderful meals. I knew that whatever dish put on the supper table at the Watson cafeteria would be good. You see, I knew who was in the kitchen. As you'll come to understand, that's important information to have.

The Boys School was—to some degree—a self-sufficient operation, meaning that a fair amount of what the students ate in the cafeteria each day came from a farm on the back part of campus. The produce was mostly vegetables—corn, peas, beans, potatoes, squash, etc.—and some of the labor involved in getting those things from the farm to the cafeteria kitchen was provided by the students after school or on Saturdays. I'm not sure that there was any payment involved although a small hourly wage may have been credited to the accounts of the participating students in the school's canteen. There were also students who helped in the kitchen, on the serving line, and cleaning up the cafeteria after meals. Those duties provided some degree of meaningful activity for them, taught some lessons about work ethic and the importance of doing a good job, and made them feel responsible for something that was important to the whole school. We talk about the value of vocational training in education, and while I don't know that any of the students went on to become chefs or even restaurant workers, I believe that they learned some skills that were of some importance to them. Finally, one of the benefits of teaching at the Boys School was that faculty and staff members were allowed to eat lunch in the cafeteria at no cost. Given the circumstances of my life at the time (see above paragraph), if I wanted more than a bologna sandwich for lunch, that seemed to be an attractive option. I would find out that I needed a little more information, however.

On one of my first days of work, one of my colleagues (a veteran Boys School teacher) asked if I wanted to eat lunch on campus. I appreciated the invitation and the company, and we walked over to the cafeteria. We stepped inside, he looked around for about ten seconds, and then he turned around and walked out. As I followed him out the door, he said, "Let's go get a couple of hot dogs." I thought it was strange for him to change his mind so quickly, but I liked hot dogs, too, so I followed his lead. A couple of days later, we again walked to the cafeteria for lunch, he stepped inside, looked around, and said, "OK, grab a tray." We had a good, country-style meal that we both enjoyed. I began to think that I'd found a great option for regular weekday lunches, and I started eating there every day. But for the next month or so, whenever the two of us went together to the cafeteria for lunch, there was no predicting what would happen. We'd walk into the cafeteria, he'd stop and look around, and—seemingly with no rhyme or reason—we'd either eat there or leave to go get hot dogs. Finally, I got up the nerve to ask him what was going on. As his mouth curled into a slight smile, he simply said, "You got to know who's in the kitchen."

It took me a while to figure out what he meant, but after some investigation I learned that when certain students worked in the kitchen or on the serving line, there was a pretty good chance that something which hadn't come from the farm might be part of your meal. There probably wouldn't be any ingredient added to a recipe that would be really harmful to a human digestive system, but—if the rumors were true—it was definitely enough to make one shudder and gag. So, I filed away another piece of Boys School wisdom in my survival handbook. My mentor's expertise was not available every day, so I decided that until I established more dependable relationships with the students who worked in the kitchen or learned to read them a little better, I'd rather not gamble on what might be in my mashed potatoes. I also was much more secure with the awareness that when I fixed myself a bologna sandwich for lunch at my apartment before coming to work, I knew who'd been in the kitchen.

Joanne Watson

15

Who's Got the Game Ball?

As I mentioned in Chapter 13, when I became the PE teacher at the Boys School, I found a lot of athletic equipment stored in the gym. Much of it was football equipment—helmets, shoulder pads, thigh pads, knee pads, two sets of jerseys, pants—pretty much everything needed to have a football team. I surmised that at some point in time, the South Carolina School for Boys had played intramural or interscholastic football. I'd already set up an intramural two-hand touch football league in which the academic classes played each other during the school day according to a round-robin schedule. While I had a class during its regular PE period, another teacher would bring his/her class out to the field, and we'd have a game. As the school's Director of Physical Education (DOPE) and Sports Information Director (SID), I also became the school sports reporter. I wrote a weekly newsletter reporting on all the games in which one of the school's English teachers rightly accused me of using every sports cliché known to man in describing the action. It was published on the school's mimeograph machine, and the students loved reading their names in the paper (for something good). As the intramural league became more popular, I became more ambitious, and it only took a little encouragement from my big boss for me to begin considering the possibility of the Boys School fielding an interscholastic team. I had no idea how much I had to learn.

Dr. Charlie Burry, Jr.

Other than intramural football at Furman, I hadn't played any organized football since I was the sixth-grade quarterback for the Carolina Elementary School Redskins. Of course—growing up in Hartsville—I'd followed the Red Foxes all my life, so I did know how football was played and had some basic knowledge of the rules of the game. I knew that I wasn't any football coach though. Thankfully, as soon as word got out on campus about maybe having a real football team, a couple of youth counselors came to me and volunteered to help coach. One had played high school football, and the other guy talked all the time about a tryout that he'd had with the Dallas Cowboys although that claim was never verified. So, I appointed one as the offensive coordinator and the other as defensive coordinator, and I would be—or have the title of—head coach. As part of those executive duties, I began calling high schools in the Pee Dee area to set up a slate of games in which the Boys School team would play their junior varsity teams. I was able to arrange, to the best of my memory, a six-game schedule. That was the good news. The bad news was that—in what I would learn over time to be part of the Boys School culture—I soon began hearing reports that my coaching staff wasn't getting along. They'd begun sniping at each other, and to make things worse, they were doing it in front of the players. Team chemistry became a huge issue and was obviously affecting our practices and preparation, and I didn't have a clue as to what to do about it. I still had much more to learn about that part of coaching . . . and a lot of other things, too.

The day of the first game—against the West Florence High School Knights junior varsity team—finally arrived. By that time, I'd discovered that the duties of the head coach also included managing all of the game logistics, as well as the preparation of the field. I'd scheduled the school's maintenance crew to give the playing field a fresh mowing the day before the game, so the grass—sparse as it was—looked pretty good. The field still had to be lined (sidelines, end zones, goal lines, yard lines, hash marks, etc.) though, and we (my PE classes and I) got started early on game day. We used chalk (hundred-pound bags of it) instead of paint, which greatly increased the time and effort involved in that job. The game was scheduled for 4:00 that afternoon, and we finished marking the field just as the West Florence bus drove onto campus. So, now that the field was ready, how about our team? I had no idea, as the assistant coaches were in charge of that. Was West Florence ready? Not only were they ready, but—with their school colors being green and gold—they looked like the Green Bay Packers getting off their bus. I was about to learn a lot more.

Game day was a huge event for the Boys School. There hadn't been a ball game on campus in a number of years, and everyone was excited. Most of the adults who worked on campus—including the big boss—came over to observe, and all of the teachers stayed after school to watch their students play. The cottages formed up in cheering sections to support their school's team. Pre-game warm ups progressed, the officials showed up, and I had a brief conversation with the West Florence head coach Sam Harrelson, who became a good friend when I came back to coach at Hartsville High School a few years later. To add to the pageantry, we had an American flag ready, and I'd arranged for someone to play a recording of the Star-Spangled Banner as the teams lined up on their sidelines. I think the Boys School chaplain even said a prayer. The team captains went out for the coin toss, and the excitement built toward kickoff of the big game. Our assistant coaches had our players fired up, I was juiced and ready to coach the first football game of my career, and the crowd was already cheering. As the teams lined up for the kickoff, the referee jogged over to me and asked, "Who's got the game ball?"

Game ball?!?! It was only then that I realized, and hoped, that the game ball was sitting on my desk in the gym. I sheepishly replied, "I'll be right back," and ran for the gym as the referee just shook his head. I delivered the game ball to him a minute or so later, the Boys School kicked off to the West Florence Packers, and I really began learning. Our defensive coordinator had played some pro football (right?), so I expected that to be the strength of our team. Well, as West Florence prepared to snap the ball on their first play from scrimmage, I realized that all four of our down defensive linemen were lined up to the right of the football. I'd watched enough football to know what an unbalanced line on offense was, but that sure was the first time I'd ever seen one on defense. While I was making an inquiry to our defensive coordinator about that strategy, West Florence ran the ball left on their first play, right into the teeth of our over-shifted defensive front. It didn't take Coach Harrelson long to send in his second play though, and it truly looked like the vaunted Green Bay sweep with Paul Hornung as they ran to their right, against air, about 75 yards for a touchdown. For the rest of the game, we at least managed to get lined up correctly—on offense and defense—and Coach Harrelson took it easy on us as West Florence cruised to a 28-0 win.

So, who's got the game ball? I kept five game balls from my 31-year coaching career—three basketballs and two footballs. The football used in the 1973 South Carolina School for Boys versus West Florence game, although I learned some valuable lessons that afternoon, isn't one of them.

16

Your Mama Wears Combat Boots

The culture of the South Carolina School for Boys in the mid-1970s was pretty unforgiving. The boys who arrived there quickly became immersed in a daily life where a survival-of-the-fittest attitude was not only an advantage, but a necessity. While classroom environments in the academic school were generally calm due to the size of classes (to the best of my memory, an average of about 12 students), an undercurrent of potential disorder was almost always present. The school day was often impacted by the arrival of new students as they found their place in the pecking order of their classes. Sometimes that went smoothly, and other times it didn't since there were always students who had some past history with others, both good and bad. Things that happened between the end of school on one day and the beginning of the next school day often carried over into the classroom, and weekends doubled the potential for those disturbances. Cottage life—as the students only spent about seven hours a day in the academic school—was the primary determinant of the school culture. That's where everybody, if they weren't already there, kicked into the survival-of-the-fittest mindset. Even though everyone who had been there a while had pretty much found his niche, the natural conflicts present in daily Boys School life rocked the boat regularly and often explosively. Depending on how conscientious and attentive the youth counselors were, cottage

Dr. Charlie Burry, Jr.

life—especially in the dark of night—often challenged both the physical safety and emotional welfare of students, particularly the most vulnerable. The bottom line was that everyone was always in a defensive, easily provoked posture; many were also hair-trigger ready to attack—verbally or physically—anyone who crossed them. Even when stopping short of violence, words were harshly, hurtfully, and frequently used.

Most students probably came to the Boys School from extremely difficult home situations. Many were from neighborhoods where shootings, stabbings, addictions, domestic abuse, hunger, drug trafficking, rape, promiscuity, and prostitution were commonplace occurrences. Some of my students who weren't even teenagers yet told me about seeing things that I'd never even imagined. Parental guidance was often missing, especially from any male influence in their lives. Some didn't even know who their fathers were, much less have a relationship with them. That left mama as the primary, and sometimes only, emotional anchor in the lives of many of our students. Beneath what seemed to be a hardened emotional exterior, mama was often the soft spot where they were most vulnerable. So, naturally, when words were the weapon of choice, insulting someone's mama was the most potent and the most painful. I saw many students fight over those words, not with tears of anger in their eyes, but with tears of hurt. It was within this culture that seemingly volumes of disparaging remarks about mama, some quite imaginative, vulgar, and even humorous, became a part of everyday language at the Boys School. "Your mama wears combat boots,"—and countless variations of that insult—were fightin' words, even to the meekest little boy on campus.

"Your mama" jokes also became popular beginning in the 1970s throughout American culture. So, as if our students weren't creative enough themselves, they found plenty of inspiration while watching television in the cottages at night:

"Your mama so ugly, she got to sneak up on a mirror."

"Your mama so old, she used to babysit Jesus."

"Your mama so dumb, she studied for a blood test."

"Your mama so fat, she got her own zip code."

We never made much headway in counseling our students to use some rational thinking in order to resist the bait of a "your mama" insult. It just seemed that the temptation to respond was too great for their level of maturity, no matter how ridiculously untrue the barb was. I also think that sort of false, misguided sense of pride was just too much a part of the Boys School culture for them to rise above it. It was as if they gained a measure of respect if they fought, and lost face if they didn't—whether they won the fight or not. The idea that it takes more courage to walk away from a conflict than to fight an adversary was something that they just weren't able to understand or weren't ready to accept. I worried that our school culture was actually teaching and reinforcing behaviors that would have much more serious consequences than losing honor roll privileges when our students were paroled and got back on the street. As I'm writing this, I'm reminded of what Red Redding, toward the end of the movie *Shawshank Redemption*, said to his parole board about rehabilitation. After 40 years in prison, he didn't think much of that idea. But as an old man, he was truly sorry for what he'd done as a young, stupid kid. So, when our students were paroled and got back home from the Boys School, maybe mama was able to talk some sense into them before it was too late.

17

Read Their Names

We remember events in our nation's history, and in our own lives, in different ways. We look at faded pictures, reread yellowed letters and newspaper articles, and we tell old stories again. We visit cemeteries, and we attend memorial services. One of the most poignant ways that we remember, and honor, lives that have been lost to tragedy is with ceremonies that include the reading of the victims' names in a slow, reverent cadence. Most of us have watched scenes from the site of the World Trade Center, the Pentagon, and the Pennsylvania countryside as the names of 9-11 victims are read on the anniversaries of that tragedy. You can visit the Vietnam Wall in Washington, DC, to read and run your fingers over the names of 58,320 heroes lost in that conflict. If you go to Boston and walk the Freedom Trail, you can see the New England Holocaust Memorial's six glass towers etched with over two million different numbers which represent the more than six million Jewish people murdered by the Nazis in World War II. It can be a healing experience when we, in some manner, see or read their names.

During the years that I was at Boys School, and for a number of years afterward, I would have a similar experience—although admittedly not as emotional—on a regular basis. In checking the roll for my Boys School classes, I looked at the names of my students twice each period, six periods a day, every day. Those names became very familiar to me, and I'd recognize some of them even today. But back then, while looking at the newspaper from time to time over my morning coffee, I would once again read their names. Occasionally, it would be on the front page, and other times it would be in a crime report in the second section. It was never for a good reason. Sometimes the name I'd read would be in the obituaries. It would make me think "I remember that boy," and I could picture him in my mind. Most often, it wasn't really surprising. But then, I'd also wonder "Did he ever really have a chance?" It was always a pensive moment for me when I'd read their names.

Why was reading their names again not surprising? I've told you about the family situations and neighborhood environments that were home to most of our students. When they got to us at the Boys School, it was just the next stop on the school-to-prison pipeline for them. If they were paroled, they usually went right back to the same situation and circumstances that led to them coming to us the first time. Not surprisingly, a lot of them did come back a second time—sometimes within just a few weeks—and they'd be right back in the pipeline, just a little further along. I've also told you about the Boys School environment and routine. Obviously, the survival-of-the-fittest culture there did nothing positive to modify the behavior patterns that had gotten the students in trouble in the first place at their home schools or with law enforcement in their hometowns. It troubled my conscience and was frustrating to know that after a student served time at the Boys School, there was still very little correlation between parole and rehabilitation. Not surprisingly, a lot of them came back to us a third time—only bigger, more hardened, more devious, and more hopeless than before—and they'd be right back in the pipeline, and even further along. I'd like to think that some of our students could have eventually benefited from their Boys School experiences, but I have to think that it was probably many years down the road, after years of

Dr. Charlie Burry, Jr.

maturity, better influences in their lives, and some perspective that we weren't able to provide. If they got the chance.

One of the names that I read again was John Henry Knight. Johnny was about 13 years old when he came to the Boys School. He had a pale complexion and a headful of long, dark, curly hair. He was an average size boy physically for his age, but his personality was very reserved. He was shy, almost meek, so he was much more of a follower than one who was more likely to be the cause of trouble. He was also a pretty good student, so it wasn't long before he was paroled. In 1975, in *The State* newspaper, I read John Henry Knight's name again. He'd been killed by Donald "Pee Wee" Gaskins, who was possibly the most notorious criminal in the history of South Carolina, claiming credit for over 100 murders. Johnny was 15 years old at the time of his death. He'd gotten involved in a crime spree with his half-brother, 13 years older, and they'd unwisely stolen a car from Pee Wee Gaskins. Gaskins tracked them down, took Johnny out into a field, and shot him in the head. Even after reading numerous articles about his death, and even while I'm typing this, it's still hard for me to imagine that happening to the boy who was in my PE class at the Boys School. How in the world did he get mixed up with Pee Wee Gaskins? I don't think that this was the connection, but ironically, Gaskins had spent five years at the Industrial School beginning in 1946 when he, too, was 13 years old. He'd been sentenced there for attempted murder after he hit a girl in the head with a hatchet. I guess sometimes it's a small world when it comes to the legacy of the Boys School, especially in the Pee Dee area of South Carolina.

A more pleasant small-world experience came my way a couple of years ago while I was picking up my truck at a body shop in Hartsville. I was having to wait a while and started chatting with another guy who was also waiting for his vehicle. The man was friendly and talkative, so I wasn't having to do much to hold up my end of the conversation. He told me about his family, his house, his work, his dog, and his truck. He finally came up for air and asked me what I did, and I told him that I was a retired educator. When he heard that, he confessed that he hadn't been a very good student at one time, but said that he'd done a lot better after spending about six months at the reform school in Florence. Naturally, that got my attention, and I asked him if he meant the Boys School. He affirmed that, and we finally figured out that he'd been a Boys School student about two years before I went to work there. In exploring that common ground with him, we discovered that our recollections of the place were pretty much the same. In thinking about that conversation afterward, it actually made me feel a little better about the Boys School and my time there. The place had made a positive difference in his life, put him on a better path, and he'd turned out okay. I just wish that I could remember his name.

Dr. Charlie Burry, Jr.

18

Why'd You Run?

When offenders were assigned to the Boys School by a juvenile court, the sentence often turned out to be for an indefinite period of time. Some were allowed to return home after an evaluation period, but usually the assignment was for at least three months. Others were serving longer sentences, and a few knew they would be with us, and then at the John G. Richards School in Columbia, until the age of 18. A handful graduated from there and went on to the Central Correctional Institute in Columbia—the big house. If a student ever tried to escape—or ran—that automatically added six months to his time. Whatever the length of the original assignment was (unless it was predetermined), most Boys School students came up for parole hearings periodically—if their adjustment and behavior (rehabilitation?) had been acceptable. These parole hearings also had an impact on the school culture, as some resulted in bitter disappointment and anger, and others brought feelings of great relief and happiness. We sometimes knew which students were having hearings, and it was easy to read their faces afterward to know the outcomes. As I learned after a while, and also as a result of one particular incident, my read wasn't always accurate.

Billy was due for his parole hearing one afternoon right after school. I knew he'd been at the Boys School for almost two years, and that was puzzling to me because—even in the brief time I'd known him—he'd always seemed to be a model student. He regularly made the honor roll, and was one of the few that—if I saw him working in the kitchen or the cafeteria—I knew it would probably be all right to eat there that day. For most students, the time leading up to a parole hearing became more tense each day. Not only would that meeting determine whether or not they'd be at the Boys School for another six months, but a number of things might happen before the hearing. Other students, envious of someone in their cottage who had an upcoming hearing, might set him up as being guilty in a situation that would get the hearing cancelled. If there was bad blood between two students, one might pick a fight with the other, knowing that would get his enemy's hearing cancelled. Occasionally, the home situation to which the student was to be released would fall through, and even though the answer from the parole committee was positive, there'd be no place for him to go. So, the days before a parole hearing were like walking across a pond on thin ice. Sometimes they made it, and sometimes they didn't. I had high hopes for Billy and looked forward to finding out the result of his hearing the next morning at school. That night, Billy ran.

When Boys School students would run, even at night, they usually were caught pretty quickly. Billy was no exception, being rounded up by local law enforcement within an hour after he was reported missing. Their account was that they'd spotted him walking down Irby Street, and when the patrol car pulled over beside him, he just walked over and waited for them to put him inside. The officers said he acted like he didn't even really want to get away. When I heard the story the next morning, I was disappointed. I figured that Billy's parole had been denied, that he'd gotten mad, and decided he'd just leave and go home anyway. Unbelievably, I found out that his parole had been approved. I was incredulous. What was he thinking? What the hell was going on? I couldn't wait for

Dr. Charlie Burry, Jr.

his two weeks in the campus jail to be over and for him to be back in the regular population again. I was going to jerk a knot in that boy.

Two weeks passed, and Billy showed back up at school. At the first opportunity, I walked him over to a bench under one of the trees, and we sat down. I'd calmed down a little by then, and all I said was, "Billy, man, what were you doing? You got your parole. You were getting ready to go home. Why'd you run?" Billy said, "Burry, I don't even know who my daddy is. My mama is a whore, and she gets high all the time. I don't ever know what I'm gonna have to eat, or even if I'm gonna have anything to eat. Half the time, I don't know where I'm gonna sleep at night because my mama might lock me out. Or one of her boyfriends might kick me out." He continued, "Here, I got a roof over my head and a bed to sleep in every night. I get three meals a day, and sometimes I can go to the canteen for candy. If I get sick, I have somebody to get me some medicine or take me to the doctor. I go to school where my teachers like me, and I shoot marbles, or play ball, or do whatever I want to do after school. I get to watch TV in the cottage at night. If I make honor roll, I get to go to a ball game or a movie that week." And then, Billy looked me with tears in his eyes and said, "Burry, you tell me. Why would I want to go home?"

Why, indeed? It was at that point that I began to understand my Boys School students a little better. I realized that there were a lot—maybe even most—of the students there who, as far as my life experience and background was concerned, came from a different world. I even began to wonder if I was tough enough to survive in such a world because I'd never in my life been hurt and beaten down like so many of them had. I also began to figure out that if real teacher-student relationships are going to exist, teachers have to know where their students come from and understand something about their life circumstances and challenges. I determined that there should be a real difference between reasonably holding people accountable for their actions and choices and blaming them for things that are beyond their control. I learned that it takes a great deal of perception to walk what is sometimes that fine line of tough love between discipline and empathy. My perception of the Boys School began to change some, too. And, I became determined to do better. As for Billy, I learned that he didn't run away from the Boys School. He just ran back to the only real home he knew.

19

He Got All of Us

Debby and I didn't have our first child until we had been married a little more than five years. We were both busy with careers—me at the Boys School and at Francis Marion, for two years at Gilbert High School, and then at Hartsville High School. Debby worked as a registered nurse at Bruce Hospital, later in a doctor's office, as a school nurse at Lexington Intermediate School, and then in another doctor's office. All of that meant long hours for both of us, and we welcomed whatever free time and relaxation that we were able manage. We were also trying to get on our feet financially, and we moved six times in the first six years of our marriage. We did have a cocker spaniel named Chuck, but he was the limit of our ambitions as far as expanding our family was concerned during those days. While you don't truly understand the scope of the responsibilities involved in becoming parents until that actually happens, we thought that we had some idea and we wanted to be sure we were ready. We had each other, and that was enough for a while.

During the first two years that I worked at the Boys School, Gregg Apartments in Florence was my address. During the first year I was single, and then in August, 1974, I carried my bride over the threshold of our first home as a couple. Our apartment was within reasonable walking distance of the Boys School and was also just a few blocks from Bruce Hospital, so the proximity to our work was very convenient. You know something by now about how my work at the Boys School was going and that I'd begun to make some progress in my thinking about teacher-student relationships. However, those relationships sometimes can be a slippery slope, and while I wanted to get to know my students better, I understood that some boundaries were a good idea regarding how much Boys School students knew about my personal life. For instance, because I wasn't interested in having any late-night visitors, I didn't want any of them to know where I lived. I always drove to school because I didn't want them to know that I lived close enough to walk. That issue wasn't a huge concern to me during the time I was single, but when Debby moved in, the distance to my work became more of a concern for us. My coaching at Francis Marion required me to be away from home at night quite a bit, so I became more cautious about sharing any information with my students that might give them a hint about those circumstances in my personal life. They did know that I was married, but that was enough.

One day, my students and I had walked back to the academic school from the gym a little early, and we were standing around outside the building waiting for the class-change bell to ring. Some of them had taken the opportunity to shoot some marbles, which was a popular Boys School pastime. It had been a fairly calm day so far, and the dynamics of that particular class were better than average, so the usual banter among the students was low-key and relaxed. One of my students got the attention of the group, though, when he asked me, "Burry, you got any children?" I replied that I did not, and then another little boy named JoJo looked up at me and said, "He got all of us." The whole group fell out laughing at that remark. I got a good chuckle from it myself, and then I said, "Yeah, you're right, JoJo. I got all of y'all." I couldn't wait to get home and tell Debby about that one.

Dr. Charlie Burry, Jr.

I believe that my concept of teacher-student relationships crossed a threshold that day when I heard JoJo's assessment of my family situation—"He got all of us." I thought a lot more about what those five words might mean on a deeper level. I think it obviously meant that JoJo had accepted me, and I believe the whole class—at least from that moment on—shared that feeling, too, along with the laughter. I believe they enjoyed thinking, at least according to JoJo, that I needed them to make my life complete. And I also believe they found some sense of trust and security in thinking that—because I needed them—they needed me, too, and I was there for them. That exchange had somehow created a bond between us, and I made the very important discovery that the feeling was contagious among my other classes. Because of the nature of the Boys School, at that time I didn't have any illusions about those bonds being in any manner lasting. Students would come and go on a regular basis, and some would do that several times, so it was a transient population. I have no idea where JoJo or any of the rest of those students might be today, so that part of the relationship is gone, as I knew it would be. But, the concept of such a bond in teacher-student relationships has stayed with me. As you can see, its beginning made enough of an impression on me that—after more than 45 years—I'm writing about it.

That brief, long-ago exchange at the Boys School may have even provided the foundation for the philosophy that I would have later in my career as a principal on what I believe to be the key in the teaching-learning process. I used to suggest to our teachers, "If you can establish mutually respectful and proper personal relationships with your students, you can teach them anything, and they'll follow you anywhere." Maybe I should have called it the JoJo Factor.

20

Short Man

JoJo was a small, skinny, light-complexioned Black boy, who was probably about 11 or 12 years old during my time at the Boys School. He had reddish hair and blue eyes, and he always talked in a hoarse, high-pitched, squeaky voice. He laughed easily, and often had a wry smile that portrayed life experience—and probably some pain—beyond his years. He wasn't the least bit athletic, and didn't care for sports at all, no doubt owing to his physical size. I doubt that he ever weighed more than 70 pounds in the time that I knew him. JoJo was a world-class player at marbles, though, and anyone who had been at the Boys School for any length of time knew not to play for keeps with him. He always had a pocketful of aggies, red devils, tigers, and turtles. Everybody in all the cottages knew JoJo, and—despite respect and compassion often being in short supply—he was a popular little guy. The youth counselors looked out for him, and nobody was allowed to pick on him. His small size seemed to have provided him with some immunity to the fighting that was so much a part of the Boys School culture. Other than on official documents, however, he wasn't known as JoJo, because he had a nickname. Everybody called him Short Man.

I was devastated one day to learn that Short Man had a congenital heart defect. Looking back on the situation now, I'm sure that his small stature—at least in part—was due to that

Dr. Charlie Burry, Jr.

condition. I'm not sure how I became privy to that information, but it was sobering. It indicated that the condition was probably terminal, and that he might have less than a year to live. I should add a disclaimer here that the part of Short Man's story that I'm telling you now came from second-hand information. I never actually saw any medical reports, but I believed then—as I do now—that the diagnosis was accurate and verifiable. It came from an official source, and it wasn't just an unfortunate rumor. Short Man's days were numbered. This news tore at my own heart. How could this little boy, already a victim of so many harsh circumstances in his few years, be dealt an even more cruel hand? This little boy who—before he was even ten years old—became a ward of the state, and now, he was probably going to die before he even becomes a teenager? I'd already seen some things at the Boys School that made me understand that life often wasn't fair, and that the carrying out of justice sometimes had unjustifiable consequences. This made me struggle further with my faith. Despite that struggle, or maybe because of it, I began to pray for Short Man. I mean that I earnestly and desperately prayed for him. I prayed for a miracle, that somehow the defect in his heart would be healed. I prayed to God that no matter what else Short Man might face in the rest of his life, not to take him so soon.

In the meantime, Debby and I had talked a good bit about Short Man and his situation. She, of course, knew of him from the "He Got All of Us" story, and that had given him a special place in her heart. Her medical training and knowledge as a registered nurse also put her closer to the situation than normal, so she knew more specifically than I did what to pray for, and I think she did that. She knew that Short Man was on my mind a lot, and she'd inquire every few days about him and how he was doing. It was during one of those conversations at the supper table that I looked at my wife and said, "I think we need to talk about adopting Short Man." She looked back at me as if I'd lost my mind, and maybe I had. I was definitely coaching with my heart instead of my head, but I wasn't ready to dismiss the idea so quickly. The major part of my thinking was the possibility that we could arrange better medical attention and treatment for him than he was getting through the Boys School and that maybe we could save his life. I hadn't gotten far enough along with the idea to consider what kind of financial cost might be involved and whether our medical insurance would cover any of it, but Debby quickly brought all of that to my attention. I had given some consideration to what Short Man's new grandparents might think of the addition to our family, and I thought—at least after a while—that the idea might fly. My parents and Debby's parents were pretty open-minded and progressive about racial relations, but keep in mind that this wasn't far removed from the 1960s. I knew there no doubt would be some social challenges that we'd have to overcome in adopting a Black child from the Boys School, regardless of how supportive our own parents might be. The big question, however—as mentioned in the previous chapter—was whether or not we were willing to accelerate our timetable in becoming parents ourselves. We prayed about the entire situation and soon found that prayers are sometimes answered in miraculous ways.

A month or so had passed, and I heard that Short Man had another appointment with his cardiologist coming up. Everybody who knew about his situation was apprehensive, fearing more bad news. I'm not sure how much he'd been told about his problem and the prognosis, but to me, his behavior hadn't seemed to change. He was still happy and laughing and shooting marbles. When I'd good naturedly joke with him about something, he'd still—pretending indignation—sputter out, "Burry, you ain't right, man!" And then, he'd give me that wry grin. So, that was the situation the afternoon when Short Man went back to the doctor. I walked into the classroom building

Dr. Charlie Burry, Jr.

the next morning, anxious for the latest report. I went straight to Mrs. Mildred Cherry's office, as she was the combination school receptionist, secretary, registrar, counselor, psychologist, and nurse—in addition to being one of the nicest and most kind-hearted people I've ever met. After a good morning greeting, I quietly asked the question, "What's the latest on JoJo?" This was the rest of our conversation:

Mrs. Cherry, after a pause: "He seems to be cured."

Me, after a pause: "Cured? What do you mean, cured?"

Mrs. Cherry: "The heart defect is gone."

Me: "What do you mean, gone?"

Mrs. Cherry: "They couldn't see any evidence of it yesterday."

Me, stunned: "So, this is—like—a miracle?"

Mrs. Cherry, with tears in her eyes: "I believe it is, yes."

I asked in a previous chapter if you believe in the power of prayer. If you've ever had any doubts, maybe this story will give you more food for thought. I'll just say this: I left Mrs. Cherry's office that morning unable to even imagine any other explanation for what I'd just been told, other than a loving and merciful God had answered my prayers. And then, I hurried outside to see Short Man—a walking, talking, marble-shooting miracle.

Section 3—
Coaching 'Em Up Better

I had a lot of learning experiences in my coaching career that ran the gamut of age groups, success and failure, and joy and heartache. My career included coaching junior high football, high school basketball, football, and tennis, and being a graduate assistant coach for a college basketball program. I was privileged to work with and know some Hall of Fame coaches, as well as some of the finest people I've ever been around. It was truly a blessing to coach with people who became some of the best friends of my life. The coaching profession is a special fraternity, and those relationships last a lifetime. Nobody except coaches' spouses and families, and other coaches, know what they put into their jobs. If you're really a ball coach, you never get it out of your blood—even when you retire—and as the years pass, you just become an old ball coach and then, an even older ball coach. When people still call you Coach, it dusts off good memories, revives meaningful relationships, and makes you feel like a young man again.

I was also fortunate to coach some incredibly talented athletes, some young men whose character and work ethic was just as outstanding, and a few who had both. I coached the sons of a number of my players, and some of my players became coaches themselves. One of my basketball teams didn't win a game all season and another one won the first AAAA Region Championship in school history. I was a varsity assistant coach in a football program that played for five state championships in 11 years and compiled a record of 107-32 during that time. I also coached in the same program when we went 13-2 one year and 3-19 during the next two years. I was hired for my dream job when I was 26 years old and fired from it seven years later. My coaching career spanned 31 years, and—despite the tough times—I wouldn't trade it for anything. When former players come back or get in touch and thank you for the part you played in their lives, it's the greatest feeling in the world. Again, if you're a real coach, that's why you do it, and it's always a win.

"Coaching 'em up better," as the old saying goes, involves an interesting, challenging, and ever-evolving combination of teaching, motivation, psychology, tough-love discipline, compassion, fixing stuff, taping people up, and the ability to laugh at almost anything. As a result of all of that, another of the great benefits of a long coaching career is that you end up with a great collection of stories. I hope you'll enjoy a few of them in the following pages.

21

Becoming a Football Coach

Thankfully, when I was hired at Gilbert High School in 1976, I was given a mulligan on my career as a football coach. Gilbert was a Class A school at that time with fewer than 300 students, and there were two varsity football coaches on the staff. I hadn't played organized football since elementary school, and I'm sure the coaches—Larry Langford (who was the head coach) and Greg Johnston—were looking for, and had possibly even recommended, more experienced candidates. Bob Whitehead was the principal, however, and—being a former basketball coach himself—he was looking for a coach whose primary sport was basketball. I was hired and, as Larry and Greg were both Coach Mooney Player disciples, I began to learn the Wing-T. That's an offense that—especially for a rookie coach—is difficult to master, and I carried a notebook—I called it my brains—on the practice field every day. I suppose that I began to show some potential as the head junior varsity coach, and Larry and Greg accepted me into the profession. We also became great friends personally, and so did our wives. It was during our first game of the season that I may have passed my first test. The game was a real display of offensive fireworks, and the score midway through the fourth quarter was 0-0. We only had about four running plays installed, and I'm not sure that we'd even practiced a pass play. We finally managed to get a drive going, and with just a couple of minutes left in the game, we were fourth-and-goal on our opponent's one-yard line. At that point it occurred to this offensive genius that we had one play—a trap play—that I hadn't called the whole game. I'd just forgotten about it. So, figuring fourth-and-goal on the one-yard line was as good a time as any, I sent the play in to the huddle. We executed it perfectly, scored what would prove to be the winning touchdown, and I heard Larry shout from the top of the bleachers, "Good call!" I honestly don't know whether he really meant "Good call," or if he meant "It's about time." I took it as a compliment, at any rate, and I never told him whether I'd just forgotten about the play, or if I was saving it for the perfect time. Anyway, maybe I was on my way to becoming a football coach.

Larry and Greg left Gilbert after that first year to pursue other coaching opportunities. Lon Armstrong was hired as the head football coach, and Jack Brewer joined him as his varsity assistant coach. Lon had played as an offensive lineman at Clemson under Coach Frank Howard, and his offensive scheme was from the more conventional I-formation playbook. So, in my second year as a football coach in a real program, I was learning my second offensive system and its terminology. Lon and Jack were both excellent football coaches, fine men, and I developed a great relationship with them, too. We would be together at Gilbert for only one year—Lon went back to Mid-Carolina High School where he'd been before, Jack moved to South Florence High School, and I came back to Hartsville High School. We stayed in touch, just the same, and Lon and I would always see each other at the July coaches clinic in Columbia to catch up. In addition to learning a lot of football from Lon, he also got me started chewing tobacco. He chewed Levi Garrett and always wrapped his chew in bubble gum to give it a sweeter taste. It only took me a few times getting dizzy from swallowing too much juice to become a Levi Garrett man, as well. So, thanks to Lon Armstrong, I added that qualification to my football coaching resume'. Sadly, Lon died in 2008 after a round of golf when he was only 68 years old. I went to his funeral to pay my respects to a good friend and see his family, and several years later I attended a football game at Mid-Carolina High School's Lon Armstrong Memorial Stadium. As I mentioned, you stay in the coaching fraternity all your life, and then some.

I got my first dose of coaching in a big-time high school football program when I came back to Hartsville in 1978. That was Johnny Roscoe's second year coaching the Red Foxes, and Lewis Lineberger, Jerry Perry, and Keith Sanders were his assistants. Dewey King was also a varsity assistant and head junior varsity coach, and I was Dewey's assistant on the junior varsity team. We all worked together during the first three weeks of practice in August, so I was with the varsity team learning my third playbook in three years. Johnny had played for Coach Billy Seigler at Hartsville, so much of what we did was from Coach Seigler's system, including the fairly unique offensive numbering scheme of having all the odd-numbered holes on the right instead of the left. I coached offensive and defensive backs, which were the position groups that Jerry coached on the varsity team. I was like his shadow and asked him a million questions—some of the same ones over and over again. He never lost patience with me or talked down to me regardless, and I owe Jerry Perry a huge debt of gratitude for teaching me most of the football fundamentals that were my foundational knowledge for coaching the game during my entire career.

A few years later, I requested a move to the junior high school football program so that I could spend more time with basketball pre-season preparation. It was at this time that I enjoyed coaching with Jimmy White, whom I'd known since little league baseball, and Hal Baldwin, who also became one of the best friends of my life. We had fun during those years, had a dominant program in the Pee Dee area, and still tell some of the old stories about those days when we get together. Lewis

Lineberger became our head varsity coach in 1984, and in 1987 I had an opportunity to move to the varsity football program as the offensive and defensive backs coach. That began what was probably the happiest time of my career. Aubrey Shaw's senior season was 1987, we won the AAAA-Division II State Championship, and Aubrey made me a pretty good coach that year. That was also the year when Dean Boyd came to Hartsville as an assistant coach. We became close friends, too, and coached defensive backs together for seven years before he embarked on a highly successful career as a head coach. We won another state championship in 1988, and I found myself fortunate enough to be part of a remarkably successful time in the history of Red Fox football. Maybe I was on the way to becoming a football coach.

As I mentioned in Chapter 5, the 1994 season was a very difficult time for our football program. After canceling the Camden game, we managed to field a team the next week in a 28-0 loss to Marlboro County in which Lewis coached from the press box. The following week, he had back surgery, and Keith was the acting head coach. Keith continued to coordinate and call defenses, and I called the offensive plays in a solid win over a good Wilson team. The next week, we played at Socastee, and I was still the play caller on offense as Lewis was recovering from surgery and was unable to make the trip. The score was close throughout the game, and as the clock moved into the last minutes of fourth quarter, we were leading by less than a touchdown. We had the ball and were driving, but we were facing a third-down situation in which we needed about seven yards that would move the chains for us and keep the clock running. The play call wasn't an easy choice. The conservative call would be a run, and even if we didn't make the first down, the clock would continue to move, we'd punt, and depend on our defense to close the game out for us. The call that carried more risk would be a pass, and if we completed it for a first down, that would probably assure a win for us. If the pass was incomplete, though, the clock would stop, we'd have to punt, and the Socastee offense would have even more time for a potential game-winning drive. The worst possibility was an interception that would turn the ball over even more quickly. The choice that I made was a play-action pass that was completed for a first down. We maintained possession, the clock continued to run, and we were on the way to a much-needed win on the road. As soon as the crucial pass was completed, Keith came down the sideline and paid me one of the biggest compliments I ever received in my coaching career. As he walked by me without even turning his head, he said, "Dropped some nuts on that one, didn't you, boy?" I can count on one hand the number of football coaches who I respect as much as Keith Sanders (that leaves four), and coming from him, that sign of respect was huge to me. Maybe I'd finally become a football coach.

Lewis Lineberger, Dewey King, Jerry Perry, Charlie Burry, Keith Sanders

22

We Should Have Cut Him

The 1990 Hartsville Red Fox football team concluded the season in the Lower State Championship game at Kelleytown Stadium with a 22-14 loss to the Lancaster Bruins, led by former Red Fox coach Johnny Roscoe. The backstory to that game is that it was the first time that Hartsville and Lancaster had played each other in an official game since Coach Roscoe left Hartsville after the 1983 season to become an assistant coach at Wofford College. Jerry Perry and Mark Strickland had gone to Wofford with Johnny, and then to Lancaster High School with him shortly after that. Ricky Brown, a former Red Fox player, was also on the Lancaster staff. Lewis Lineberger became head coach of the Red Foxes in 1984, and Keith Sanders stayed in Hartsville as our defensive coordinator and offensive line coach. I had also coached with Johnny, Jerry, and Mark in Hartsville, and both teams were always together at St. Andrews College in Laurinburg, North Carolina, for pre-season camp, so the personal feelings between the coaching staffs were interesting, to say the least. Lewis and Johnny had traded game tapes and talked on Saturday after our third-round games, and Johnny—being a master psychologist—had already started trying to get in Lewis' head. When our coaching staff met on Sunday afternoon to begin game planning for Lancaster, we were all interested to know what Johnny's take on the game was. Lewis relayed a part of their conversation in which Johnny had said, "After Friday night, things will never be the same between us."

Keith's retort to that was, "Well, hell, if he feels that way about it, let's just start right now." That was the tone, at least superficially, going into the game. I should add that after that bitterly fought Lower State Championship game, as well as a number of other highly competitive Hartsville-Lancaster games over the years, things between us are the same. We all remain very good friends and enjoy each other's company every time we get together.

The 1990 Bruins were powered by one of the best high school running backs that I've ever seen play, a guy named Tracey McGriff. He was a big tailback—to the best of my memory—standing probably 6'4" and weighing at least 230 pounds. That made him about eight inches taller and 65 pounds heavier than our biggest defensive back. As I watched game tape of McGriff against previous opponents, I was hopeful that our defensive linemen and linebackers could get him slowed down enough so that all our defensive backs had to do would be to come up and finish off the tackles. If he broke the line of scrimmage or got into the open field, and our little guys had to tackle him one-on-one, the physical mismatch would be daunting. I kept watching tape on him over and over trying to figure out how we were going to get him on the ground. I saw that when a tackler would hit him high, the guy just bounced off, and McGriff would hardly slow down. But then I began to notice that when a tackler hit him low—not on his thighs because they were like tree trunks—but below the knees, he went down quicker. So, I started saying to myself, "We can't tackle him high; we have to cut him." There was one problem with that, however.

I coached fundamentals hard because that's the way I'd learned the game from the coaches I'd worked with in the past. That was the basis of my knowledge of the game, and I wanted to do a good job in that area so that Coach Langford, Coach Armstrong, Coach Roscoe, and Coach Lineberger would be pleased with my work as an assistant coach. I remember a conversation I had with Lewis and Keith one night in Laurinburg at the beginning of my first year as a varsity assistant when I'd told them that I didn't want to be a weak link on the staff. They'd both told me, "Charlie, just coach the fundamentals, and you'll be fine." So, that's what I did with individual fundamentals and team concepts as well. Offensive backs worked on hitting the hole, reading their blocks, protecting the football, and running low behind their pads. Quarterbacks worked on taking snaps, and perfecting their steps, handoffs, ball fakes, and pass drops. Defensive backs knew that their three basic rules were "Don't get beat deep, don't get beat deep, and don't get beat deep." And most important, when tackling "Stay on your feet and keep a wide base, keep your eyes up and never, ever duck your head, hit high and wrap up, get your head across on an angle tackle, chop your feet, and work your hips to drive the ball carrier back." Those are examples of the things I'd been taught and what I knew, and that's the way I coached.

Hit high and wrap up, huh? Against Tracey McGriff? That was my conundrum, and—despite what I was seeing on tape—I stuck with the fundamentals. Looking back on the situation, I know now that I just was not confident enough in my football instincts to go against the book and tell Lewis and Keith what I thought. So, all week in preparation for Lancaster and Tracey McGriff, I never gave our players the option of hitting him low and cutting him. You see that all the time in the game now, so much so that some of the great running backs and receivers have become adept at hurdling tacklers when they go low. Well, Tracey McGriff was good, but he wasn't that good. I think that's probably one time when my lack of playing experience did hurt me as a coach. Maybe if I'd known first-hand what it felt like to run into an armored tank on a football field, I wouldn't have been so insistent about asking our players to do something that they had very little chance of being able to do. If any of

Dr. Charlie Burry, Jr.

them are reading this now, I hope they'll forgive me. It was a great game, and both teams left it all on the field that night. Still, I can't help but wonder, "Could we have been playing Union for the AAAA State Championship the next week if I'd coached our players to cut Tracey McGriff?"

So, what lesson did I learn? The big thing is that you still absolutely want to have high expectations of your players, students, and teachers. You want them to do the very best that they can possibly do, and you have to remember that sometimes that's more than what they think they can do. But you can't just set the bar and say, "Jump higher," without giving them the means to do so. You can't demand that they do something that doesn't make sense or that they're just not capable of doing. Sometimes you've got to have enough confidence in yourself to change course, go against the book, and come up with a game plan that is more appropriate for especially challenging circumstances. Sometimes—to give yourself a chance—instead of tackling high, you have to cut 'em.

23

You Realize How Lucky We Are, Don't You?

I was fortunate to coach with Lewis Lineberger for 26 years—seven years during Johnny Roscoe's tenure as head coach, and then for 19 years after he became head coach in 1984. When I became principal of Hartsville High School in 2004, I had been one of Lewis' varsity assistants for 17 years. Lewis Lineberger is one of the finest coaches—and finest men—that I have ever known. While our relationship is not the same as it once was, I still consider him to be one of the best friends of my life. When I became principal, one of the most difficult issues I faced was the state of our football program. During Lewis' tenure as head football coach, a 14-year period of 147 wins and only 40 losses had been followed by a six-year period of 22 wins and 45 losses and only one winning season. During my first year as principal, our record was two wins and nine losses. I knew if the Red Fox Renaissance that we were promoting was going to be taken seriously, I had to make a change in the leadership of what was arguably the most visible part of the school to much of the community. It was one of the most difficult decisions of my life personally, and by far the most difficult decision of my professional career. I believe today, as I did at the time, that it was the right decision. I do regret the timing of it—the first week in March—but that's a story for another day. As the situation has played out over the years, though, all parties have benefited. Jeff Calabrese came to Hartsville, revived the program, and has compiled 161 wins in 16 years. Lewis went to Johnsonville where he again experienced success and had a team play for a state championship in 2012. He retired after the 2017 season with 253 wins, and he has been honored with several athletic Hall of Fame inductions. His 41-year coaching career was truly remarkable.

At the height of our success, from the State Championship win over Airport High School in 1981 through the State Championship game loss to Walterboro in 1997, the Red Foxes were one of the most dominant football programs in South Carolina. During those 17 years, we played for State Championships seven times and won three (1981, 1987, and 1988), and played for Lower State Championships three other times. It was always our goal to still be practicing on Thanksgiving, because that meant we were playing for a Lower State Championship the next day. Obviously, those playoff runs included a lot of big games in earlier rounds, many of them at Kelleytown Stadium. The buildup to all of the playoff games was always bolstered by great excitement among the students and faculty at school, as well as tremendous support from the community. During the pre-game warmup periods for those games, the assistant coaches went about running the drills to prepare their position groups, and Lewis oversaw all the activity. We all had feelings of nervous anticipation, but the assistant coaches had an outlet for that extra energy. Lewis was always stoic—jaw set and eyes focused. Even when he shook hands with the opposing head coach, you could sense the intensity in his manner.

Prior to the warmup period when the players were in the locker room, there were a few minutes when the coaches would walk the field, make last-minute checks of personnel groupings, and look over the game plan. It was at some point during that time that I'd walk over to Lewis, offer him a chew—even though I knew he already had one—and say, "You realize how lucky we are, don't you?" The first time I did that, he looked at me as if I'd lost my mind and said, "What the hell are you talking about?" I was trying to loosen him up some, and I'd broken through his aura of intense concentration—and he didn't like it. I ventured on to say, "This is a huge game, and there's going to be a packed stadium. We're playing against a great team with a lot at stake—winner advances, loser packs up the equipment for the year. The game is on the radio, and there will even be some television coverage. The excitement and the noise are going to be unbelievable. It's going to be an incredible atmosphere. What we should remember is that there are a lot of coaches who go through their entire careers, and they never have an opportunity to coach in a game like this. We do tonight, and we're lucky to be a part of it." I'm not sure Lewis bought all of that, because his response was something like "Yeah (spit), right." I do think he thought about it some more, however, and finally he would acknowledge that I had a good point. Especially since I persisted in doing it, and when he saw me coming, he couldn't walk away fast enough to avoid me.

So, what's the life application here? I think it's in a lesson that was frequently reinforced to me by Sandra Gaskins, a long-time school counselor at Hartsville High School. Sandra cared deeply about her students and the school, had boundless energy, and got more done in a day than most people did in a week. While I was principal, others would sometimes come into my office and say, "We've got a problem," or "You're not going to believe this." When Sandra would come in, she would always say, "Dr. Burry, I have an opportunity for you." I'd roll my eyes for sure, but I did appreciate her putting a positive spin on whatever we needed to talk about. I believe when you think about a situation that way, the approach that you take toward resolving it tends to be more effective and acceptable to everyone

Dr. Charlie Burry, Jr.

involved. Progress, especially in problematic cases, often isn't made without a little discomfort or even pain involved. In that regard, difficult situations are actually—as Sandra would say—opportunities to make things better.

Every ball game in life is an opportunity for a win. Sometimes it's a first-round game against a fourth-place team from another region, and it's pretty easy. Then as you advance, the game might be against an undefeated region champion, and it's a lot tougher. What is always the case as you move through the play-offs is that the greater the challenge is, the greater the reward will be. If you're really fortunate, the games involve opportunities that can truly make a difference in people's lives, and those hold potential for the most satisfying wins. Those are the games that people in the education profession coach in every day. Those are the times when, if you want a career that is truly meaningful, you realize how lucky you are to have that opportunity.

Charlie Burry, Lewis Lineberger, Keith Sanders

24

Laurinburg in the Rearview Mirror

Laurinburg is a small city in eastern North Carolina about ten miles from the South Carolina border and about an hour's drive from Hartsville on Highway 15. It's a fairly progressive city and is the county seat of Scotland County. Laurinburg is also home to St. Andrews University and its beautiful campus. All that sounds pretty nice, right? Believe it or not, there are many young men who played football for Hartsville High School between 1977 and 2003 who hate the place. Some of them still don't even like to drive through there (right, Tony Gainey?). There are others who blanch when they hear the name, and a few whose Post Traumatic Stress Disorder symptoms return when they are reminded of the place. The toughest of them just shake their heads. You see, that's where the Red Foxes went to camp each year for the second week of pre-season practice, and it was the first time we'd practice in full pads. We loaded up all the equipment we had—blaster, bridge, blocking chute and boards, two-man blocking sled, ropes, stand-up dummies, shield dummies, forearm pads, weights, bars, and benches, and the kitchen sink—on a big truck that followed the players' bus up there. A few times, we managed to get the use of an 18-wheeler tractor trailer truck, and we even took the seven-man sled. It was quite an effort to move our entire operation, but it was important to have a productive week of camp, and we were going to have everything we needed to do that. We left all the mamas, daddies, and girlfriends at the Hartsville High gym at 2:00 on Sunday afternoon and headed up the road to Laurinburg. Everyone anticipated a week of fun described by the veteran players in all manner of horrific and sadistic ways, especially to the younger guys who'd never been to camp before. Upon arrival, we unloaded the equipment truck, moved into the dorms, and then headed to the cafeteria for supper. At 7:00 that night, we were on the field for a two-hour practice in shorts, shoulder pads, and helmets. Then it was back to the dorm for bed to await the first practice in full pads and the Oklahoma drill on Monday morning. Some of the younger players didn't sleep.

Monday was the first of two days of practicing four times a day. The schedule was a one-hour practice at 6:00, breakfast, a three-hour practice at 9:00, lunch, a three-hour practice at 2:00, supper, and a one-hour practice at 7:00. In our spare time, position group meetings and weight-lifting sessions were worked into the schedule. And then, we did it all over again on Tuesday, and Thursday was the same. Wednesday was different because that was the first scrimmage of the week against other teams, and that was also the day (and the only day) that parents and families could visit. They would start arriving after practice at about noon, and the coaches would transform into rational human beings for a couple of hours. The scrimmages started at 2:00, and every team at camp (sometimes as many as eight or ten) would be going against another team on four or five different fields. It was quite a spectacle with the parents, families, friends, and cheerleaders crowded around the sidelines. The scrimmage sessions were scheduled for three hours, and by the end of that time, most of the camp visitors had departed for home. That left supper and another practice at 7:00 to review the scrimmage. We sometimes eliminated the early Thursday morning practice, depending on how we'd done in the scrimmage, and then Friday was another scrimmage-day schedule. Finally, we'd scrimmage again on Saturday morning, load up, and head home. I used to ask Jerry Perry at the beginning of each week if he knew of any other profession in which a grown man could spend a week at summer camp and have so much fun. He couldn't think of anything.

One enjoyable part of camp for me was getting to spend time with friends who were coaching other teams and making new acquaintances on other coaching staffs. During water breaks at our practices, I'd sometimes walk over to the field next to ours and observe other coaches running drills with their players or teaching fundamentals. Especially during the first few years, I'd go over to the Lancaster dorm at night to talk football with Jerry Perry, who was still a mentor to me. As often as I could at a meal, I'd talk with Fred Edwards, who coached the defensive backs for Summerville High School. Fred always patiently entertained my questions and was never hesitant to share anything that I wanted to know about the way he coached the Green Wave secondary. I haven't seen Fred in many years now, but I appreciate him to this day. A special opportunity was available if we finished our practice a little earlier than Summerville, and I'd be able to stop on the way off the field to listen to Coach John McKissick talk to his team. If you don't know this, Coach McKissick—with 621 wins and ten state championships in a 62-year career—was one of the all-time legendary high school football coaches in the nation, and certainly in South Carolina. His 621 wins is still the most by any football coach at any level—high school, college, or professional. It was a privilege to listen to him speak at any opportunity, and I was fortunate to fall in beside him as we walked back to the dorms after breakfast one morning. As was his nature, he wasn't talking about himself, but was asking about me and my career in coaching. This was in 2002, and—thinking of myself as having become a veteran coach at almost 51 years of age—I offered that this was my 25th football camp. Coach McKissick reflected a moment and said, "My first football camp was in 1952." Realizing that was the year after I'd been born, I adjusted my perspective a bit on what it meant to be a veteran football coach. I still consider it an honor to have talked with him that day.

Things weren't always so cordial between Hartsville and Summerville, however. The Green Wave was the absolute heavyweight champion of South Carolina high school football at the time, and Hartsville—while building a great program of its own—was merely a challenger. But, reflecting the attitudes of our head coaches—Johnny Roscoe and Lewis Lineberger— we weren't going to back down from them an inch. In 1990, we were scrimmaging Summerville in one of the Wednesday afternoon affairs, and the action was intense. It reached a fever pitch when Phillip Coe—one of the best tailbacks I ever coached—ran a sweep around our left side. The Summerville defensive player came up to make the tackle, and Phillip—all 155 pounds of him—ran over the guy and knocked his helmet off, similar to the famous Jadeveon Clowney hit against Michigan in the 2013 Outback Bowl. Our team went absolutely crazy, and Summerville was furious at the embarrassment. After another big hit a few minutes later, a huge brawl broke out between the teams. It lasted for several minutes, and at one point while Randy Wheeler (who later played for the USC Gamecocks and Miami Dolphins) was on top of a Summerville player, I was on top of Randy trying to get him off the guy. It was like riding a bucking bull in a rodeo, and I didn't make the eight-second count, either. We finally got all the skirmishes stopped and continued the scrimmage but were chagrined to find a couple of big pictures of the fight on the front page of the sports section of the Laurinburg newspaper the next day. My good friend, Steven Steele, who is currently principal of Berkeley High School, was a player on that Summerville team. He may have a slightly different version of this story.

So, what's the Laurinburg lesson? I think it's the axiom that "iron sharpens iron." A Laurinburg football camp with the Hartsville Red Foxes was an experience not soon forgotten. It was unquestionably hard—our coaches intended it to be that way—and undoubtedly much more difficult than football camps are today. Some former players who have served in the military claim that Laurinburg was tougher than boot camp. We took some boys to camp, though, who came home several steps closer to being men. Camp built a bond between players on our teams that couldn't be forged in any other way. Those who survived camp are part of a brotherhood in which they can proudly claim membership. And, like me, they've got some stories to tell. Nevertheless, by the end of the week when I drove that bus out onto Highway 15 South, we were always glad to see Laurinburg in the rearview mirror.

25

The Best Halftime Talk Ever

Motivation is an interesting concept, and it's a key part of coaching. It's important because coaching often involves persuading athletes to do—or attempt to do—things that are hard to do, that they might not want to do, or don't think they can do. Even the most coachable athletes sometimes need encouragement to summon the extra effort needed to be successful. I still have an inch-thick folder of motivational ideas that I collected during my career: things like (even though I'm not from Alabama) the Auburn Creed. Those words still get me fired up when I read them, so thank you Renny "War Eagle" Johnson for that. The poem entitled "If" by Rudyard Kipling is another example, as is the poem "Dream Big" (author unknown) that I gave to my oldest daughter during her senior year of high school. The catch to successful motivation techniques is—while a story or quote might be appealing to the coach—it's also got to be motivating to the players and occasionally those two things don't correlate. The coach is usually plenty motivated, but it's the athletes who are on the field or court competing. The coach has to figure out what motivates the players.

Great coaches are sometimes known for pre-game talks that have their players storming out of the locker room with their adrenalin pumping. History made note of Knute Rockne's "Win One for the Gipper" speech to his Notre Dame team. Vince Lombardi was known for his ability to motivate his Green Bay Packers. There are some great examples of pre-game speeches in Kenny Chesney's video for his song "Boys of Fall" that give me chill bumps every time I watch it. I heard Johnny Roscoe and Lewis Lineberger give some good ones. On the other hand, I was witness to one that failed to connect. The coach was relating a story about a football player who had suffered an injury to a finger during the first half of a game. The injury was so severe that the player being able to participate in the second half was ruled out by the team doctor. The player was pleading for anything that could be done that would get him back out on the field. The doctor, in jest, suggested that the only thing that could be done was to amputate the finger. Hearing that, the player said, "Cut it off, doc!" Upon that climactic ending to the coach's story, there was a couple of seconds of silence. Then, a voice from the back of the locker room said, "Naw, man." Obviously, the spell was broken, and the story fell flat. I managed to keep a straight face at the time, but I'm smiling even as I type this now. With motivation, sometimes you hit a home run, and other times you swing and miss.

One fundamental piece of coaching that is often the subject of pre-game talks is an emphasis on doing the little things right. There's a television commercial these days in which the scene is the parking lot of a grocery store. There is a single shopping cart in the middle of the parking lot, and the message is something like "If you can't trust people to put a shopping cart in the right place, are you going to trust them to do something really important?" The point is, of course, that doing the little things right is important. That's especially true in athletics, and it's true in most occupations. Proper blocking technique in football and proper shooting technique in basketball require attention to detail. Making change correctly is important for a cashier. Playing as a defensive back in football or hitting a backhand properly in tennis require proper footwork. Following directions is important for a truck driver. Baseball pitchers and golfers grip the ball and the club properly. Filling a prescription correctly is important for a pharmacist and the customer. I've watched another television commercial showing football players running sprints, sometimes called gassers. They're required to start on one line, sprint to touch another line some distance away, sprint back to the starting line, and repeat those sprints a number of times without stopping. The commercial shows all players touching each line except one guy, who instead touches about a foot short of the line. Again, the point is that doing the little things right is often the difference between winning and losing.

Halftime talks are important, too, but usually involve more teaching than motivating. When I was coaching, there was a chalkboard in the locker room on which the coaches would sometimes diagram adjustments to blocking schemes, changes in defensive alignments, what our opponents were doing on offense or defense, etc. Anything of a motivational nature usually came under the heading of closing remarks. Our normal routine was for Coach Lineberger to speak, then for each position coach to take his turn at the chalkboard, and Coach Lineberger would summarize with some points of emphasis. One night at Kelleytown Stadium, we'd played poorly in the first half of a game, and all of our coaches were disgusted with the effort, execution, and pretty much everything that we'd gotten from the team in the first 24 minutes. Our staff gathered outside the door of the locker room, and Coach Lineberger asked each coach for input. When it was Keith Sanders' turn to speak, he didn't say anything, but you could tell he had something on his mind. Little did any of us know what it might be.

The coaching staff walked into the locker room, and before Coach Lineberger could say a word, Coach Sanders grabbed the wheel. He proceeded to go on a blistering ten-minute rant, hardly pausing to take a breath, about . . . our players not picking up the bars of soap off the locker room shower floor at the gym! I still don't know how it was possible for anyone to elaborate on the subject of leaving bars of soap on the shower room floor with such eloquence and emphasis, but Keith Sanders did it that night. And he did it with such passion (if you know Keith), that no one dared to even say a word, much less interrupt him to tell him that halftime was almost over. The coaches exchanged a few incredulous looks, but quickly turned our attention back to the speaker of the house in order to stay out of the line of fire ourselves. Finally, one of our student managers—not realizing what was happening—burst into the locker room, looked at Coach Lineberger and pointed to his watch, signaling that it was time to get back on the field for the second half. Coach Lineberger stepped forward and said, "OK, let's go." Not one word had been spoken about football.

We came from behind to win the game. Our team played with much greater effort, enthusiasm, and attention to detail than we had in the first half. We did the little things right, and it made a world of difference in the quality of our play. There are still a lot of times when I consider the topic of motivation and doing the little things right—especially in regard to athletics. It's then that I often remember the lesson that Keith Sanders taught in the Kelleytown Stadium locker room that night about picking up the soap off the floor in the shower. It was the best halftime talk ever.

Keith Sanders

Dr. Charlie Burry, Jr.

26

I Got Four in My First Three Games

As you've read in some previous chapters, I began my coaching career with my primary interest in basketball. I did that for 12 years while also getting my feet wet as a football coach. Basketball was my first love, however, and for those 12 years, that's how I thought of myself. I'd played for and coached with Tim Watson for four years before I became a head coach, and he was my coach, teacher, mentor, and a second father figure to me. I adopted much of his coaching philosophy, copied many of his offensive and defensive principles, and—in all honesty—tried to be too much like him early in my career. One of Coach Watson's memorable characteristics was his apparent dislike for the gentlemen who officiated the games. I don't think that he truly harbored any personal animosity for referees (except maybe one or two), but I often heard him say that the shirts referees wore should have horizontal stripes instead of vertical ones. When I was in college and came home for weekends or holidays, I would usually get together with some former teammates for a visit at Coach Watson's house. With that audience, he would regale us with the latest tales of his run-ins with basketball referees, and Mrs. Watson would always chime in with, "Tim, I can't believe you said that to that man. You must have lost your mind." Looking back on those visits now, I'm fairly certain that those stories were embellished a good bit for our entertainment. For better or for worse, though, that was the attitude toward referees that I had inherited when my career as a head basketball coach began at Gilbert High School in 1976.

Fast forward with me to 2013, when Dr. Eddie Ingram became superintendent of the Darlington County School District. I'd been principal at Hartsville High School for nine years, and one of the first things he told me was, "Charlie, I've already heard what a great job you do, and you can stay here as long as you want." That was reassuring to hear from my new boss, and we hit it off well. We had several things in common, and one was his own career as a high school basketball coach in North Carolina. He understood the value of athletics and extracurricular activities in the school culture and once told me that if he was starting a new high school, the first two people he would hire would be a head football coach and a band director. So, while Dr. Ingram was very involved in and supportive of our primary mission of academics, we also enjoyed some chats about basketball and coaching. He had some good stories about his seven years as a basketball coach as well, and he enjoyed talking about that part of his career. He dropped by a Red Fox basketball game one night, and we were standing at the end of the court exchanging observations. The game was getting a little chippy, and we began talking about referees. Dr. Ingram then said, "You know, Charlie, I got four technical fouls called on me in seven years." My response to that was, "Well, Dr. Ingram, I hate to tell you this, but I got four in the first three games I ever coached."

I slowed down considerably after that inauspicious start, or I probably wouldn't have kept my job. I'd estimate that I got technical fouls about six or eight times a year and maybe deserved a few more. The rules today call for a coach to be ejected from a game after two technical fouls. At the time I was coaching basketball, however, the limit was three—so I had a little more leeway. That was a good thing with one official who

Dr. Charlie Burry, Jr.

was assigned to our games regularly. Whenever he would nail me with a technical foul, he would always come over to our bench and stand right in front of me, just waiting for me to say something else. I didn't have the self-discipline to resist that kind of temptation, so I always got a second technical in very short order, and I think he enjoyed it. Ironically, this gentleman was one of the better officials we had to call our games, and we had a great relationship on and off the court—except when I thought he'd missed a call. It took me a while to understand that you seldom got the best of those guys in an exchange, and I learned that in an embarrassing way in a game at Hillcrest High School. We had a veteran official that night who actually refereed college games regularly, as well as high school contests. I was peeved at him about a call, and was giving him the stink eye while he used a towel to mop up some water on the floor. When he finished and walked toward the scorer's table, I called out—with as much sarcasm as I could muster—"Hey, Bill, you missed a spot!" Without a word and barely a glance my way, he sailed that towel towards me from about 15 feet away. I had my hands in my pockets in an innocent posture, and before I could react, the towel wrapped around my neck. The Hillcrest crowd, which had heard and seen everything, went wild as I sheepishly mopped up the spot that I'd called to his attention. My reputation with referees apparently followed me into the principal's office, and one night we had an official for a game with whom I'd had pretty frequent run-ins while I was coaching. I was on duty that night and was standing against the wall at the end of court near the free throw lane when there was a break in the action. This official was standing about five feet in front of me, and I jokingly said, "You know, James, I don't think we've ever been in a gym together when you didn't call a technical foul on me." He looked over his shoulder and said, "Well, the game's not over yet."

With the benefit of hindsight and a good many more years of maturity, I began to understand that I'd have been a much better coach—and hurt my teams with fewer technical fouls—if I'd had better composure. I don't think I learned soon enough in my basketball career that you can't be mad as hell at a referee—or about anything else—and do your job as a coach. There's nothing wrong with being intense about coaching, but you've got to be able to think unemotionally and rationally about what you're trying to get your players and team to do, and what your opponent is doing. Some technical fouls are strategic in terms of motivating your team, but I doubt many of mine were that well-planned. Thankfully, I believe that I developed a more acceptable level of composure by the time I became a principal. I think most of our teachers recognized that I was unquestionably intense about my job, but they also saw a calm demeanor, even in stressful situations. Our administrative team and administrative assistants saw my temper occasionally, but it was almost always within the confines of my office. There are a lot of similarities between coaching a team and being the principal of a school, and I believe that I was a lot better principal than I was a basketball coach. I occasionally watch games now and see coaches whose sideline behavior is—let's just say, not very well-composed—and I say to myself, "I can't believe that used to be me."

Dr. Charlie Burry, Jr.

27

It Can't Be as Bad as Last Time

At the beginning of my first season as head boys' varsity basketball coach at Gilbert High School, we played Batesburg-Leesville High School on two consecutive Saturdays. Batesburg-Leesville is a small town less than 20 miles from Gilbert, and is famous as the home of Shealy's BBQ Restaurant. Although not the natural rival that Pelion was to Gilbert, it was a game that attracted local interest and meant a good gate for each school's athletic department, especially on a Saturday night. Not lost in those circumstances, at least to me, was the fact that Batesburg-Leesville High School was a Class AA school whose student population was considerably larger than our Class A enrollment. The Panthers had an outstanding basketball program, and the team was coached by Gary Phillips, who—in the small world of coincidences—is the uncle of Clark Phillips, who later played basketball for me at Hartsville and married my sister, Emily.

The first game was played on our home court, the school and community were excited about the matchup, and I thought that I had our Indians prepared for the challenge. Halftime had the Panthers ahead by a score of 40-12. Coach Phillips took his foot off the gas from there, and I think the final margin was around 30 points. We licked our wounds on Sunday and had good practices and two more games the next week. The team seemed to be making progress, and we'd put the previous Saturday night massacre behind us. The next weekend, it was our turn to visit the Panthers. On the bus trip to Batesburg-Leesville, I was sitting beside our assistant coach, Bob Wilkinson, and he asked me what I thought our chances were. I quietly replied to him, "Well, I don't know, but it can't be as bad as last time." About three hours later, the Panthers had once again scored 40 points in the first half. We had ten. It was like we were playing against five Apache helicopters. On the way out to the bus after another thrashing, Bob said to me, "Well, coach, you were almost right."

As you may suspect by now, it was a rough year for the Gilbert Indians. We were a very young team due to losing some veteran players who had trouble adjusting to a new, young coach who was trying to change the culture of the program. We had a playbook about half an inch thick, a million charts, and rules for everything. I've second-guessed myself about some of those control and discipline issues, wondering if I could have salvaged a few of those young men instead of blowing the whole program up and starting over. At any rate, the result was that we had only two seniors on the team, and we played the majority of the season with what was really a junior varsity squad. Most of the time, our 14 and 15-year-old guys were going against players three or four years older and more experienced. Compounding that issue was the fact that we were playing in a realigned conference that included four teams who had moved down in classification from Class AA to Class A but still had larger enrollments than Gilbert High School. In addition to our Lexington County rival Pelion High School, I got to know the roads to other schools like North, Wagner-Salley, Williston-Elko, Hunter-Kinard, Jackson, St. Angela, Chapin, and Cardinal Newman. That first year was a crucible for a young team and a young coach, and we won only two games. The second year, we won six games—beating Chapin, St. Angela twice, and Pelion twice. We won a conference tournament game and played much closer games in losses than the year

Dr. Charlie Burry, Jr.

before. That was done with pretty much the same players, who were then ninth and tenth graders, and I believed we had built a solid foundation for my third year at Gilbert. I was convinced that it would never be as bad as last time again. But, as Bear Bryant once said, "Mama called."

The Hartsville boys' varsity basketball job came open when Gordon Jackson left after only one year for Boiling Springs High School in Spartanburg. I was excited about the possibility of coming home, coaching at my alma mater, and moving up the ladder to a Class AAAA job. On the other hand, I was terribly torn about leaving some young guys at Gilbert who had given me all the effort and loyalty they had, and with whom I'd established very close relationships. It was July before Duke Hucks, the Hartsville High School principal, called to offer me the job. As much as Gilbert had come to mean to me, and as much as I appreciated the support of my principal, Bob Whitehead, and as late as it was, I couldn't pass on the opportunity that Hartsville offered. Mama had called, and Mr. Whitehead was gracious enough to release me from my contract with Lexington School District One. We had a team dinner at our house in Lexington shortly after that, and I told my players that I was leaving them. There were a lot of hugs and tearful goodbyes before the evening was over.

The first year at Hartsville wasn't much easier than the first year at Gilbert had been. Coach Jackson was a good coach and had started building a good foundation, but the veterans on the team were playing for their third coach in three years. We won eight games and lost a bunch of close ones. I was teaching two new courses during five of the six class periods each day, coaching junior varsity football, and trying to find time to do some pre-season basketball work. Debby was still living in Lexington because we hadn't sold our house yet, so I was going there, or she was coming to Hartsville every weekend.

Circumstances were pretty rough. It was in the middle of that first season when I noticed that Gilbert was scheduled to play at Cardinal Newman High School in Columbia on a Saturday night. I went to see my old guys play, and play they did. I was emotional and proud as I watched them win convincingly against a team that would have beaten us soundly a couple of years before. As soon as the game was over, Dudley Lybrand—who had become almost like a son to me while I was at Gilbert—sprinted up into the bleachers and jumped into my arms. There were more tears—happy ones—and hugs before I headed back to Hartsville.

Those two years at Gilbert will always be special to me, and I won't ever forget my guys there. Dudley Lybrand and Kenny Schofield made me proud by becoming coaches themselves. Billy Crout has raised a fine family in Gilbert. Von Hite ran virtually in the Boston Marathon last year, and Jeff Keisler graduated from Georgia Tech where he played football. Bird Lybrand has one son who is an educator and another who's starting a career as a country music singer. I keep up with Tony Heslewood on Facebook, and I wish I knew where Tommy Brock, Joe Harmon, Jerry Harris, Ricky Isreal, Danny Jones, and Preston Kennedy are. Sadly, Russell Kennedy and Squeak Lybrand have passed away. I like to think that those boys learned a little about basketball and life from me, and I believe they'll always remember the black, high-top Chuck Taylor basketball shoes that we wore. They taught me a few things, too, and reinforced the portions of my coaching philosophy about persistence and a positive attitude. They taught me that saying, "It can't be as bad as last time" isn't the right way to look at things. Instead, I learned to say, "It will be better next time." And for them, because they kept believing and kept working, it was. I know, because I saw the Gilbert Indians win that Saturday night at Cardinal Newman High School.

Dr. Charlie Burry, Jr.

First Gilbert Team 1976-77

28

I'm Gonna Pick a Fight with Coach Thomas

The Hartsville Graded School was founded in Hartsville in 1900 on the present site of Pride Park on South Sixth Street. It was renamed the Darlington County Training School in 1918 before relocating down and across the street about six blocks in 1921. The school was renamed Butler School in 1939 for the Reverend Henry H. Butler, who was principal of the school from 1909 until 1946. Butler High School continued to be the predominantly Black high school in Hartsville until a consolidation—which was really an assimilation—with the predominantly white Hartsville High School in the 1982-83 school year. Butler High School continues to have a proud tradition in Hartsville thanks to the loyalty of its graduates and supporters and especially the Butler Heritage Foundation. Several of its buildings have been renovated, or are currently undergoing renovation, for community use with the goal of the campus being a key part of progressive civic and cultural development in the South Hartsville area. The recently established Butler Academy will add further emphasis to the importance of the Butler High School legacy in Hartsville for generations to come.

The Butler Tiger athletic program had a strong tradition of its own, primarily due to the leadership of Coach Theodore (T. B.) Thomas, Jr., for 32 years. While he also coached football and baseball, it was his basketball program that was most renowned. His teams won more than 800 games, captured 16 conference championships, and won 20 tournament titles. His Tigers won two State Championships and finished second in the state four times. After Coach Thomas retired from the Darlington County School District in 1982, he served on the Hartsville City Council for 23 years and served as mayor pro tempore until retiring from public service in 2007. The T. B. Thomas Center at Byerly Park was named in his honor, and I was privileged to make these remarks when the basketball court in the new Hartsville High School Arena was dedicated to him and Coach Pat Hewitt in 2011:

"Coach Thomas was truly an iconic figure in high school athletics in South Carolina and competing with him was very difficult. His Butler Tiger teams were always tough, and the Butler Gym was an intimidating place to play. More important, though, was his positive example and impact as an educator of young people and his leadership in city government. The noble character of Coach Thomas is woven into the very fabric of our community and has made Hartsville a better place."

When I returned to Hartsville in 1978, Hartsville High School and Butler High School had never before competed in athletics. My welcome-back-home moment came when I got my first look at the 1978-79 basketball schedule, and there were two games between the Red Foxes and the Tigers slated for early December. Gordon Jackson, the Hartsville coach before me, thought that Hartsville-Butler games would be good for basketball in the community, and he'd scheduled them. However, one of the things that he left behind for me was a letter written to him by our principal, Duke Hucks, addressing several items that he'd suggested to improve the basketball program. In response to Coach Jackson's recommendation that we schedule Butler, Mr. Hucks had written that he would support that idea, but "there is a good chance that we might be embarrassed." We played

Butler three times in my first season. The first game was in our gym, and the place was packed with fans by 5:00 for the first of two games (girls and boys) that would start 90 minutes later. As Coach Jackson had predicted, a Hartsville-Butler rivalry would indeed be good for basketball in our community. Butler won a close game that night and did embarrass us a few days later in their gym. We defeated them in another close game for the championship of the Darlington County Christmas Tournament during the holidays. Obviously, that was a huge win for us.

We played the Tigers three more times during my second season, following the same pattern as before—we lost a close game in our gym and got blown out at their place. That set the stage for another Hartsville-Butler matchup in Darlington for the Christmas Tournament title. As I've mentioned before, the Butler Gym was a very difficult place for a visiting team to play, and I believed that the large margin of defeat in our games there had been due to—at least in part—our team being intimidated by the environment and the Butler team. I was determined not to allow that to happen again in the finals of the Christmas Tournament, where there again would be a sell-out crowd in Darlington. I decided that I was going to show our players, and everybody else in the gym, that the Hartsville Red Foxes weren't going to back down from anybody. So, while our assistant coach, Hal Baldwin, and I were talking before the game, I told him, "I'm gonna pick a fight with Coach Thomas tonight."

I certainly didn't mean an actual physical fight, but it was my intention to get into an argument with him that would turn the emotional tide of the game in our favor. Coach Thomas was fairly active during games (as I was), often walking down the sideline in front of the scorer's table between the team benches. I decided that the first time he did that, I was going to go after him. It was just a few minutes into the first quarter when I had my opportunity. He was in front of the scorer's

Dr. Charlie Burry, Jr.

table instructing his team, and I hustled down there, got right beside him, and started yelling at the referees to get him back in front of his bench where he was supposed to be. I think at first Coach Thomas was shocked at my impertinence, but not for long. We immediately engaged in a nose-to-nose, emphatic discussion about who belonged where, and what we were going to do about it. The whole gym went bonkers, and I had my stage. The referees didn't know what to do. After about ten seconds, though, I felt someone tugging on my arm. It was one of our players, Danny Nicholson, and he was saying, "Coach, Coach, that's alright. Calm down, Coach, it's OK." I turned around towards him, and he'd gone pale and looked like he was scared to death. I believe he thought I was going to get us all killed, and the rest of the team was looking at me like they'd been sentenced to death by firing squad. When I saw that, I knew that the emotional swing that I was trying to create wasn't going to happen, and I returned to our bench to pick up the pieces. I still think it might have worked if I'd gotten some more backup from Hal, but I guess he thought I was crazy, too. The Tigers went on to win in overtime, and I respectfully shook hands with Coach Thomas after the game. We played four more times during the next two years, and Butler won all of them. So, my career record against Coach Thomas was one win and nine losses. I never felt too badly about that, though, because he won about 90% of his games against every other coach, too. The lesson that I learned from that night was "Don't pull on Superman's cape." I left unused most of my more imaginative motivational ploys from then on and stuck to coaching basketball.

Coach Thomas and I developed a good friendship over the years, and every time we met, we shared a cordial hand-shake and some encouraging, heartfelt words. We never talked about that night in Darlington when a young whippersnapper dared to challenge a legendary coaching figure, and he may not have even remembered it. After I became principal, I also enjoyed working with Mrs. Thomas on some National Day of Prayer services, and she was most appreciative of our school's participation in those events. I was saddened by the passing of Coach Thomas in 2014 but I am always encouraged by the memory of his contributions to the education profession, our community, the lives of young people, and my life as well.

T. B. Thomas, Pat Hewitt, Charlie Burry, Phyllis Griggs

29

Basketball Cybernetics

I enjoyed attending coaches clinics during my 31-year career in athletics and was able to hear some truly legendary coaches speak. It was an awesome experience to actually see in-person and listen to coaches like John Wooden, Dean Smith, Bob Knight, Jim Valvano, and Mike Krzyzewski share their knowledge of basketball. At football clinics, I was privileged to hear coaches like Danny Ford, Steve Spurrier, Joe Paterno, Lou Holtz, and Mack Brown make presentations. The first South Carolina Coaches Association Clinic that I ever attended put me in the audience for a session with Hubie Brown, who had just been named coach of the Atlanta Hawks professional basketball team. I was amazed at the depth of Coach Brown's knowledge of the game (as well as his colorful language), and I continued to follow his career at several more coaching stops, as a television commentator for NBA games, and I was able hear him at a couple more clinics. I'd come home from clinics with pages and pages of notes about coaching philosophy, teaching individual techniques and skills, and offensive and defensive schemes. I certainly couldn't implement all of it but I usually found bits and pieces that would fit into what I was trying to do with my own program.

One clinic that my basketball players wished I'd not heard about was at Clemson in 1980 when Bill Foster was the coach there. I'd asked Hal Baldwin to go to the clinic for me, and being a Clemson graduate, he was happy to oblige. He came back from that clinic with an idea called depth jumping, which allegedly was something the Russians were using to train their athletes at the time. The concept involved using two boxes for which the dimensions were about 24 inches on each side. One box was also 24 inches high, the other one was 30 inches high, and they were built on a platform about two feet apart. The idea was for the athlete to stand on one box, jump down onto the platform, and spring back up onto the other box. The player would turn around, jump down and bound back up again, and do about ten repetitions of the sequence back and forth. They'd be jumping down 30 inches, springing up 24 inches, jumping down 24 inches, and bounding up 30 inches. I quickly bought sheets of plywood and the other lumber that I needed to build the apparatus and moved it into the weight room. The Hartsville High School basketball program had adopted Russian technology to be on the cutting edge (which came to have a double meaning) of improving the jumping ability of our players. It was a physically challenging routine, especially jumping up to the 30-inch-high box. It was mentally challenging as well, especially after not jumping high enough, missing the box, and barking one's shins on the edge of it. Just ask Robbie Jordan and Mark Howle.

Another innovation that we implemented in our basketball program was designed to improve free-throw shooting. Making foul shots is a crucial part of the game and is often the difference between winning and losing. In addition to having a sense during the game about how your free-throw percentage is impacting the score, all you have to do is look at the stat sheet after a game, and if you've lost by five and made only eight out of 20 free throws, it's obvious what shooting only 70% from the foul line would have done for your team. Therefore, shooting free throws was an important part of our practice routine, and we tried to simulate game situations as much as possible.

Two or three times during a practice, we'd take a time-out from whatever drill or scrimmage situation we were in, put two players at each of the six baskets, and each of them would shoot ten free throws, two at a time. They were to go through their normal free-throw shooting routine, and managers would record the number made by each player. They got a brief rest and a water break during that time, and we were still getting something productive done. At the end of practice, we'd have one player—chosen by a coach or the team—go to the foul line with the game on the line. The situation was that we were down by one point with no time left in the game, and the player had a one-and-one opportunity. If he made both shots, practice was over, and we'd won. If he made the first shot and missed the second, the team ran a wind-sprint, and another player went to the line. If he missed the first shot, the team ran two wind sprints, and another player went to the line. We'd shoot free throws until we won. The importance of good free throw shooting led us to the concept of basketball cybernetics.

Stan Kellner was a legendary high school basketball coach at Brentwood High School in Long Island, New York, from 1965 until 1978 and also coached at C. W. Post College until 1981. In 1978, he published *Taking It to the Limit with Basketball Cybernetics*. I bought the book and became a disciple of positive thinking and positive visualization in athletics. The concept is that if athletes, in practice or prior to a game, will mentally visualize themselves being successful—running a kickoff back for a touchdown, hitting a curveball, making a game-winning free throw, or hitting a crucial golf shot close to the pin—they'll be more likely to do it successfully during the actual competition. A person's mind, being like a computer, can be programmed with a positive image of something occurring, and then replicate the programmed positive mental image during the actual mind-to-muscle transfer of executing the movement. I decided to apply the concept of basketball cybernetics to free-throw shooting. I explained the idea to my team at the beginning of practice one day, and I described the process that they were to follow during our foul-shooting sessions that day. They were to step to the free-throw line without a basketball, close their eyes, go through their normal routine, execute the motion of shooting a free throw, follow through with the shot, and mentally visualize the ball—the made shot—going through the net. They were to repeat that sequence ten times.

When we got to the first practice period for free throw shooting that night, I was really interested to see how it would go. I briefly explained the process of positive visualization to the team again, and they went to their baskets to shoot their ten shots. The period was eerily silent as all 12 players—at the free throw line with their eyes closed—went through their routines and shooting motions without basketballs. I'd been walking around quietly and observing during the period, and as most of the guys were finishing up, I stopped by a player who had completed shooting and visualizing his ten successful free throws. I decided to test the effectiveness of my teaching and said to him softly, "How many did you make?" He whispered back, "Six, Coach." I just stared at him for a moment, shook my head, and walked away.

As you can see, it took a while for us to fully implement basketball cybernetics in our program. Once we were able to practice a little more with the concept, although I no longer have the data to prove it, my recollection is that it did help us improve our free-throw shooting in games. As a coach, I continued to believe in the benefits of mental preparation and positive visualization in all sports. Some players just saw things a little more quickly than others.

Dr. Charlie Burry, Jr.

30

Just Keep Your Eyes on the Road

After the 2001 football season, when our team finished with a record of 3-8 and failed to make the playoffs for the fourth consecutive year, I volunteered to coach the boys' tennis team that spring. The reason I did that was because Emet Reyes, who was in charge of the weight program for our football team, was also coaching the tennis team. Because of tennis practice and matches after school, he was unable to be in the weight room as much as he wanted to be when many of our football players were doing their lifting and conditioning. We were having trouble getting our players to work out regularly, and for those who were there, the supervision and intensity was not what it should have been. The situation was obviously hurting our football program. I figured if Coach Reyes didn't have the tennis team to worry about, he could be in the weight room full-time after school and our off-season conditioning and weight-lifting program would improve. He agreed to give up tennis in order to help the football program, and I became the coach.

I had never coached tennis before, but I had played in high school. Until the time I was a senior, we'd had very good teams with George Goudelock, Sid Segars, McKeever Hunter, and Jeff Boyd playing in the top four positions. I played fifth or sixth. When those guys graduated, Ken "Frog" Hughes and I moved up to the top two spots on the team. Needless to say, we were playing against much tougher competition, and our team wasn't as successful as we'd been in the past, but Frog and I got a lot better. I just did tennis recreationally, however, and never took any private lessons, went to any camps, or learned any of the finer points of the game that would have made me a more fundamentally sound and strategically adept player. I ran around my backhand whenever possible, got by on my athletic ability, and knew how to keep score. I probably hadn't played tennis half a dozen times since high school, and I had to go up into the attic to find my old wooden racquet. That was the background that I brought to my new position as the Hartsville High School boys' tennis coach in 2002.

I did know one thing as a tennis coach, though, and that was—just like in any other sport—if you were in better physical condition and more mentally tough than your opponent, you had a much better chance to win. So, I determined that our tennis team was going to have those fundamental characteristics, even if we didn't have anything else. We had our first team meeting, and that's when our players learned of our four-week pre-season conditioning program that we'd complete before any of them ever picked up a racquet at a tennis practice. We met five days a week at 6:00 in the morning in the gym. Each day they completed about 45 minutes of fast-paced agility and conditioning drills, I gave them a protein bar and a carton of orange juice for breakfast and told them that I'd see them an hour later to begin the school day. It was unlike anything they'd ever been through before, and a couple of them made the mistake of eating and drinking something before a workout. They only did that once, though, and everyone gradually adapted to the demands. And, we got into shape.

It was at the first practice on the tennis courts that I quickly saw that I was going to be a "Do as I say do, not as I do" coach. Our top four players—BJ Bariska, Justin Evans, Edward Reames, and David Reynolds—were very good, and I knew if I got on the court with any of them, that I'd just embarrass myself. I began researching drills that would either build or reinforce basic fundamentals and strategies, and I put the team through those paces every day. I knew from my own tennis career that you get better by playing better people, so our challenge matches—in addition to determining our lineup—brought about improvement. Those matches were usually highly competitive, especially among the top four players. I also accepted an offer from Scott Cameron in which he recruited adults from the community who were outstanding players to come to our practices. Our players learned quite a bit in their matches against those men, who most of the time gave my guys more than they could handle. I remember one match in particular when my old teammate, George Goudelock—over 50 years old at the time—completely outclassed our best player.

As you know by now, I became a tennis coach at a pretty good time. Another coaching axiom that runs true across all sports is that "It ain't the Xs and the Os, it's the Jimmies and the Joes." What that means is that most of the time good—or great—players make more difference in the success of a team than coaching does. It's the same thing that I quickly learned as a principal—that just like great players can make you a pretty good coach, great teachers can give you a chance to have a great school and be a pretty good principal. That fundamental truth was made clearer to me early in that season with words of wisdom from my good friend and coaching colleague, Hal Baldwin. Hal had coached the tennis team a few years earlier, so on the day we were traveling to Camden for a pre-season scrimmage, I dropped by his classroom to ask if he had any advice for me. He just looked at me in the perfectly classic Hal Baldwin deadpan manner and said, "Just keep your eyes on the road."

I kept my eyes on the road during that season, got our team to all of our matches safely and on time, and got us back home again every time. I filled out the lineup card according to the results of our challenge matches, and did my best to assure that our players comported themselves well and with good sportsmanship. We finished the regular season with a record of 12-2 and were Region 5-AAAA Co-Champions. We defeated Wando, Hilton Head, and Spring Valley in the playoffs, and then lost to Richland Northeast in the AAAA Lower State Championship match. It was the best season that a Hartsville High School boys' tennis team had achieved in many years, maybe ever. All of the success can be attributed to outstanding players, great community support, and a rookie coach who was smart enough to just keep his eyes on the road and let the players play the game.

2002 Red Fox Tennis

Dr. Charlie Burry, Jr.

Section 4—
Something Better in Mind

We seek improvements in our lives because we've had experiences with which we're unsatisfied, we've seen things that interest or inspire us, or we see a better way of doing things. When we're 12, we can't wait to be a teenager, and then teenagers want a driver's license. High school and college students are impatient to graduate, not realizing those are some of the best years of their lives. Engaged couples are anxious to get married, buy a house, and a few years later they're excited about the prospect of their first child. Everybody wants to move up the career ladder and make more money. Adventurers want to travel and see the world. Older folks might look forward to retirement. Some people might want to write a book and then write another one. Others just want peace of mind and happiness. While there's certainly merit to being content with the current state of things in our lives, there's also a danger in complacency. As long as we balance ambition with some patience, though, there's not anything wrong with having something better in mind. And then, we also have to learn that the grass is not always greener on the other side of the fence.

I worked at summer jobs for which I was grateful, but they made me realize that there was something better out there. I had to hitch rides for two years back and forth to college, and that made me want to own a car. Apartment life was great for a while, but my wife and I wanted a house. I watched a lot of sports on television, and that made me want to see the

Boston Garden, Wrigley Field, Fenway Park, and The Masters golf tournament in person. I liked fishing, and grew to appreciate just being on a pond, a creek, or a river. I enjoy solitude, so I'm content in the woods or on a mountain. Debby likes being at the beach. Because my youngest daughter, Caye, wanted something better, I flew to London. Following are some stories about a few experiences that occurred in my life because I began to have something better in mind.

Dr. Charlie Burry, Jr.

31

Two Summers in McBee Were Enough

The first job I had other than at my dad's dime store was in the packing shed at McLeod Peach Farm on Highway 1 east of McBee, about a 15-mile drive from Hartsville. Rick Clanton, Gregg DeWitt, Frog Hughes, and I made the trip six days a week during the summer of 1968. I drove my dad's 1957 Metropolitan one week, and Rick drove his family's Volkswagen Bug the next. We arrived at work by mid-morning, because the pickers needed time to get the first load of peaches of the day to the packing shed. We worked every day until all the peaches that had been picked that day had been culled and graded, packed in boxes, run through the cooler, and loaded onto trucks for shipping. My job was usually at the end of the cooler, which was an enclosed conveyor belt operation about eight feet wide, four feet high, and 50 feet long. As the boxes slowly moved along about four or five abreast, ice-cold water rained down on the peaches until they came out at my end. As the boxes came out of the cooler, I put a top on each one, and shoved it down another roller-type conveyor belt to the guys who were loading the truck. Loading the truck was the best paying job, but it was repetitive heavy lifting all day long inside a refrigerated truck, and only the more experienced guys got to do that. Sometimes if there was bad weather and the pickers had to stop work, the work in the shed got caught up, and we stopped, too. That only meant we had to work later into the evening, though, because the pickers got paid by the load, not by the hour. When they weren't picking for whatever reason, they weren't making any money. Rick, Gregg, Frog, and I made 60 cents an hour. If we stayed for the entire summer until all the peaches had been picked, we were promised a bonus of a nickel for every hour we worked all summer. As that meant another 25 or 30 dollars—the equivalent of a week's pay—at the end of the summer, we did that. Keep in mind, though, that the cost of living was a little different then. Gas, for instance, was about 25 cents a gallon, and you could buy a movie ticket for the same quarter. The Metropolitan gas tank held eight gallons, and I could fill it up for less than two dollars. I could drive almost two weeks on a full tank since the Met's four-cylinder engine got about 40 miles per gallon. An extra bonus was that we were allowed to eat all the peaches we wanted while we were at work, but that got old pretty quickly. None of us were eating many peaches by the end of the summer, and I think Mr. McLeod knew it would work out that way. We brought sandwiches from home for lunch each day, and if we were told to be back in an hour or so, we'd go to a pool hall in town to eat and shoot pool. We were all so bad that the owner of the place said he should charge us by the hour instead of by the game.

That was my summer of 1968. The McLeod family treated us well, and we were all glad to have jobs and some extra money. Job satisfaction wasn't high on our list of priorities, so we were fairly content even though the work was repetitive and boring. We also knew that work in the packing shed was seasonal, and none of us saw much of a future as peach farmers or migrant workers. If we weren't thinking that way at the beginning of the summer, I think by the end of the peach season, all of us had a taste for something better.

Better for me in the summer of 1969—right after I graduated from high school—was work at Mafco Textured Fibers, Inc., which was also east of McBee on Highway 1 where the A.

O. Smith Water Heater plant is now located. The Mafco plant was still being completed during that summer, and I think they were short of workers. I interviewed for about two minutes with the personnel director and was hired. My peach farm buddies from the previous summer had found other employment, so I again made the drive north on Highway 151 to McBee and turned right on Highway 1 every day, six days a week. The work week was 60 hours, from 7:00 AM until 5:30 PM, Monday through Saturday, with 30 minutes for lunch. My hourly pay rate more than doubled from the peach farm to $1.25 per hour, so I was making $75.00 a week. In the first part of the summer, I was assembling machinery on the floor of the plant, and I don't think I ever figured out exactly what I was supposed to be doing. In my defense, I don't recall my job ever being explained to me very well either. At any rate, I was moved to another job pretty quickly. Mafco was a polyester manufacturing plant at that time and part of the process was thin fiber threads running through vertical heated grooves. There was a bank of these heated grooves, each groove four or so inches apart, that was about 50 feet long. My job was to walk up and down a platform walkway in front of that bank of heated grooves to be sure the threads kept moving. If any of them ever got hung up for any reason the fiber thread would scorch inside the groove, similar to food burning in a frying pan. The machinery would be stopped, and I had a squirt bottle of cleaner that I would shoot from a couple of feet away down the length of the groove until all of the brown, burned fiber was washed out. Then the machinery would be turned back on, the operation would resume, and I'd be walking up and down again looking for scorched fiber. I did that for ten hours a day. There was a break in that action for a few days during the summer when I was part of a crew that was assigned to sweep the parking lot in front of the plant. We'd gotten word that some of the big bosses were coming in for an inspection, and the local plant managers wanted everything looking good. To them, that meant the parking lot, too, which at that time was about the size of two football fields. Each crew member was given a push broom as leaf blowers apparently hadn't been invented yet. If you recall, McBee is in a part of our state known as The Sandhills, so there was plenty of action for us with those push brooms in that parking lot during the next several days. If I hadn't been convinced already, that assignment swept away any ideas that I may have had about a future with Mafco Textured Fibers, Inc.

So, what did I learn from my two summers in McBee? I learned that my future wasn't in peaches or any kind of farming for that matter. I also learned that I didn't want to work ten hours a day for six days a week at minimum wage. Although I didn't apply myself to my studies at Furman nearly as well as I should have, peaches and polyester made me realize the value of an education. Those summers helped me understand that all honest work is good and noble, but that I needed to have something better in mind.

32

Meter Reading for CP&L

The next summer I continued my upward mobility in the job market as I became a meter reader for Carolina Power & Light Company, which later became known as Progress Energy, Inc. It was by far the best summer job I'd had, and I was fortunate to keep it during the entire time I was in college. I even worked one year during the Christmas holidays when I was home from school. The Hartsville CP&L office was a great place to work, and Mr. Lyn Poe was the manager. Curly Pate and Jim Sweatt were the servicemen, and Wayne Earn and Charles Smith were the meter readers who trained me. Elijah Hayes, whose sons I later coached in football and basketball, also worked in the office. I would occasionally go to Cheraw to read meters for their office, and Mr. Bill Griggs, who was a former Hartsville serviceman, was the manager there. Mr. Poe and Mr. Griggs were fine men, and it was a privilege to work for both of them.

I don't think the process for determining electrical usage has changed much since those days. There's an electrical meter on the side of houses and buildings, and readings are still taken at a certain time each month of the number of kilowatt hours showing on the meter. The reading from the previous month is subtracted from the current reading, and a bill is sent for that month's electrical usage. The service area of each office was divided into geographical routes, and a meter reader walked the city neighborhood routes in which the houses and businesses were close together, and drove a truck if the route was in a rural area. The walking routes usually had around 500 meters to be read in a day, and the rural routes had about half that many. The routes were carefully sequenced so that travel between meters, whether walking or driving, was most efficient. Image was important, so I wore long khaki pants and a collared shirt. I had more hair back then, so I didn't wear a hat. A comfortable, sturdy pair of boots was a must for handling the miles of walking, and also for kicking at attacking dogs. Meter readers carried a book of cards, each one about three-by-eight inches, and there was a card for every address and meter on a route. Two or three pencils were carried, too, as each reading was recorded by filling in small bubbles on the card that corresponded with each of the five numbers showing on the meter. Meter readers also carried a receipt book, as part of the job was to collect past-due electric bills. Finally, it was necessary to carry a screwdriver and a pair of pliers. If there was a bill that was two or more months past due, and payment couldn't be collected, the meter reader turned the electricity off at the residence or business. As you'll see in just a minute, that's where the job could get really interesting.

Other than the summer heat, the most hazardous part of meter reading was encountering dogs that objected to tres-passing strangers. Coming around once a month just wasn't often enough to establish good relationships although I did quickly learn which ones just barked and which ones would try to take my leg off. One of the most aggravating situations was when a dog's owner would stand there telling me how sweet the dog was, and that it only barked and never bit anyone, while at the same time the little angel was latching onto the front of my shin. A dog might be man's best friend—and I've had some that I truly loved—but the opposite relationship was usually the case with meter readers. I was bitten by dogs at least twice each summer that I worked and once by a pony. One of the scariest and most dangerous situations I encountered was when I was working in Cheraw. I was on a walking route in a neighborhood one morning when a pack of five dogs attacked me. They were swarming and snarling and snapping all around me, coming closer all the time. I was kicking at them, and had my document book in one hand and pliers and screwdriver in the other, swinging and trying to keep them off me. I knew if I went down they'd tear me apart and I knew better than to turn and run, so I was slowly trying to make my way down the street to get away from them. I suppose that I finally landed enough kicks and blows for them to give up, or either they just got tired, but not before one leg of my khakis had been torn off. I got some strange looks during the rest of the day as I finished the rest of my route wearing half a pair of short pants.

Other interesting situations sometimes developed when a customer would tamper with a meter. Part of my training included checking the security of the lock that was on each meter box. That was because some people would cut the lock, remove the meter, and substitute a spare meter that had managed to come into their possession. They'd use the spare meter for a couple of weeks, put the real one back in and replace the lock when it was time for the meter reader to come around on the route, and their kilowatt hour usage for the month would magically be about half what it should have been. I drove up to a house on a rural route a couple of days earlier than usual one month, and when I walked to the meter box, the meter had been removed and replaced with some heavy-duty jumper cables. I'd obviously caught the electricity pirates red-handed with their scheme, so they sheepishly handed over the meter. I put it back in place, installed a new lock, and confiscated the jumper cables. I believe that CP&L randomly spot-checked that customer for a few months after that.

My most vivid meter reading memory is of a situation with a past-due bill, when—instead of the payment—I almost collected a 30-30 caliber bullet. I was again reading a rural route when I drove up to a trailer for which payment for electric service was two months late. I knocked on the door, and a big man—wearing nothing but a pair of short pants—answered. I politely explained the problem to him, and he told me in no uncertain terms that he had no intention of paying the bill. I then informed him that I'd have to turn the power off to the trailer. He said, "Do what you have to do, then." I went back to my truck, got my pliers and screwdriver, and walked over to the meter box which was on a pole about 20 feet from the front door of the trailer. I was standing in front of the meter box when I heard the sound of a click behind me. I turned back towards the door, and the gentlemen had leveled down on me with a 30-30 rifle—and had me in his sights. He said, "Boy, if you touch that meter, they'll carry you away from here." That's when something better came to my mind because I could feel my legs shaking inside my khaki pants. I slowly backed away and walked back toward the door as the man lowered the rifle. To shorten the story a bit, I'll tell you that—believe it or not—I talked the man into paying the bill. I found out while talking with him that his problem was with someone in our office who'd failed to get back in touch with him about a service issue. He was trying to gain some leverage by withholding payment on his bill. I told him that I would certainly get that information to the proper person at the office, and he wrote a check for the full amount. I'm just thankful that he didn't shoot the messenger.

Dr. Charlie Burry, Jr.

33

The Hitchhiker and Old Blue

When our daughters were students at Furman, we moved them back and forth to Greenville in our cars and using vans that we borrowed from Steve and Paula Terry and from Lee and Margaret Lanier. Our cars were loaded with clothing and personal belongings, and the vans—with all of the seats removed except in the front—carried things like rugs, futons, televisions, stereo systems, and the other basic necessities of life for young ladies who were attending college away from home. Move-in day was always an adventure, and a first-floor room assignment was a blessing, especially for the manual laborers. I used to suggest—only half-jokingly—that Furman ought to have EMS on standby for all of the middle-aged dads lugging stuff up and down two or three flights of stairs. By the time room setup was complete, computer connections were established with the network, parking permits secured, and it was time for mom and dad to leave, it had been a full day. I don't mean to make light of these moments, because having a child move away to college—whether it's the first time or the fourth time—is always an emotional, watershed event in the life of a family. It was that way in 1998 with Beth, it was again in 2004 with Caye, and it was in 1969, too.

When my parents helped me move into McGlothlin Hall at Furman University as a freshman in the fall of 1969, I carried everything that I had in a suitcase and a couple of cardboard boxes. There was no television or stereo to hook up because I didn't have either of those things. The room was furnished with two beds, two desks and wooden chairs, and two other slightly cushioned chairs. A linen service was available for bed sheets, pillow cases, and towels, so I didn't need to bring any of those items. There was a sink and mirror in the room; and communal showers, urinals, and toilets were located down the hall. Two telephones, located in booths halfway down the hall, served everyone on that floor of the dorm. There was no need for a parking permit because freshmen weren't allowed to have vehicles on campus, and I didn't own one anyway. A bus service was available for travel between Furman and downtown Greenville, but that area wasn't anything like the shopping, dining, and entertainment district that it is today. A couple of movie theaters and the locals cruising up and down Main Street were about the most exciting things you could find. You might be asking by now, how'd I make the trip home for a visit? Beth and Caye used to say that the distance between Hartsville and Greenville was perfect—close enough for them to get home when they wanted to come, but too far for mom and dad to make a surprise visit. But remember, they had cars, and I didn't. It wasn't practical for my parents to make two round trips to Greenville in one weekend, and I couldn't always find a ride with Bill and Pat (Twitty) Shelley, who were seniors. Bus or train service wasn't a convenient option, either. So, I hitchhiked.

Hitchhiking in the late 1960s and early 1970s may have been a bit uncertain, but it didn't hold near the potential danger that it does now. I won't pick up a hitchhiker today, no matter how innocent or needy the individual appears to be, much less think of doing it myself. When I was in college, however, hitching rides was a common and acceptable means of transportation, and there was no shortage of people who were more than happy to pick up riders. Jim Martin, whom I'd played basketball against when he was at McClenaghan

High School in Florence and who was also a Furman freshman, and I hitchhiked together several times. We'd just catch a ride or walk out to the Poinsett Highway entrance to the Furman campus, stick out our thumbs, and we'd be home four or five hours later. Sometimes we'd need only a couple of rides; other trips required three or four depending on our luck. On the return trip, my parents would take me to Exit 98 (Lugoff-Elgin) on I-20, let me out, and head back to Hartsville. The reason they took me there was because the section of interstate highway from Exit 98 on to Bishopville and Florence hadn't been built yet. My younger sister, Emily, says that she used to look out of the back window of the car as my mom and dad drove away with tears in her eyes until she couldn't see me anymore. I met a number of interesting people who picked me up, including a minister who preached to me for about 100 miles. I did catch a ride home with a couple of sketchy looking guys once, and I had them let me out about half a mile from my house because I didn't want them to know where my family lived. I will tell you that it was a good feeling to see a car's brake lights come on as it passed and then pulled over to the side of the road, and I never hesitated to jump in.

My Greenville-to-Hartsville transportation became more dependable during my sophomore year after I pledged a fraternity. Fulton "Big Cat" Elvington, who was from Nichols (near Mullins), was one of my new brothers, and he was always willing to have me ride along on his trips home, since Hartsville was on the way to Nichols. Actually, I didn't just ride along, as Fulton required me to be his chauffeur while he snoozed in the back seat of his Plymouth Roadrunner. Jane Hursey, recently retired Assistant Superintendent for Human Resources in the Darlington County School District, was a freshman from Darlington, and she usually rode shotgun. After dropping me at my house in Hartsville, she'd drive on to Darlington to her house, and then Big Cat was on his own the rest of the way. On

Sunday afternoons, Jane and Fulton would pick me up, and we were on the road back to Furman. I think Jane still has fond memories of those trips today.

By the end of the summer before my junior year at Furman, I had something better in mind. I'd saved enough money from my meter reading job to buy a car of my own, and my dad went with me to a Newsome Ford used car dealership that was across the Highway 151 Bypass from where Pam's Restaurant is now. With my dad as chief negotiator, I paid about $1,500 for a 1967 Ford Falcon Sports Coupe. The engine was six-cylinders, and it had a manual, four-in-the-floor transmission. I used to love the sound it made when I was coming off Poinsett Highway onto the Furman campus and downshifted to second gear. The color was navy blue, and Debby and I affectionately nick-named it "Old Blue." Old Blue provided me with dependable transportation for almost three years, and during that time I may have even picked up a few hitchhikers. Just like today, paying it forward in some manner made the world a better place.

34

Gregg Apartments and King Avenue

When I went to work at the Boys School, my first home address was at Country Club Apartments near Five Points and just off of Cherokee Road in Florence. It was a nice place, but the only thing really country club about the complex was that it had a swimming pool which I never had time to use. After I'd been there only a short time, I learned from Steve Taylor—one of my new teacher colleagues—that a place had become available in Gregg Apartments where he lived, which was on South Dargan Street and only about a quarter mile from the Boys School. The same company owned both complexes and graciously allowed me to move, even though the rent—$80 a month—was less than what I was currently paying across town. My second new Florence address in as many months was two stories with a living room, dining room, and kitchen downstairs, and two bedrooms and a bathroom upstairs. The apartment buildings—which still exist today—were fairly old even at that time, and were in a pretty setting of big, stately oak trees. The neighbors were all good people about my age or just a little older, and it was a comfortable social atmosphere. After I'd lived there a year, Debby and I got married, and she fit right in with everyone. It wasn't long before we had our first baby, a blonde cocker spaniel named Chuck. We enjoyed him, even when he howled at the train whistles about half a block away, and he was no trouble except for the time he ate our income tax returns. We jokingly referred to Chuck as our son, and it wasn't until we were talking with an insurance salesman one night that we realized how it had become second nature for us to do that. We'd made reference to Chuck in that manner a couple of times during the conversation when the gentleman asked who kept our son for us while we were at work. It dawned on us then, even though Chuck was right there in the living room with us, that the salesman thought we also had a human son. I decided we were too far down the road at that point to back up, so I casually said, "Oh, nobody, we just leave him out on the back porch." For some reason, the salesman quickly brought his presentation to a close and seemed to be in quite a hurry to leave. We never got a visit from Child Protective & Preventative Services (the precursor to DSS), so apparently the man decided to just let sleeping dogs lie.

Nothing lasts forever, though, and the original group of neighbors began to move out as they bought houses. We all had something better in mind. Our good friends who lived in the apartment adjacent to ours—the front doors were at right angles to each other and shared a front porch that was about five feet square—were among the first to go. A young woman who appeared to be single moved in and became our new next-door (literally) neighbor. After just a short while, we noticed that she seemed to be at home most of the time, frequently had company, and that most of her visitors were men. It was definitely a party-type atmosphere that was quite a bit different from the quiet couple who had lived there previously. Chuck didn't adjust well, either, and once he awakened us with his excited and insistent barking from the back porch in the middle of the night. I looked out of the upstairs bathroom window to check on him and saw a large white object moving quickly back and forth behind our apartment. Upon closer investigation from the back porch, I discovered that Chuck was barking at a large white turkey that our neighbor had tied to our clothesline. The turkey, which had apparently been kidnapped, was scared out of its mind and was running up and down the clothesline while Chuck went crazy. I brought Chuck inside, and everyone settled down for the rest of the night. When I got up the next morning, the turkey had either escaped or was being held for ransom at another location. There were other disturbances as well, like the Sunday afternoon that our neighbor got into a fight with one of her visitors in our front yard. She was wearing very short cut-off jeans and a bikini top, and as her antagonist left, he ripped off her bikini top and took it with him. That seemed to upset her quite a bit more, so she ran screaming and cursing after him, and threw a brick at his car as he peeled out. The straw that broke the camel's back, however, came when Debby arrived home from work one afternoon just as two male visitors were concluding a visit with our neighbor. The guys said something suggestive to Debby as she was unlocking our door, and she just ignored them. Not appreciating the slight, they proceeded to address her further with some vulgar and abusive language. By the time I arrived home, they had long departed, which was probably fortunate for me. I did, however, write a letter to our rental company that night threatening to sue them for violation of the portion of our lease guaranteeing the peaceful occupancy of the property—sharing with them the details of my displeasure. I delivered the letter the next morning, and that afternoon a representative of the company served our neighbor with an eviction notice. It wasn't long before we moved out, too, as we definitely had something better in mind.

Better for us at that time was located on King Avenue in Florence, which was in a quiet neighborhood with tree-lined streets. We'd found a small and attractive brick house that had been built in the 1940s for sale. It had a screened porch on the side of the house, a nice breakfast nook at the back of the kitchen, beautiful azaleas in the shrubbery beds all around the house, and a fenced back yard for Chuck. We signed a mortgage for $24,000, and our house payment was $180 a month.

We were only there for a year, however, before the Boys School was moved to Columbia, I took a job at Gilbert High School, and we moved to Lexington. A couple's first house is always special, though, and we were very proud of it. Debby did a cross-stitch of our King Avenue house that we had framed, and it hangs in our house today. There was only one strange thing about our new home. It was haunted.

One night not long after we'd moved in. Debby awakened, sensing that something was in our bedroom with us. When she opened her eyes, she saw what appeared to be a human figure at the foot of the bed. She was trying to call out or shake me awake but she was too frightened to make any noise or move. The figure then moved down her side of the bed, reached out, and touched her arm. The touch was warm to her skin, and then the apparition disappeared. Debby and I believe that it was a friendly ghost, someone from the house's past history welcoming us to our new home. We were glad that rather than trying to frighten us away, it had something better in mind.

King Avenue House

35

The 1985 Final Four

When I became a student at Furman, I got a taste of college basketball up close when I became a member of the freshman team. I didn't play much at all but managed to score points in Clemson's Littlejohn Coliseum and Georgia Tech's Alexander Memorial Coliseum. I had a front row seat for the varsity game when Furman's Joe Brunson outrebounded the entire South Carolina Gamecock frontline of Tom Owens, Tom Riker, and John Ribock in a 59-56 loss to a Frank McGuire team that had begun the season as the top-ranked team in the nation. At that time, Furman played its games downtown in the Greenville Memorial Auditorium, and I loved playing there because the portable floor had tremendous spring. Perhaps the best part of my Furman basketball experience, however, was the friendship that I developed with Steve McCammon, a varsity player who treated me like a real person, instead of just a lowly freshman. I've never forgotten his kindness and respect. Bob Dotson was my coach, and Frank Selvy—an All-American player at Furman who once scored 100 points in a game (the NCAA Division I record) against Newberry College—was the varsity head coach. Coach Dotson later became one of Denny Crum's assistants at Louisville for many years. Alan LeForce, who later had a highly successful career as college head coach, was also one of Coach Selvy's assistants. Coach LeForce was the head coach at The College of Charleston during the time that I was a graduate assistant coach at Francis Marion College.

During all this time, I'd dreamed about attending the ACC Tournament and the NCAA Final Four. I haven't made it to the ACC Tournament yet, but in 1985, the other part of my dream came true.

While I was coaching basketball at Hartsville High School, I joined with several other high school boys' coaches to form the Pee Dee Area Basketball Coaches Association. Our purpose was to gain publicity for our players and our teams and increase interest in high school basketball in the area. We met once a week at a restaurant in Florence to select Players of the Week and compile statistics for the week, and a couple of members of the media were usually there. We also had a banquet at the end of the season that was attended by Player of the Year candidates and other honorees and was covered by a local television station. The 1985 banquet was on Wednesday, March 27th, before the weekend of the NCAA Final Four in Lexington, Kentucky. Butch Estes, who had just been named as the new head coach at Furman, was our keynote speaker. Lewis Hill, who was the head coach at Francis Marion College, was also in attendance. I found myself seated beside my good friend, Tommy Johnson, who was the head coach at West Florence High School, and we were seated between Butch and Lewis. They were discussing their plans to drive to Lexington the next day, and Tommy and I were listening with more than just passing interest. Butch must have sensed that and said to us, "We've got some extra room in the van, why don't you guys go with us?" Lewis overheard him, and he said, "I've got space in my hotel room for two more people, and you're welcome to stay with me. Come on and go with us!" Tommy and I could hardly believe our ears and suddenly, we had something better in mind than going to school the next day. I went to a pay phone in the restaurant to call my principal, and told him I had a once-in-a-lifetime opportunity and needed to take personal leave through Tuesday (the championship game is played on

Dr. Charlie Burry, Jr.

Monday night) of the next week. Thankfully, he granted my request, as did my wife when I got home a couple of hours later.

The next morning, having absolutely no idea 12 hours earlier what I'd be doing, I was on the way to Lexington, Kentucky, and the spectacular Rupp Arena for the 1985 NCAA Final Four. The scenery was beautiful as we passed mile after mile of horse farms, Kentucky bluegrass, and sparkling white fences. The van was like a rolling coaches clinic as Tommy and I listened to Butch and Lewis talk basketball, and we occasionally offered opinions of our own. Upon crossing the Tennessee border, we were soon reminded that Kentucky is a basketball state, and when people there talk about ball, unlike in South Carolina, they're not talking about football. Tommy and I managed to make our way into several events for college coaches the next day, including the practices for all four teams, and we rubbed elbows with some basketball icons that we'd only seen on television. We were also able to visit a horse farm and saw those beautiful, powerful, and expensive animals up close. We couldn't find tickets for the two semi-final games on Saturday, so we watched on television from our hotel room as Villanova defeated Memphis State, and defending national champion Georgetown topped St. John's. On Sunday afternoon, we went to the College All-Star Game that is held in conjunction with the Final Four. The venue for that game was the old Memorial Auditorium, home to Coach Adolph Rupp's great teams before Rupp Arena opened in 1976, so seeing that iconic building was a treat. Best of all, we were able to score tickets for Monday night's championship game between the Wildcats and the Hoyas, coached by legends Rollie Massimino and John Thompson.

On April 1, 1985, little did Tommy and I know that we were about to witness what would be quite possibly the greatest NCAA Championship Game in history. The only other game that comes close is Jim Valvano's North Carolina State team upsetting Houston's Phi Slama Jama juggernaut in 1983. Villanova was a huge underdog, but they played what many basketball experts refer to as "The Perfect Game"—shooting 78%—and defeated Georgetown by a score of 66-64. It is still— 36 years later—one of the greatest upsets in college basketball history. My vantage point for this amazing game was at mid-court in the fourth row of Rupp Arena's upper deck across from the team benches. When I watch games on television from that venue today, I always locate that seat and remember when I was there and what I saw. It was one of the greatest sports experiences of my life, and I'll always be grateful to Butch Estes and Lewis Hill for giving me that opportunity. I still smile when I think of that night in Florence at the Pee Dee Area Basketball Coaches Association banquet when I didn't have anything better in mind than going to work the next day, but Butch and Lewis sure did.

Dr. Charlie Burry, Jr.

36

Make a Bucket List

Athletics has been a big part of my life for almost as long as I can remember. I was blessed when Mr. Hubert Twitty picked me to be a member of his Exchange team in Hartsville's Dixie Youth Baseball League when I was nine years old. I learned more baseball from Pee Wee Reese and Dizzy Dean on Falstaff's Game of the Week, but thankfully, not the English language. Around that same time, when my family lived on Oak Avenue in Hartsville, a guy named Daulton Keith lived across the street. Daulton was a running back on the Hartsville High School football team, and he became my idol. He wore jersey number 33 for the Red Foxes, and at a time when most football helmets had only a single-bar facemask, his helmet had two because he wore glasses. Daulton had a basketball goal in his backyard, and on Saturday mornings Jimmy Bell, Johnny Barfield, and Jim Shelley—Red Fox teammates—would come over to his house to play two-on-two. I'd sit on the grass in my front yard and watch them for as long as they played but never gathered enough courage to venture across the street for a closer look at my heroes. Within two or three years, I'd begun playing basketball myself with a group of guys, and on Saturdays and Sunday afternoons after church we'd sneak into the gym that was behind the three-story high school building on the corner of Carolina Avenue and Eighth Street. We were always able to find an unlocked window, and we played until the police came by and ran us out. The first organized basketball that I played was when I was in the ninth grade, and I managed to make the varsity team, coached by Mike Reidy, the next year. I played for Cliff Malpass during my junior year, and then Tim Watson was my coach when I was a senior. During my junior year in high school, I took a United States History course with Mrs. Lib Howle that I enjoyed, and I subsequently declared a history major two years later at Furman when Bob Dotson was my coach on the freshman team.

I believe that those two interests in my life—athletics and history—caused me to develop a special affinity for the old, tradition-laden sports venues that I'd seen on television over the years. I loved the parquet floor in the old Boston Garden where Bill Russell and John Havilcek played. I thought the ivy-covered outfield walls at Wrigley Field in Chicago where Ernie Banks always said, "Let's play two!" were beautiful in the summer. I tried to imagine standing on top of the Green Monster left-field wall at Fenway Park in Boston and looking down on the diamond where Ted Williams and Carl Yastrzemski became legends. Dodger Stadium in Los Angeles—although fairly recently constructed in 1962—was where my hero, Sandy Koufax, pitched. I wondered if I could stand the cold at Lambeau Field in Green Bay where Bart Starr and Paul Hornung played for Vince Lombardi. When I watched *The Bucket List* in 2007, that caused me to have something better in mind. I made a bucket list of my own, and I'm still working on it.

I checked the Boston Garden off my list in 1992 when Hal Baldwin and I made a weekend trip there for two games. Our dear friend, Beth Bass, arranged that trip for us, and we were able to tour the Garden while we were there. We visited the home team locker room—surprisingly small and sparsely furnished—where K. C. Jones gave his pre-game speeches and Bob Cousy laced up his black high-top basketball shoes. We dribbled basketballs on the same parquet floor where Sam

Jones and Dennis Johnson led Celtic fast breaks and made shots at the same goals on which Larry Bird drained his jumpers. We took pictures of the championship banners and retired numbers hanging from the rafters and imagined the Garden ghosts that are said to haunt opposing teams. We sat on the same bench where Red Auerbach lit up his cigars when the Celtics had clinched another win.

In 2014, I was able to check Wrigley Field off my list, at least partially. I'm going to have to make a return trip because we went in April, and the ivy wasn't green yet. The grass was though, in the same outfield where Billy Williams and Andre Dawson ran down fly balls, and on the same infield where Ryne Sandburg played second, and Ron Santo played third. Although way before my time, Wrigley was also home to Hall of Famers Grover Cleveland Alexander, Hack Wilson, and Rogers Hornsby, and it was awe-inspiring to know that the stadium was celebrating its one hundredth birthday when we visited. I ate a world-famous cheezborger at the original Billy Goat Tavern, where you can "butt in" any time. My daughter, Beth, and I were Bleacher Bums that sunny afternoon, and when I go back, I don't want to sit anywhere else.

Fenway Park in Boston earned a check mark in 2019 when I watched the Red Sox defeat the New York Yankees. We went on a tour of the stadium in the afternoon, saw every corner of the place from all vantage points, and got a running commentary on its history. I did stand at the top of the Green Monster, just as I'd imagined, and it was an amazing sight. We got a close-up view of the red seat in the right field grandstands that marks where a Ted Williams' 502-foot fly ball landed in 1946 that is still the longest home run ever seen at Fenway. Later that night, when Beth, Clay, and I entered the stadium and made our way to our seats just a few rows up from the left-field foul line, I felt as if I was walking into a dream. I could visualize Carlton Fisk dancing down the first-base line, waving his home run fair just inside the left-field foul pole to win Game Six of the 1975 World Series, and I could see Luis Tiant on the mound turn his back on the hitters during his windup. Best of all, we sang Neil Diamond's "Sweet Caroline" along with the crowd before the bottom of the eighth inning.

A more convenient trip that should be on every true base-ball fan's bucket list is to a venue with which you may not be familiar. Asheville, North Carolina, home of a minor-league team called the Tourists, is about 40 minutes from our cabin near Saluda. The Tourists play in a ballpark named McCormick Field that was constructed in 1924. The stadium is built into the side of a mountain, and you can't imagine a more picturesque setting. Because of the setting, the right field wall is only 300 feet from home plate, which would be a short poke for a home run were it not for McCormick's 36-foot monster wall of its own. The stadium's history includes appearances by Babe Ruth, Lou Gehrig, Jackie Robinson, and Henry Aaron, and even though its original wooden bleachers were replaced by concrete in 1991, you can still feel the tradition.

I've got a few more places to visit—I haven't been to Dodger Stadium and Lambeau Field yet—and I hope to be able to travel again when we get COVID under control. I also want to go to a Notre Dame home football game and attend an Army-Navy football game on the West Point campus. I want to see a University of Kansas basketball game in Phog Allen Field House and watch a game in Hinkle Field House on the Butler University campus in Indiana, where part of the movie *Hoosiers* was filmed. I hope to make another trip across the big pond the next time The British Open is played on the Old Course at St. Andrews, and I'd love to be in the center court grandstands at Wimbledon one day. Finally, I hope you've been making your own bucket list—if you don't already have

Dr. Charlie Burry, Jr.

one—while you've been reading this, and it certainly doesn't have to be about sports venues. I also want to visit the Mark Twain House in Hartford, Connecticut, go on a riverboat tour from Hannibal, Missouri, and return to the Ryman Auditorium in Nashville, Tennessee. Remember, it's always good to have something better in mind.

Beth Burry-Jackson and Charlie Burry at Billy Goat Tavern

37

Joining Arnie's Army

As I think back on my memories of my dad—he died almost 25 years ago—I don't recall his taking much leisure time until later in his life. In our early years in Hartsville, he couldn't afford that, as he was working at least 60 hours a week trying to turn the Hartsville 5 & 10 into a business that would support his family. He also did some moonlighting by building and installing fixtures, counters, and display cases for other retail businesses in neighboring towns. I've already told you a little about his interest in fishing, but after we moved to Hartsville, he started playing golf. I imagine the reason he became interested in that hobby was because of some of his business colleagues who played. Dan Coker, who owned and operated Fifth Street Cleaners was an excellent golfer, comes to mind. My dad only took the time to do that because all of the businesses in downtown Hartsville closed on Wednesday afternoons at one o'clock during those years. That was the only time he played golf, and I'm sure he wouldn't have done that if he'd had to keep the store open. He'd usually let me tag along to play with him, and I had a small, canvas golf bag with four sawed-off wooden clubs. My dad's clubs had steel shafts, but they had a wood veneer to make them appear to be like the hickory shafts from which golf clubs were originally made. Steel shafts began making an appearance in the 1920s, and this was in the early 1960s, so you can imagine how old those clubs must have been. The Hartsville Golf Club (now Hartsville Country Club) at that time was a nine-hole course, and Mr. Art Townley was the golf pro there. Like many part-time golfers and golf fans, my dad's favorite professional golfer was Arnold Palmer. He was popularly called "The King" and was the first superstar of televised golf in the 1950s. Palmer, Jack Nicklaus, and Gary Player were known as "The Big Three" during the 1960s, and they popularized and commercialized golf around the world. My dad played golf on Wednesday afternoons, and on Sunday afternoons, he watched on television as Arnie won tournaments, most notably, The Masters.

I had maintained a mild interest in golf myself, playing occasionally in high school and then bringing my clubs to Furman once I had a car in which to transport them. As I began my coaching career, I found little time to play golf and became more of a television fan of the sport. I did play golf on the morning of the day I got married, however, and my bride still points out my sunburned face in our wedding pictures. The four major golf tournaments—the U. S. Open, the British Open, the PGA, and The Masters—were must-see TV for me. The Masters became a particular favorite because it's played every year at Augusta National Golf Club in Augusta, Georgia, which is just across the South Carolina state line. The tournament's close proximity to Hartsville—just a little more than two hours away—moved it up near the top of my bucket list, and I wanted to take my dad with me. Tickets to The Masters—even back then—were extremely hard to come by, though, and every spring for two or three years I'd asked around town about borrowing a couple of passes for one day of the tournament without any luck.

People that I talked to suggested I go to a day of the practice rounds on Monday, Tuesday, or Wednesday instead of the actual tournament; so, on Tuesday, April 7, 1987, I made a trial run. I left Hartsville at about 7:00 AM and was on the hallowed grounds of Augusta National before the dew burned off the grass. At that time, practice round tickets were first-come/first-served, and all you had to do was pay $15 for a credential, and you were in the gallery. Today, you have to be a lottery winner to be eligible to purchase tickets, and I've been shut out for ten straight years since Jimmy Harrell and I went in 2011. But in 1987, I was amazed by the perfectly manicured fairways, lightning-fast greens, smooth-as-glass ponds, huge banks of azaleas in full bloom, the thundering roars of the patrons echoing through the tall pines, and seeing up close the golf pros that I'd only seen on television. Augusta National is located on Washington Road in Augusta, an area not unlike any other thoroughfare of strip malls in America, but when you walk through the gates, it's like stepping into another world. While I was there that day, I spent a few minutes at the practice range within arm's length of Augusta native Larry Mize listening to him talk with friends, never dreaming that five days later, I would watch on television as he chipped in from 140 feet on the second sudden-death playoff hole to win the tournament. It was a wonderful day, and I made up my mind before I left that my dad was coming back with me the next year.

We arrived around 9:00 AM on the first Tuesday in April 1988, and I was a proud son to be able to provide such an experience for my dad. He was every bit as taken by the beauty and the tradition of Augusta National as I had been when I saw it for the first time. We hung around the practice putting green for a while, saw old-timers like Sam Snead, Billy Casper, and Julius Boros, and then meandered over to the tenth tee. As we walked on down to the 11th hole and Amen Corner, where the tournament is often won or lost on Sundays, I could sense a spring in my dad's step. We spent some time sitting in the bleachers behind the 12th tee watching the players come through, and then walked on out to the outer reaches of the course. By the time we got back to Amen Corner, it was time for a couple of the famous Masters pimento cheese sandwiches for lunch. After that, we walked past the Eisenhower tree and back up to the 18th green and the clubhouse. I knew my dad was enjoying himself, but I could sense a bit of anxiety, too. The fly in the ointment was that we'd seen Jack Nicklaus, Gary Player, and many other great golfers, but Arnold Palmer hadn't shown up yet. An hour or so later, still no Arnie, and I could tell my dad was getting tired because the course has a lot more hills than the way it appears on television. I think he was about ready to suggest that we call it a day, when we spotted a crowd coming our way surrounding none other than The King. At that moment, my dad caught his second wind, and he had something better in mind than going home. We became loyal foot soldiers in Arnie's Army for the rest of the afternoon. His biggest thrill, I think—and mine, too—was when Palmer was walking up a fairway within about ten yards of us. There were just the two of us at that spot outside the ropes, and my dad— almost like a little kid—called out, "Hey, Arnie!" The great man looked over, smiled, gave a little wave, and replied, "Hey, how ya doin'?" Arnold Palmer, God rest his soul, had spoken to my dad, and that was all we needed to top off our day.

38

Catfishing and Coon Hunting

After a ball game on Friday night, if you're looking for something to do besides sitting around the house all day Saturday, I've got another idea. If the grass needs to be cut, and you're looking for a good reason not to do it, here's a suggestion. If your wife has a shopping trip planned, and you need something far more important to do, look no further. When you've just drawn an unlucky card out of the honey-do jar on a Saturday morning, try pulling this ace from up your sleeve. Or, if your television won't get anything but Hallmark movies after supper, here's a good way to change the channel. When your 30-minute afternoon nap turns into a two-hour snooze, and you can't get to sleep at night, you might as well do this. If your doctor has prescribed more exercise for you, try taking this kind of walk instead of getting on the treadmill. When you're feeling like your evenings are just too boring, this kind of nightlife will provide some excitement. If any of the things I've just mentioned ring true to you, I've got something better in mind. You need to go catfishing on the Big Pee Dee River, or you ought to get with some guys and go coon hunting. I've done both, and either one will cure what ails you.

My catfishing colleagues from back in the day were Harvey Drawdy, Stan Drawdy, Harmon Baldwin (RIP), Hal Baldwin, and Jimmy Harrell. Harvey was a long-time principal of Pate Elementary School in Darlington before retiring. Stan is one of Harvey's sons (Rick is the other) who coached for a long time in Darlington and Hannah-Pamplico, and he's in real estate now. Harmon Baldwin was the director of Parks and Recreation in Darlington for 43 years and was also on the Darlington County School Board. Hal is one of Harmon's sons (Andy is the other) who coached and taught with me in Hartsville for a number of years and is one of my best friends. Jimmy Harrell is a veteran of a long coaching career in Society Hill and Darlington, a state championship coach in basketball and baseball, and one of my best friends. Our Saturday would begin with breakfast at the B & B Restaurant in Darlington where we'd decide who would fish with whom that day. What I really mean by that is who would have to take Jimmy in his boat because he was bad luck and never caught any fish. Three of us would sit at a table and match quarters, and the odd man had to take Jimmy. Whoever that was would always feign disgust, Jimmy would pretend to be all indignant, and we'd all have a good laugh to start the day.

We put our boats into the Big Pee Dee River near where Highway 34 crosses the river going east out of Darlington. There's a horseshoe bend in the river not far from the landing where it's a little shallow and rough, but after that my jon boat easily handled the trip upriver. Harvey was our expert guide, having fished the river for many years, so all three boats headed to where he thought a good catfish hole might be. If no one had been able to find any spoiled shrimp or other kind of rancid meat in the freezer, we used worms for bait. Catfish, being bottom-feeders, aren't at all particular about what they eat. Catfishing isn't hard, either, as all you do is bait a hook on a weighted rig that will allow the bait to float about three feet off the bottom of the river, throw the rig out downriver, rest the rod on the side of the boat at about a 45-degree angle, and sit back to watch the tip of the rod. When the tip of the rod starts to jump, that means a catfish (or an eel) has picked up the bait.

If you're awake and paying attention enough to notice when this happens, you set the hook (hopefully) and reel in a nice catfish. When you're ready to take the catfish off the hook, it's good to grab it with your thumb and second finger behind its two spines because getting stuck with one will sting for a while. If you happen to catch an eel instead of a catfish, it's best to just cut your line and let it drop back in the river. Taking an eel off a hook usually results in the eel wrapping itself around your arm—which is not a pleasant experience—and it's even harder to get one off your arm than it is a fishing hook. Hopefully, the end of the day results in a catch big enough for a good fish fry or catfish stew. The best thing about catfishing, though, is it leaves plenty of time for conversation. Harvey and Harmon, being a little older, were absolute fountains of knowledge about local politics, social issues, education, and sports, and they knew plenty of good jokes, too. I still appreciate their wisdom to this day, and the opportunity to sit on the river with them for a few hours on Saturdays was a true blessing.

I'll have to confess now that I've only been coon hunting one time, and it was probably 30 years ago. I am familiar with coon dogs, however, having attended several Coon Dog Day festivals in Saluda, North Carolina. They are fast, good-looking scent hounds with an average weight of about 65 pounds, and they come in a variety of colors. Harvey was an avid coon hunter as well as a fisherman, and I think Stan and Hal had coonhounds at the time, too. On this particular hunt, we went into the woods at night because, well, apparently that's a good time to hunt raccoons. It was also cold that night, so those of us who didn't have dogs were in charge of building and tending a large campfire. The hounds were turned loose, and they headed into the woods to search for the scent of their prey. Coon hunting at this point consisted of standing around the campfire, trying to stay warm, and listening for the dogs to bay. Experienced coon hunters can tell by the sound of their dogs baying when they're still on a chase or whether they have the racoon treed. Once a raccoon is treed, the real hunters followed the sound to retrieve their dogs and bring them back to the fire. Those of us who were just along for the fun kept the fire going. I recall the eerie sight of Hal coming back through the woods to the fire with his dog on a leash, both of them illuminated only by the searchlight on the miner's helmet that he was wearing.

As you've probably figured out by now, coon hunting—at least for me—was not even as strenuous as catfishing, and standing around the campfire was much like sitting in a boat on the Big Pee Dee River. But the opportunities were just as ripe for listening to the knowledge and humor of the older men, and the conversations were just as rich with their wisdom. For me, although I did like to catch fish, catfishing wasn't about coming home with a full cooler, and coon hunting wasn't about treeing a raccoon. I had something better in mind, and that was relaxing, learning from, and having fellowship with good friends and men for whom I have the greatest respect.

39

In the Middle of Nowhere

At some point in my life, I figured out that there's a difference between being lonely and being alone. I don't know that any-one likes the bereft feeling of loneliness, especially during the difficult times of life. From time to time, we all need someone who'll listen to us, empathize with us, and share our sorrows. Family and dear friends often provide the medicine that we need to ease the pain of loneliness in those times. It's also important to be able to share the joys of life with others. For example, picture Jim Valvano immediately after his Wolfpack upset Houston for the 1983 NCAA National Championship, rac-ing around the basketball court looking for someone to hug. Coach Valvano certainly didn't stay lonely for long, but in the stark reality of life's truly trying times, loneliness can be crushing. It's usually not a matter of choice, and if it is, it's not healthy. On the other hand, being alone—although not always—is more often a matter of preference. We can choose to be in the company of others or not. We can go out to a restaurant, or we can pick up supper and bring it home. The silence of reading in solitude can be the soothing comfort that we need after a hectic day of work. Listening to music alone, even if it's using earbuds, means you don't have to worry about anyone else liking country music. Being alone can summon relaxation that eases our minds, massages our muscles, and seeps into our bones. It's certainly a matter of personal preference, but in some circumstances, the idea of being in a place which is isolated from the rest of the world can be just about the best feeling you can have. About 25 years ago, with something a little better in mind, I found such a place.

Leon and Betty Coward have a vacation home near the edge of the Blue Ridge Mountains near Saluda, North Carolina, that is aptly named Mountain Refill (because Leon is a retired pharmacist). They graciously allowed Debby and I to use their place a couple of times a year, starting back when I was still coaching football. After the pressure of what sometimes was a 15-game season, a few days at Mountain Refill were just what the doctor ordered. I remember the first time we went there, the thing that struck both of us most was the silence. There was absolutely nothing to hear, only the silence. And, even after a beautiful sunset when the cicadas started chirping and the whippoorwills began calling, the darkness of only a starlit sky was comforting. During those years at Mountain Refill, I began dreaming of having a place of our own like that. I must admit here that I used the phrase "I began dreaming" in the previous sentence because while Debby enjoys the mountains—at least when it's warm—she much prefers the beach. Anyway, about six years ago, I was able to convince her to build the log cabin in the mountains of which I'd dreamed. Our place, also near Saluda, is located on Next To Last Road, which is just off of The Last Road. I'll save you the trouble of trying to locate it on MapQuest or a GPS because you won't find it. And, if you come to our cabin, you're either looking for us, or you're lost. There are a couple of neighbors within 100 yards or so of our cabin, but you can't see their houses from our place when the leaves are out, so it is very much a feeling of quiet solitude. The first time that Hal and Donna Baldwin visited us there, I met them at the Saluda exit on I-20, and they followed me on the rest of the eight-mile trip to the cabin. When we got there after the last two miles on a gravel road, Hal climbed out of his truck and sarcastically asked, "Don't you think you could have found a place a little more out of the way?" You'd have thought that we were in the middle of nowhere.

I can assure you—after a trip that our family made about six years ago—that you don't know the real meaning of the phrase "in the middle of nowhere" until you've been to Arizona. In the spring before our 40th wedding anniversary, Beth and Caye suggested a special trip to celebrate the occasion and asked us where we'd like to go. I pulled out my bucket list and soon settled on the Grand Canyon. Debby had never been there, either, so we started looking at flights to Phoenix. Our anniversary is in August, so even though we were hesitant about visiting Arizona in the summer, we decided to go in July before I became immersed in the start of the school year. Our rationale for that timing was helped by an understanding that the dry heat (due to the lack of humidity) in that part of the country— even though the actual temperature may be higher—doesn't seem as oppressive as in South Carolina. So, we flew to Phoenix and spent the first two days of our trip in Scottsdale, resting from the flight, being tourists, and adjusting to the time change. The next day we drove north to Sedona to view the amazing red rock canyon formations for which that area is famous. We had an Airbnb cabin rented for several days, so we were able to set-tle in comfortably to enjoy the spectacular scenery and sunsets. My one piece of unsolicited tour guide advice is that if you ever visit Sedona, be sure to take a helicopter ride through the red rock canyons for an absolutely amazing experience. Sedona is a vibrant arts community and known as a spiritual haven, and there are numerous other interesting things to do and places to see, including the Chapel of the Holy Cross, Cathedral Rock, and a sunset at the Airport Mesa.

The southern rim of the Grand Canyon was our primary destination, and that is about a two-hour drive north of Sedona, so we scheduled that for a day trip. After getting off I-40 west of Flagstaff, traveling up Highway 64 to the Grand Canyon is without a doubt the most desolate territory I've ever seen. The only consistent sign of humanity was the wildlife fencing along both sides of the highway to keep animals from crossing. Other than that, what we saw in every direction was miles and miles of desert, sagebrush, and cactus. Every few miles, far out in the distance, we'd spot a little single-wide trailer baking in the sun. I couldn't imagine living in a place like that, or what those people did to support themselves, or how they even survived in that environment. The specter of that degree of solitude is what caused the thought to first cross my mind about not knowing the real meaning of "in the middle of nowhere" until you've seen that part of Arizona. The view was actually a bit unsettling to me, and I checked both the gas and engine temperature gauges on our rental car frequently.

Having said all of that, the Grand Canyon was positively astounding. I don't care how many pictures you've seen of it, the first time you view it in person literally takes your breath away. The majesty of it, the colors, and the realization of how it was sculpted is almost too much to comprehend. We all took dozens of pictures, and Debby and I have one of them—an amazingly clear shot from my cell phone, enlarged, matted, and framed by Scott Hupfer—hanging in our den to commemorate our trip to the Grand Canyon. It represents a wonderful memory, one that we'll always be deeply grateful to our girls for sharing with us. Every time I think of Arizona, though, I also remember a different perspective—and, in all honesty, probably a representation unfair to the beauty of that state—of what it's really like to be in the middle of nowhere.

Beth Burry-Jackson, Debby Burry, Caye Burry

Dr. Charlie Burry, Jr.

40

The Burrys Are Coming!

On April 18, 1775, Paul Revere, William Dawes, and Samuel Prescott rode through the night to warn American colonists that British troops were crossing the Charles River in preparation for a march on Lexington and Concord. That event was immortalized in the poem "Paul Revere's Ride" by Henry Wadsworth Longfellow. Longfellow's use of poetic license taxes the historical accuracy of his composition: because the mission depended on secrecy, Revere did not actually shout the fabled phrase, "The British are coming!" Yet the midnight ride of Revere and his two friends did successfully warn people within 25 miles of Boston of the British invasion. Almost 189 years later, on February 7, 1964, another British invasion of America (ignoring the War of 1812) was initiated when The Beatles landed at Kennedy Airport in New York. Two days later, the band appeared live on *The Ed Sullivan Show* in a televised performance watched by an estimated one-third of the entire United States population. During the next three years, other musical acts from the United Kingdom made successful American debuts in what became known, officially, as the British Invasion. Then, some 54 years after The Beatles' American debut, the Burry family—led by Caye Marie Burry—launched a return invasion of England. Caye, Colin (Caye's fiancé), Beth, and I landed at London's Heathrow Airport on July 10, 2018, and we encountered only token resistance from customs agents and airport security. Apparently, they didn't have any advance warning from a Brit's midnight ride that the Burrys were coming. This all transpired because Caye, just as the American patriots did in their desire for independence, had something better in mind. Here's how it happened.

Caye graduated magna cum laude from Furman University in 2008 with a major in Communication Studies. She spent a couple of months in Hartsville after graduation and then moved to Cleveland, Ohio—mainly because that was where Beth was living at the time, and the economic crisis of 2008 made living with family an appealing option. She had also spent the previous summer in Cleveland exploring a potential career path in journalism, and after working for the music editor at the now defunct *Cleveland Free Times* and stumbling into an abruptly vacated internship position at the Rock & Roll Hall of Fame and Museum, she decided to return to further her career in nonprofit development instead. She worked full-time for Junior Achievement of Greater Cleveland as a Program Coordinator, recruiting volunteers and raising money for K-12 financial literacy programming for students in northeast Ohio. Her communications degree served her well in each of these positions, but she was seeking more professional fulfillment (and, truth be told, a warmer climate). After two years in Cleveland, she relocated to the nation's capital, seeking both employment and a place to live. Her courage and initiative were rewarded with some good fortune, and she found both employment and housing in DC pretty quickly. She continued her work in nonprofit fundraising, eventually forging a path in full-time grant writing thanks to the mentorship and support of a fellow colleague at Washington National Cathedral. That path proved short-lived, however. Caye admits that she never relished asking people for money, and unfortunately, that was one of the essential functions of the job. She has always had a creative nature, and that led her to explore a long-held interest in interior architecture and design. She got her foot in the door of that industry with

Dr. Charlie Burry, Jr.

CallisonRTKL, a global architecture and design firm, as a marketing and public relations writer. It was during that time that she identified an interior design school that would allow her to earn her degree while maintaining her current employment in DC. The school was KLC School of Design in London, England. Caye Burry had something better in mind, and her own British invasion had begun to take shape.

Over the course of seven three-month-long terms, KLC provided Caye with training in residential and commercial design and general business practices. She learned the entire design process, including conceptual design, spatial planning, building construction, and the study of materials and finishes. The program was built around a series of portfolio projects intended to give students an experience comparable to the inner workings of a real design studio. All of that was the easy part. The distance learning—meaning across time zones and the Atlantic Ocean—had its inherent challenges, including highly frustrating technical glitches that occurred regularly. The instructors pushed hard, and the curriculum encouraged independent learning; anyone with insufficient drive and commitment would inevitably fall short. The in-person instruction obviously took place on the KLC campus in London, so Caye traveled there quarterly with all her portfolio materials in tow for comprehensive course seminars. The challenges posed by distance learning—when we were accustomed to most of our interactions being face-to-face—exacerbated by the logistical difficulties demanded a degree of persistence that I find hard to even imagine. There were many tearful, late-night phone conversations, mostly between Caye and her mom, during which the best we could offer from 400 miles away was: "Just hang in there, baby girl; it'll all be over soon."

After two and a half long years, however, the end was in sight. We booked our flight from Dulles International Airport near

DC to Heathrow to attend the graduation ceremony of Caye Marie Burry from KLC School of Design. I'd never been across the Atlantic Ocean, so a trip to London was doubly exciting for me. It's a taxing trip physically, so unfortunately Debby's fibromyalgia didn't allow her to go. The first thing we did upon arrival was retire to a Yotel sleeping pod in the airport for a three-hour nap to recover from the flight. That might be the best three hours of sleep I've ever had in my life. We then traversed the 15 miles—um, 25 kilometers—to our Airbnb in the Maida Vale neighborhood of west London, caught our breath, and headed into the city. Caye and Beth were leading the excursion, so the first place we ended up was the world-famous Liberty Department Store, where Debby's souvenir gift was purchased (first things first). The next day, we visited the Tower of London to see the Crown Jewels, which reminded me that I also needed to purchase an anniversary gift sometime soon. We proceeded on foot to the River Thames and took our pictures in front of the real London Bridge. The following day, we ate breakfast in Hyde Park (they didn't have grits), visited Buckingham Place (the Queen wasn't available to see us), and sampled lunch at multiple food stalls in the famed Borough Market. One evening, I ordered shepherd's pie in an honest-to-goodness English pub, The Scarsdale Tavern, where we watched the English soccer—um, football—team's televised World Cup semi-final match. We also visited the awe-inspiring St. Paul's Cathedral and viewed centuries of British history, including Poet's Corner, in Westminster Abbey. The day after KLC commencement, we traveled about 75 miles northwest of London to the Cotswolds, which features beautiful rolling terrain with mile after mile of centuries-old stone fences. Shopping, sightseeing, and lunching in the quaint village of Moreton-in-Marsh were the perfect ways to decompress.

While I saw many wonderful landmarks in and around London that I'd previously only read about or seen in pictures,

Dr. Charlie Burry, Jr.

I'd be remiss to gloss over the real reason for the trip. Caye's graduation was the culmination of a dream come to fruition through unbelievably hard work and diligence. It was a celebration of sorts for Colin, too, for his patience, faithful support, and deeply caring love, without which Caye would have been lost. They got married in October following our trip, and Debby and I are incredibly proud of both of them. Fittingly, one of my best memories of the trip is witnessing Caye's happy dance upon opening an email with her first job offer from an interior design firm only two days after graduation. After a couple of job changes—one due to the pandemic—she now works as an interior designer at the United States Department of State Bureau of Overseas Buildings Operations. Time will tell if this will be a long-term gig, but one thing I know—she usually has something better in mind. Whatever it might be, maybe our family will get another trip out of it. I think I'd like to invade France or Italy next time.

Charlie Burry, Beth Burry-Jackson, Caye Burry, Colin Sloand

Section 5—
This Had Better Be a Joke

I've known Jimmy White for what seems like most of my life. We played Dixie Youth Baseball against each other—he was on the Moose team, and I played for Exchange—and our friendship continued through our days together as members of the Hartsville High School graduating class of 1969. College sent us separate ways—Jimmy went to Newberry College while I attended Furman—but our career paths brought us together again when I came back to our alma mater in 1978 to teach and coach. Jimmy made it back to Hartsville a few years before I did, and by the time I returned he had already begun to establish himself in a baseball coaching career that would lead to more than 500 wins, two state championships, and Hartsville High School's baseball facility being named in his honor. He was an excellent football coach as well, whose teams at Hartsville Junior High School helped build the foundation of the Red Fox program at the high school. Jimmy is also well-known as part of the radio broadcast team for Red Fox football today.

I got to know Hal Baldwin when he came to Hartsville to teach and coach three years after his 1976 Clemson graduation. Even though he has roots in Darlington as a St. John's Blue Devil, he soon adopted Hartsville as home, and he's been here ever since. Hal taught at Hartsville Junior High School for a number of years with Jimmy before they both moved to the Social Studies department at the high school. Hal and I coached football together for several years, but I owe him my greatest debt of gratitude for coaching the junior varsity boys' basketball team and assisting me with the varsity team during that time. He was an outstanding coach in both sports, probably kept me from getting more technical fouls than I did, and was unfailingly loyal. Hal also did a wonderful job in the classroom, and his students loved him. One of his former students contacted me on Facebook a few months ago inquiring about how to get in touch with him. Hal's former student is a teacher herself now, and she wanted to let him know that she tries to teach her classes in the same ways that he taught her. I don't think there could be a greater compliment for a teacher.

Having said all of that, I must also tell you that Hal Baldwin and Jimmy White are the two most accomplished and imaginative practical jokers that I have ever known. Paul Newman and Robert Redford in the 1973 movie *The Sting* were only amateurs by comparison. The fact that these gentlemen happen to be two of the best friends of my life has resulted in my own reputation being somewhat sullied, merely through guilt by association. I can't count the number of times that I've been unfairly accused of being the perpetrator of practical jokes when in truth, one or both of them have been the true culprits. To make matters worse, they've even sunk so low as to make me the target of their hilarity at times when I've lowered my guard. Finally, the fact that their own wives have fallen victim to their shenanigans only solidifies their well-earned reputations. Should there be any doubt about these two jokers, I'll present evidence of the above charges in the following chapters and let you be the judge.

Dr. Charlie Burry, Jr.

Jimmy White, Charlie Burry, Hal Baldwin

41

Exhibit A: Toothpaste in My Shoes

Coaches clinics are fertile ground for practical jokes, as are football camps. While clinics are certainly purposeful and beneficial in terms of learning more about coaching, those events are also times for relaxation and catching up with old friends. I think that I sometimes learned more from conversations outside the lecture halls between sessions than I did inside. As I've mentioned before, the coaching fraternity produces lifetime relationships, and the camaraderie is especially enjoyed. I don't think I've ever known a coach who didn't have a good sense of humor, even though some mask it pretty well. The intensity inherent in coaching, even in high school, requires opening a pressure valve from time to time and enjoying a good story or a funny joke is a good way to do that. You also get to know people better when you live with them for a few days—sometimes better than you'd like. I'm reminded of a clinic when one of our coaches slept in the bathtub with a blanket and pillow because his roommate snored so loudly. The down time in the hotel rooms after lectures was particularly ripe for practical jokes, especially if Jimmy White and Hal Baldwin were around. Football camp is much more intense than a clinic, but the potential is still present for some levity. Most of the time, the fun was pretty clean.

A number of years ago during the last week in July, the Hartsville High School coaching staff was attending the South Carolina Athletic Coaches Association (SCACA) Clinic in Columbia, which at that time was held in the old Carolina Inn hotel on Assembly Street. Jimmy and Hal were rooming together, and I was rooming with Dean Boyd who was coaching at Hartsville at the time. We had some spare time after lunch one day, and we all decided to walk a few blocks over to the State Department of Education Rutledge Building so that Jimmy could check on a certification issue. As we walked along the sidewalk, Jimmy started complaining about his feet being hot. We reminded him that it was July, and that everything was hot, but he kept talking about his feet. An hour or so later when we'd gotten back to the Carolina Inn, it was obvious that Jimmy was in some discomfort. We went up to our rooms where he anxiously removed his shoes and discovered the problem. Earlier in the day, someone had squirted Close-Up toothpaste into his shoes. It was the cinnamon red gel-type toothpaste, so Jimmy's socks had turned red, and it was the cinnamon ingredient that was burning his feet. We all fell out laughing as he headed to the bathtub to wash his feet in some cold water. Fortunately, he'd brought along another pair of shoes, which he carefully checked each time he put them on the rest of the time we were there. Dean finally confessed to being responsible for the prank, and if you know Jimmy White, you can bet that he had already begun planning his retaliation. I just didn't think that I would be one of the targets.

A couple of weeks later, we were at football camp in Laurinburg, and our coaching staff was staying in a suite of dorm rooms. We closed and locked our doors only when we were going to the practice field, so access for anyone who had mischief in mind was pretty easy. It was Wednesday and Parents' Day, which meant that the first big scrimmage of the week was scheduled for 2:00 that afternoon. We knew we'd be going against Summerville for a good portion of the afternoon, and Coach John McKissick's Green Wave was still the measuring stick that we used to gauge our program's progress, so all of us were fired up about that. There are a lot of unknowns about the first scrimmage of camp, however, and Dean and I were a little antsy about how our defensive backs would do against Summerville's passing attack. We left the dorm a little after 1:00 for the practice field to supervise stretching and calisthenics, to run our players through some agility drills, and to prepare our position groups for the scrimmage. The crowd of parents and others who had come from both communities had already begun to gather around the edges of the field, and you could feel a bit of excitement in the air.

Strangely, I could also begin to feel a bit of moisture inside my shoes. I didn't pay much attention to it at first because I certainly had other things on my mind, and I didn't notice Jimmy White and Hal Baldwin watching me, either. The scrimmage began, and right from the start the action was intense and the coaching was aggressive on the part of both teams. After each of our offensive plays, I was moving quickly to the ball to coach up our running backs, and then getting back to the huddle to hear the next play call. While we were on defense, Dean and I were both running around in the secondary, talking to our corners and safeties about their alignments, reads, run support angles, and pass drops. I also began to notice a squishy feeling inside my shoes, and I started looking for Jimmy and Hal. They were on the sidelines, and every time I looked their way, they appeared to be either closely watching the scrimmage or totally engaged in conversation with others. They were playing their innocence to the hilt, and it was a while before I could catch Jimmy's eye. When that happened, it was just too much for him, and he and Hal both burst out laughing.

Meanwhile, the toothpaste had started to foam up and seep out of the mesh portions of my shoes. To make things worse, the grass had been mowed earlier that day, and grass clippings had begun sticking to the foam. After another 30 minutes or so, in the middle of the biggest scrimmage of the week, my feet resembled a couple of Chia pets. Even our players had started to notice, and I was getting questioning looks. By that time, my buddies couldn't conceal their glee. They were giggling like a couple of kindergarten kids, and every time I walked close to them, I was cursing them under my breath. Thankfully, they'd used Crest and not Close-Up toothpaste, so I was able to finish the scrimmage without taking my shoes off and going barefoot.

The upside of their toothpaste trick was that it put me on offense again, and both of the scoundrels were extremely wary for the rest of the week. Sometimes knowing that a thing is going to happen—but not knowing when—is worse than the actual event. That's the position they were in, and I enjoyed it while I could. What goes around comes around, and they knew it. The other good thing was that for a couple of weeks, my toenails were sparkling white, and my feet had a smell of minty freshness. I could have been in a toothpaste commercial.

42

Just What's the Meaning of This?

For better or for worse, I've learned a lot from Hal Baldwin and Jimmy White over the years about the fine art of planning, engineering, and executing practical jokes. While the ability to create embarrassing scenarios for others just seems to come naturally to them, it might take other less gifted folks years to develop those qualities and master the techniques. You'll find keys to success in the following list:

1.   One should be imaginative and able to see the potential for a good joke in even the most common circumstances. For instance, most people wouldn't see that potential in an ordinary tube of toothpaste.

2.   Such an imagination should be coupled with a high degree of resourcefulness, as an accomplished joker must be able to use almost anything as a prop, bait, or tool in constructing the desired scenario. Again, a normal person wouldn't think of a pair of running shoes as being a key piece in a practical joke.

3.   A devious mind, however, instantly connects those two components—toothpaste and running shoes—to formulate a prank that has lived in infamy, been retold many times over the years, and now even has made its way onto the pages of a book.

4.   The factor that separates the consistently successful jokester from the rest of the field, however, is nerves of steel. When a sting is playing out perfectly, just the

Dr. Charlie Burry, Jr.

slightest hint of nervousness or indecision can cause the whole enterprise to fall apart. Even when one is running the ultimate bluff, you've got to act like you know exactly what you're doing and that you absolutely belong right in the middle of the situation.

5. The final characteristic of a truly elite prankster is the ability to keep a straight face, or better yet, feign the same shock and surprise that has overcome the victim. Escaping from the situation with the guise of innocence intact is the pinnacle of accomplishment. Nobody does it better than my two friends, and I am truly envious of their talent.

Those of us in the minor leagues often need a stroke of luck to set the stage for a caper. That happened to me years ago when an opportunity just fell into my lap, and I was simply unable to resist the temptation it offered. I was helping my dad at his bookstore with adding some shelving to the display areas, and he had purchased some used fixtures from a bookstore owner in Charleston. He rented a 16-foot Ryder truck for me to drive to Charleston and bring the shelving units back to Hartsville. In preparing to leave, I spent a few minutes with a pre-trip inspection of the truck. As I was checking the mirrors, familiarizing myself with the dashboard gauges and indicators, and adjusting my reach to the gas and brake pedals, I noticed something under the seat on the driver's side of the cab. What must have been mistakenly left there by a previous customer was a Polaroid picture of a scantily clad woman seductively posing in what appeared to be a motel room. I started to throw the picture away, but then—as I remembered that I'd be going to the July SCACA Clinic the next week with Hal and Jimmy—I had second thoughts. My mind had unavoidably and irretrievably begun to work like theirs, and I realized what potential the picture might have. The wheels were turning, and I don't mean just on the truck.

The three of us departed for Columbia and the clinic the next week with me driving my wife's Dodge station wagon. Upon arriving at the Carolina Inn, we found that the three of us would be rooming together with one of us sleeping on a roll-away bed. That was no big deal, and when we moved in, we matched coins to determine who had the roll-away. We enjoyed the clinic as usual, attending lecture sessions during the day, catching up with coaching buddies from other schools, and going out for supper at our traditional spots. We were all on our toes about examining our shoes for toothpaste every time we put them on, making sure our beds hadn't been short-sheeted, and checking before we went to bed that none of our colleagues had left a request for a 5:00 AM wake-up call at the desk for us. On the day of departure, it was time to put my plan into action. Before leaving for the clinic, I'd shown Debby the Polaroid picture that I'd found in the Ryder truck. Needing someone's handwriting unlike my own, I requested that she autograph the picture for me. My suggestion was that she write on the picture something like "Hey, Jimbo, thanks for a great time! Love ya! Crystal." She did it perfectly. While Jimmy was showering, I showed the picture to Hal, and when he noticed Jimmy's dirty clothes bag on his bed, he immediately saw the potential for combining those two components. I saw the gleam in his eye, however, and began to have second thoughts. We both knew what trouble the scheme might cause for Jimmy if his wife, Rita, were to find Crystal's picture in his clothes bag. Hal didn't seem to be overly concerned about that possibility, and as a matter of fact, he said, "Wouldn't it be great if we could be there when that happens?" So, he pulled the trigger, and the dirty deed was done. We both kept straight faces all the way back to Hartsville.

Dr. Charlie Burry, Jr.

The remainder of this story is a second-hand account, related by Jimmy, regarding what happened in the White household later that night. Jimmy was lying on the living room floor and was playing a board game with his son, Bill. Rita was preparing to put a load of dirty clothes in the washing machine and opened Jimmy's clothes bag that he'd had at the clinic—the one into which Hal had put Crystal's picture. Within moments, Rita was in the living room, and something seemed to have upset her. She flipped the autographed picture of Crystal down on the floor in front of Jimmy and spat out, "Just what's the meaning of this?" Jimmy, immediately realizing that he was the victim of a prank by his clinic roommates, burst out laughing. Unfortunately, that reaction didn't seem to be very effective in answering Rita's question. Jimmy was perceptive enough to sense this, and he suggested, "You know who I've been rooming with all week, don't you?" Rita, knowing that the only prankster more notorious than her own husband was Hal Baldwin, gave a big exasperated sigh, shook her head, and walked out of the room. She couldn't wait to see Hal and tell him in a crystal-clear way just how funny she thought he was.

Jimmy claims that the aftermath of the episode has actually worked to his advantage. He says from that point on, no matter what kind of shenanigans of which he might be suspected, all he has to say is "I was with Hal Baldwin and Charlie Burry," and he's awarded a get-out-of-jail-free card. Somewhere, though, "Crystal" and her friends are still enjoying a good laugh.

43

Six Sisters in a Hot Tub

I mentioned in the previous chapter that Hal, Jimmy, and I had ridden together to the SCACA Coaches Clinic in Columbia in my wife's Dodge station wagon one year. Coincidentally— and as proof of the dangerous double-crossing nature in the world of practical joking—at the same time the Crystal plot was being hatched, there was more mischief afoot on the part of my riders. I suspected as much because of a recent fishing trip with the two of them, when—a day or so after the trip—a foul odor alerted me that part of our catch had been left under the seat of my truck. While the summer heat made the stink even worse, at least I was able to ride with the windows down for a month or so. With that memory fresh (well, not exactly) in my mind (and also in my truck), when we returned home from the clinic, the first thing I did was to search my wife's vehicle. I was not surprised to find, under the front seat on the passenger side, a pair of lacy, red panties. I knew that I had narrowly averted at some point the difficulty of Debby throwing the panties down in front of me and demanding "Just what's the meaning of this?" in much the same manner that Rita requested that information from Jimmy about Crystal's picture. I could have easily offered Jimmy's same excuse and been fine, however, as our wives always were aware of the possibility of such shenanigans. Hal got married a little later in life than Jimmy and I did, but it didn't take Mrs. Baldwin long to learn to be on her toes when—imme- diately after their wedding ceremony—the bride was briefly kidnapped by one of the groomsmen. Anyway, as their pant- ies plot was being deconstructed at a later time, I was glad to find out that Hal and Jimmy had encountered a bit of an embarrassing moment themselves while obtaining the panties at K-Mart in Columbia. When the cashier gave the two of them a questioning glance about their purchase, Hal—pointing at Jimmy—said, "They're for him." I would need two pairs of lacy, red panties, however.

About a week later, packages addressed to Mrs. Baldwin and Mrs. White arrived via US Mail at their respective residences. As you might guess, the parcels each contained a pair of red panties. Also enclosed was the following letter from the Travelodge Hotel management in Columbia on official letter-head stationery.

Dear Mrs. Baldwin/White,

We at Travelodge enjoyed providing accommodations for you and your husband on your recent trip to Columbia. The enclosed item was found by our housekeeping service while cleaning your room on Thursday afternoon, and we are pleased that we can return it to you.

We are also pleased to inform you that the bed which collapsed during the night Wednesday is still under warranty, and there will be no additional charges to you and Mr. Baldwin/White for those damages. We wish you a speedy recuperation from your back injury and hope it will not give you too much trouble in the future.

As we mentioned when you and your husband checked out, our legal department may contact you regarding the damaged Jacuzzi. It was also under warranty, but only if being used according to the manufacturer's specifications. The maximum capacity of that model Jacuzzi is four adults, and you, your husband, and your six sisters all being in the tub at the same time definitely voids the policy. It appears at this time that the replacement cost to you and Mr. Baldwin/White will be approximately $3,750. In order to avoid litigation, please remit that amount via certified check payable to Travelodge at your earliest convenience. You may send it to our address here in Columbia.

Your husband mentioned that he makes frequent business trips with you to our city, and we hope that you will be staying with us again in the near future.

Sincerely,

U. R. Welcome

Manager

Travelodge—Columbia, SC

As you may have noticed by now, a common theme in the Baldwin-White-Burry practical joke competition is the men attempting to get each other in trouble with their wives. Extreme care must be used in such endeavors, however, because women—and especially those who are married—have senses of humor which are highly unpredictable and quite often the opposite of men. The safest approach for men attempting to walk this minefield is to do so in the company of at least two other couples. For example, jokes and television dialogue that husbands find absolutely hilarious are often met with teeth-sucking and eye-rolls by their wives. This disdain can be lessened somewhat if it's shared, and the three ladies can shake their heads in sympathetic agreement and say something like, "Can you believe we married these fools?" Miscommunication is also better defended when three couples are on trips together, and the men decide to stay in the car while their wives go inside a store to shop. When the ladies come back outside, they have a tendency to think that the car should be in the same place

Dr. Charlie Burry, Jr.

in the parking lot as it was when they left, and just can't seem to understand their husbands' amusement in watching their puzzled looks as they search the parking lot. As the wives' confusion quickly turns to ire, though, men know that it's best to have some company in the foxhole. In another instance, after a wonderful evening of three couples enjoying a meal together, the men can commiserate while their wives watch videos of birthdays, weddings, and other family gatherings instead of professional wrestling. And, if a wedding video somehow becomes mislabeled, when an episode of *The Andy Griffith Show* comes up on the screen instead of the wedding ceremony, the men's feigned surprise in unison makes their claims of innocence even more believable. As a final example, when three couples are ordering their meals in a restaurant, and one husband points at his wife across the table and says to the waitress, "That one's with me," the other two men immediately exploding in laughter quickly helps to ease the tension created by such an insensitive reference.

I've finally come to the determination that there are two predominant factors in explaining such behavior among husbands. One is the cumulative effect of watching too many episodes of *The Three Stooges* during childhood. The second is simply peer pressure—in other words, "Boys will be boys." When a couple of jokers like Hal Baldwin and Jimmy White get together, they just can't help themselves, even when their wives and their wives' sisters are along with them on the trip.

Whites, Burrys, and Baldwins

Dr. Charlie Burry, Jr.

44

Testing Partners

While the business of educating our young people is vitally important to the survival and prosperity of our country, culture, and society, the seriousness and professionalism of that occupation—just like anything else—benefits from a good laugh occasionally. The environment of a large high school provides fertile ground for those opportunities and Hartsville High School was no exception. The large number of people who work there, along with the hundreds of working parts of such an operation—policies, procedures, schedules, etc.—regularly creates circumstances which may need only one additional ingredient to become candidates for *America's Funniest Home Videos*. For example, teachers received memos requiring them to perform their lunch duty from the roof of the gym. Coaches arrived in the morning to find their office furniture completely rearranged. Birthdays were celebrated with visits from The Grim Reaper. Vaseline smeared on door handles created some greasy situations. Professional development reading assignments from *Dick and Jane* and *The Berenstain Bears* were given to faculty members whose undergraduate degrees were from The Citadel, Wofford College, and Newberry. The advent of electronic communication increased the prank potential exponentially, and some of the more ambitious efforts even made it to the district office. Interestingly enough, almost all of the practical jokes on the *HHS Top Ten List* occurred prior to 2004.

When I retired as principal of Hartsville High School in 2018, a few of my friends remarked that they knew of my association with Hal Baldwin and Jimmy White, and they wondered why I never played any practical jokes like they did. I told them that as principal, I hadn't been in much of a joking mood for the last 14 years. I did laugh at funny situations, like the time Gina Easterling rescued me when I got my necktie caught in a new paper shredder, and it began reeling me in. I used to jokingly call Von Cranford "Ms. Hardhead" when her asthma was bothering her so much that she was having difficulty breathing, yet she still insisted on coming to work. I'll admit that I truly enjoyed posting a picture on Facebook of Phyllis Griggs putting gas in her vehicle when she ran out in front of the school. I thought the Class of 2018 filling the hallways with balloons one night during the last week of school was a great senior prank. Students were incredulous during morning announcements one Monday when I expressed my sincere condolences to Coach Lewis about his Dallas Cowboys losing in an especially frustrating manner the night before. Unfortunately, I didn't allow those lighter moments to occur for me very often while I was principal. I was intense, maybe too much so, about my job. I worked long hours, and that never changed from the first day I walked in that office until the day I walked out for the last time. It was important for me to be tough, composed, and never blink in emergency situations, and I was diligent about projecting that persona. While my tenure as principal was absolutely the most rewarding time of my career, I had a lot more fun when I was a school counselor.

One of my responsibilities during the last 14 years that I was a school counselor, after Ray Petty retired, was being school test coordinator (STC). That meant attending all of the district-level in-service meetings at which testing procedures were reviewed and testing materials were issued. I always came back to Hartsville High School with a truck load of test booklets,

Dr. Charlie Burry, Jr.

answer documents, exceptional education modified materials, and other accessories—all to be stored in a secure location until I returned them to Darlington after a couple of weeks. I did that at least three times a year, and that didn't include preparations for the SAT and ACT. The STC was responsible for creating all of the testing logistics—modified daily class schedules, test administrator and monitor assignments, test site assignments, class coverages for teachers who were administering the tests, distribution and return of testing materials, and the certainty that we had enough calculators, plastic rulers and protractors, cassette tape players and earphones, and 11 million sharpened pencils, all with erasers. As I mentioned earlier, though, the working parts of such an operation created other opportunities.

Leading up to the spring administration of the Exit Exam one year, I had become aware of some friction between Coach White and another teacher whose classroom was located on the same hall as his. I'll call her "Ms. Smith." Ms. Smith reportedly had cut the line in front of Coach White one morning at a copy machine and had been rather unapologetic when he brought the indiscretion to her attention. That was the beginning of a feud that—while never becoming unprofessional—obviously rankled Coach White, especially when Hal and I would express our truly heartfelt concerns about how he and Ms. Smith were getting along. As I was working on test administrator assignments for the Exit Exam and pairing teachers together whose classes would be combined in one test site, it occurred to me that Coach White would probably enjoy being paired with Ms. Smith for the three days of testing. I figured it might be an opportunity for them to bury the hatchet. When the packets of Exit Exam information were distributed at the test administrator meeting one afternoon, it didn't take Jimmy long to notice the White-Smith pairing. As the meeting concluded, as expected, I noticed him not-so-patiently waiting for an opportunity to speak with me. With sincere regret, I told him that the assignments had been based purely on logistical considerations, that we were too far along in the process for his assignment to be changed, and that we had to overcome personal issues for the good of our students.

What I didn't tell Jimmy was that his packet of materials contained a special test site assignment sheet, and that he wasn't really partnered with Ms. Smith. I knew that he would appeal to others—Hal, Paula Terry and the other counselors, and Kaye McElveen, who was principal at the time—so they were all in on the scam and had special sheets to match his. They played their parts perfectly each time he went to one of them to plead his case. Finally, on the day before testing was to begin and after several days of anguished appeals, the trap was ready to be sprung. Jimmy was in Paula's office (which was next door to mine) making one last-ditch appeal, and I walked in and sat down with them. We let him go through his spiel again, and I must admit that he'd prepared his case well. He'd even included suggestions for alternate test administrator pairings. I expressed my concern and asked Paula to let me look at her test assignment sheet (the real one). I studied it for a minute, and then said, "Jimmy, I don't see what the problem is." He grabbed the sheet from me, spent a few seconds looking at it, and then compared it to his sheet (the fake one). A few more seconds passed, and then you could see his face fall when Paula and I started laughing, and he realized that he'd been played. That look was absolutely priceless. I can see it in my mind now as I write this, and I'm smiling and enjoying it all over again. He threw the papers on Paula's desk, looked at me and said, "You son of a . . . gun," and stalked out. Every once in a while, the grasshopper gets the best of the master, and now—many years later—we both laugh about it.

45

Don't Hang Up! This Is Not a Joke!

Hal Baldwin and I have taken a lot of trips and ridden a lot of miles together over the years. Many of the trips were on official business. We left Hartsville after a football game one Friday night and drove to Chapel Hill in order to attend a basketball coaches clinic on Saturday and Sunday. We drove to Conway 39 years ago to see the first-ever Beach Ball Classic championship game when Christ the King High School from New York beat Sumter High School. We made trips to Charleston to take the Hartsville High School basketball teams to summer camp at The Citadel. Hal was driving our team bus to South Florence late one afternoon when all the lights went out, and was in the driver's seat another time in Darlington when the entire gear shift lever pulled loose out of the floorboard. We made trips all over the Pee Dee area, to the beach, and to Columbia to coach basketball games. Other trips, because we are good friends as well as fellow coaches, were for pleasure. Hal pulled his camper to Clemson for football weekends. We're both country music fans, so we went to Columbia to see Martina McBride at Colonial Life Arena, sat on the third row at a Merle Haggard concert in Columbia Township Auditorium, and heard John Prine sing "It's a Big Old Goofy World" at the North Charleston Performing Arts Center. We fished in Lake Ashwood near Bishopville, Lake Darpo between Darlington and Society Hill, Lynches River, and the Big Pee Dee River. We visited our good friend, Jimmy Harrell, a number of times at his apartment in Darlington during his months of recuperating from a terrible fall in the gym at Rosenwald High School. Other rides that we took during the time that I was coaching basketball were therapy trips for me. Especially after losses—and there were plenty of them most years—we'd leave the gym in one of our trucks and just drive. Although most of the time we stayed on the back roads in Darlington County, we didn't have any particular destination in mind other than peace of mind. Sometimes we'd talk, and sometimes we'd just ride. Most of the time we'd get home pretty early, but occasionally we'd get home pretty early in the morning.

The trip that I'm going to tell you about took place at least 40 years ago, and you'll see why that historical context is important in just a minute. We'd been out riding in Hal's truck and were on the way back to Hartsville on the 151 Bypass when we had a flat tire. Hal had a good spare and changing a flat certainly was something that we'd both done a number of times before, so we didn't expect any problem. The spare was carried underneath the truck bed near the rear of the vehicle, as is the case with a lot of trucks today. Rather than the tire being lowered by cranking a cable, though, it rested on a metal arm the width of the tire, and one end of the metal arm was lowered in order to release the spare tire onto the ground. The end of the metal arm was usually secured by something like a wing nut and was pretty easy to release. The manner in which the spare tire could be released was very convenient, but it was also convenient when someone other than the owner of the truck needed a spare. That was the reason that Hal had installed a padlock on the end of the metal arm. He confidently produced the key to the padlock from the glove compartment, and shortly after that we discovered that the padlock was rusted so badly that the key wouldn't work. We needed a hacksaw to cut the lock off, and neither one of us knew of one that was within walking distance.

Dr. Charlie Burry, Jr.

Here's where the historical context is important. Cell phones hadn't been invented yet. The only way to make a phone call while you were on the road was to stop at a business to ask to use a phone or to find a pay phone booth. Pay phone booths were usually located at convenience stores, fast food restaurants, or busy intersections, and it cost a dime to make a local call until 1981 when the Bell Telephone Company raised the cost to a quarter. We knew of a pay phone booth just down the highway at a car repair shop, so we started walking. It was during our stroll that we discovered that the only pocket change we had between us was a dime. One. Dime. This is where more historical context is important. It was during this era of practical joking that late night prank phone calls were a staple of the trade. They were made solely for the purpose of awakening someone from a sound sleep, and the usual tactic for combatting such an aggravation was to forcefully hang up on the caller, with or without a word of advice. It was too late to call my wife, and Hal wasn't married yet, so the next person on our list was Jimmy White. We knew what his immediate reaction would be, however, the very second that he heard either one of our voices on the line at that time of night.

We reached the phone booth, and it was Hal's dime, so he made the call while I held my breath. The first thing he said as soon as Jimmy sleepily answered was "Don't hang up! This is not a joke!" Thankfully, he stayed on the line as Hal explained our predicament. He agreed to come to our aid, but he said he didn't have a hacksaw. Hal and I conferred for a moment, and I said, "Tell him to come on. I know where one is." Jimmy arrived a few minutes later, picked us up, and I asked him to drive to my house. The catch was that the hacksaw I was thinking about wasn't at my house. It belonged to my dad, and I knew it was hanging on the wall inside the garage at my parents' house, which was about 50 yards down the street from my house. We quietly eased into the driveway at my house, and I quickly walked to my parents' house. Fortunately, my folks owned a cat, and they always left the garage door open about a foot so that Tippy—who was an outside cat—could get in and out at night. I thought there was enough room for me to slide under the door without raising it anymore and surely awakening someone other than Tippy. So, there I was flat on my back, squeezing under the garage door of my parents' house in the middle of the night, hoping that my dad wouldn't come out the back door and shoot me. I made it in, found the hacksaw, and made my escape.

Back at Hal's truck a few minutes later, the rest of the operation was pretty simple: cut the lock off, change the tire, drop me off to pick up my truck at the gym, and we were home free. Other than being a bit bleary eyed at school the next day, the only other painful repercussion was Hal and I owing Jimmy a favor. The statute of limitations has passed on this story now, so I feel safe telling it, and relating—at least figuratively, since this happened 40 years ago—the following lessons. First, don't put a padlock on your spare tire. Second, carry more than one dime in your pocket. Lastly, and most important—if you have to make a late-night phone call to a friend for help, and your reputation as a prankster precedes you, be ready to say, "Don't hang up! This is not a joke!"

46

Oh, Come on! Be a Good Sport!

Sports rivalries provide great material for practical jokes, since just about everyone has graduated from—or at least attended—a particular school, or has a favorite hometown, college, or professional team. Others may have adopted such an allegiance for one random reason or another, even if it's just temporary. In fact, I remember a student who came into the Hartsville High School counseling office one time asking for a particular college application because she liked the colors of the school's athletic uniforms. I pulled for the Washington Nationals in the 2019 World Series because Caye lives in DC, and I've been to a game at Nationals Park. I pulled for the Chicago Cubs in the 2016 World Series because Beth once lived in Chicago, and I've been to a game at Wrigley Field. I now frequently wear a Boston Red Sox hat because I checked a Fenway Park visit off my bucket list in 2019. When I was a boy, I loved the Los Angeles Dodgers, and my hero was Sandy Koufax. Jimmy White was a big Mickey Mantle and New York Yankees fan, and I still enjoy talking with him about the 1963 World Series in which the Dodgers swept the Yankees in four games. He doesn't have much to say about it. If you've read Life Lessons . . . Principally Speaking, you know of my loyalty to the Boston Celtics and how Bill Laimbeer of the Detroit Pistons narrowly escaped paying a dear price for that one night in Boston. The key factor regarding the relationship between sports and jokes is that, because most people have a favorite team (or teams), they also have a rival (or rivals) that they love to hate. Therefore, when a rival becomes the butt of a joke, the humor has wide appeal. The enjoyment of a good zinger is almost universal even if people don't have a direct stake in the matter. Sometimes jokes cross the line of good taste, however, and discretion must become the better part of mirth. At other times, the pranks reach the pinnacle of originality, imagination, and hilarity.

Without a doubt, the most intense college rivalry in South Carolina, which even transcends athletics, is between the Gamecocks and the Tigers. The best practical joke in that rivalry—and maybe anywhere, anytime—that I know of occurred on November 11, 1961, when 50 members of the Sigma Nu fraternity at USC, dressed as Clemson football players, went onto the field at Carolina Stadium for pre-game warmups. They had an insider at Orangeburg High School and had borrowed their orange and purple uniforms and equipment, and they'd practiced their routine for weeks. As the Sigma Nus came onto the field impersonating the Tigers, the Clemson fans cheered wildly and their band broke into their fight song, "Tiger Rag." Then, as a frat member comically disguised as Frank Howard (the Clemson coach) appeared on the field, the imposters transitioned from their practiced, precision warmup drills into a pantomime of foolish stunts and antics. At that point, the Clemson fans and students knew they'd been pranked. They came pouring onto the field, and a full-scale melee ensued. The prank was reported in newspapers as far away as the *Los Angeles Times* and the *Detroit Free Press*.

Probably the group most well-known these days for their sports-related antics is the Cameron Crazies at Duke University basketball games. They camp outside Cameron Indoor Stadium in an area known as Krzyzewskiville (named for their coach) for weeks in advance in order to secure game tickets and then they harass visiting teams unmercifully. Their highly imaginative cheers are well-choreographed and—due to extensive research on the visiting team—are often specifically aimed at personal issues related to opposing players. Once, following the arrest of a North Carolina State player for stealing pizzas, the Crazies showered the court with pizza boxes when he was introduced as part of the starting lineup before the game. Without a doubt, however, the most irreverent group was the Columbia University Marching Band. They were the first to adopt the scramble band style and were followed in that manner by most Ivy League bands, as well as the marching band at Stanford University. The Columbia University band, however, has a history of being banned from other college campuses for inappropriate and controversial performances related to social and political issues of the day. Most recently, in September 2020, the band's leadership—known as the Bored—voted to dissolve the organization in the face of charges of offensive behavior. Compared to those kinds of activities, the thefts of the mascots of the Army (mule) and Navy (goat) teams before their annual football games seem mild.

On the local front, this Furman alumnus has been subjected to endless harassment from graduates and fans of The Citadel, Wofford College, and Marshall University. Those experiences with the Dogs from Charleston began during my freshman year at Furman when Citadel cadets invaded our campus with gallons of blue paint. Later in my freshman year, I was subjected to considerable verbal abuse from Citadel cadets while sitting at the end of the Furman team bench during a basketball game in McAlister Fieldhouse. Later, in 1995, I felt it was only fair that I should retaliate by enrolling Shannon Faulkner in each of Madge Zemp's classes at Hartsville High School. Also, just last year I acknowledged Citadel graduates Booster Windham, Skip Gering, and Chip Ellerbe by promoting a special coloring book edition of *Life Lessons . . . Principally Speaking*. The Dogs from Spartanburg have taken plenty of bites out of me, too, many of them by Tony Gainey, Hartsville High School business education teacher and baseball coach. Then there's Lyn Joyce, who once worked as the Hartsville High School community liaison. Both of her children are Terriers, too (if only they'd gone to Furman!), and she never misses an opportunity to take a shot at me on the rare occasion of a Wofford win over Furman in any sport. Thankfully, Bob and Ginny Hayes both retired, so I was spared the sight of them parading around the HHS campus in their ugly, green Marshall Thundering Herd attire.

At the high school level, it didn't take me long after moving to Hartsville to become aware of the rivalry with Darlington. One of my early Hartsville memories is of riding by the old high school on Carolina Avenue and seeing cardboard tombstones with the names of each starter for the St. John's Blue Devil football team. Many years later, when Darlington High School came into being with their Falcon mascot and purple and silver colors, they began calling their stadium and gym "The Falcon's Nest." I liked referring to those places as "The Purple Pigeon Perch." Greg Harrison took my harassment pretty well while he was Darlington High School principal; we had a good relationship, and I once answered his Ice Bucket Challenge for a charitable cause. When Greg moved to Charleston, and Cortney Gehrke took over for him, my gentlemanly manner curtailed any such needling directed at her. Of course, the underlying message of this chapter is that good sportsmanship and genuine respect should always be present in a rivalry of any kind, and we always emphasized that at Hartsville High School. But we seldom passed on an opportunity for a good joke, either.

Greg Harrison and Charlie Burry

47

Spiderman

I imagine that most people, if they'll admit to it, have—or at least have had at some point in their lives—a phobia about something. I used to have a phobia about flying. It was somewhat illogical since my dad had piloted B-52s in the Army Air Corps during World War II and had kept his pilot's license for a long time after the war. I'd actually flown with him a few times when he'd borrowed a friend's plane at the Hartsville Airport. It was still a consideration, however, when Hal Baldwin and I were planning a trip to Boston in 1992. After looking at train schedules and figuring out that we could get to Boston about ten hours more quickly by flying instead of riding Amtrak, we booked tickets out of Douglas International Airport in Charlotte. Knowing of my fear, Hal graciously showed his compassion as a friend not long after we entered the terminal when he asked if I wanted to visit the airport chapel before going to our gate. I let him know how much I appreciated his consideration, but passed on prayer, at least at that point. I'm a lot better about flying now, and have made a number of flights in recent years, and even one trans-Atlantic flight. So, I guess you could say that I've conquered my aerophobia.

Another common phobia is entomophobia, which is the fear of insects. We had a football coach who worked with us at Hartsville High School for a number of years who was afraid of insects. This was entertaining for the rest of the coaching staff, especially when we were at camp in Laurinburg as early August seemed to be the peak time for June bugs in that area. June bugs are large, flying beetles, and it can actually be a little startling when one lands on your shoulder. We always knew what had happened when, in the middle of practice, this coach would suddenly start dancing madly around in circles, flapping and swinging his arms. He would also become upset when another coach would walk up to him, open a hand, and allow a June bug that had been caught to fly up in his face. We tried not to do that more than a couple of times during each practice. Crickets were often found in the grass, and they would also send him into a conniption, especially when one was thrown on his chest. It was a good thing that I could run faster than he could. Other phobias include ophidiophobia, which bothers folks who believe that the only good snake is a dead snake. Caye won't consider going zip lining with me because of her acrophobia, which is a fear of heights. My wife, Debby, who is a retired registered nurse, definitely doesn't have hemophobia—a fear of blood, or aichmophobia, which is a fear of needles. Some people always take the stairs instead of an elevator because they're claustrophobic. Please don't turn off the lights on anyone who has nyctophobia, or advise anyone who has glossophobia to join *Toastmasters*. And then, there's arachnophobia—the fear of spiders—which brings us to a guy named Jack Fairly.

Coach Fairly came to Hartsville from Michigan in the mid-1980s to teach the shop class at Hartsville Junior High School. He also coached junior varsity football and assisted with the baseball program. Jack is a wonderful guy, and while he was in Hartsville, he cared deeply about the young people with whom he worked, was well-liked by everyone, and did a great job coaching. While being a northerner, he adapted well to southern life, liked the warmer weather, and grew to love chicken bog. The great challenge that he faced while being in South

Carolina was being a member of the same faculty at the junior high school with Jimmy White and Hal Baldwin. They welcomed Jack, and they became great friends, but his status as a first-year teacher/coach and his trusting nature made him highly susceptible to their practical jokes. They used to say pranking him was like taking candy from a baby. Naturally, I didn't condone such shenanigans, and I tried my best to protect Jack when I was around. Then one day, Jack made a huge mistake. He let Jimmy and Hal know that he was afraid of spiders.

Suddenly, it seemed as though Jack's classroom was infested with spiders of all kinds—real ones and fake ones, big ones and little ones, dead ones and live ones, fuzzy ones and spindly ones. They appeared in his work area, his desk drawer, his locker, his car, and everywhere else that would frighten the bejeebers out of him. Jack rented a house some distance out of town in the Auburn community, and even there he wasn't safe. Jimmy and Hal somehow got access to his house one day, and laid their trap. It was around Halloween, and they'd bought one of the big, black, rubber spiders that were easy to find in any discount store. They attached the spider to a short length of monofilament fishing line, taped the other end of the line to the bottom of the toilet seat in Jack's bathroom, and closed it. They then verified with a series of trial runs that when the toilet seat was raised, the spider would come up out of the water swinging from the end of the line. According to their notations of the test results, the sudden appearance of the spider was quite impressive. While there were no eyewitnesses to the culmination of the prank, Jack's account of the event left no doubt that the spider jumping out of the toilet had scared the . . . well, you-know-what . . . out of him.

Jack left Hartsville after a few years to return to Michigan—if I'm not mistaken—to a teaching and coaching job at his old high school where he eventually became head football coach and athletic director. I truly don't think the practical jokes had anything to do with his leaving, and I believe he'll readily tell you today that he has fond memories of Hartsville and his friendship with Jimmy, Hal, me, and a lot of other people here. He's been back to visit two or three times in the years since, and it's always been great to see him. When Jack left South Carolina, though, he made one final mistake. In his move back to Michigan, he somehow managed to leave his briefcase behind. When he contacted his Hartsville friends to locate it and ship it to him, Jimmy was more than happy to oblige. If you've been paying attention, you can easily guess what happened—another big, black, rubber spider attached to a short piece of fishing line which was taped underneath the top of the briefcase, so that when it was opened, out came the spider. The booby-trapped briefcase was shipped, and word that it had been received was eagerly anticipated. Jack's priceless reaction, heard in a phone call shortly after delivery, was "Dang it, you guys, you got me again! From 700 miles away!"

48

Yard of the Month

Oscar Wilde once said, "Imitation is the sincerest form of flattery that mediocrity can pay to greatness." As proof of Mr. Wilde's theory, a pretender to the throne would occasionally emerge in Hartsville to challenge the true masters of the art of practical joking. While these attempts might be given a grade of A for effort, the results usually fell far short of the standards of creativity and ingenuity required to achieve true and lasting fame in the field. Also, illustrating the inexperience and lack of foresight of the novice jokers, they always failed to anticipate the repercussions of their futile foolishness. Revenge was always exacted in a swift and sure manner by the superior forces who were only temporarily stymied. In other words, in the end, the cream always rose to the top—even if things got off to a rocky start.

I drove a black 1985 GMC S-15 pickup truck for about 13 years. At some point during that time, when Steve and Paula Terry were living on College Avenue in Hartsville, it developed a peculiar problem. Steve and I had gone somewhere—probably fishing—and I'd left my truck parked in front of their house. After we returned that afternoon, and I was pulling away from the curb to go home, I noticed a grinding, rattling noise coming from my truck. I stopped, got out, and looked under the truck for something that was loose or dragging. I didn't find anything, but I noticed Paula standing at her front door watching me. That was my first clue that something was fishy besides what Steve

Dr. Charlie Burry, Jr.

and I had caught that day. I waved, shrugged my shoulders, got back in my truck, and started off a second time. I heard the noise again, so I stopped and this time raised the hood to look at the engine. Paula noticed my strange behavior, so she came out to see what was wrong and express her concern. I didn't see anything amiss under the hood, and everything seemed to be working, so I decided to drive home. As I left with my truck sounding like a cement mixer, Paula—with a big smile on her face—waved a friendly goodbye. It was only about a mile to my house, but the faster I went, the louder the noise was. By the time I drove in my driveway, I knew that I had to find out what was wrong, and why I only heard the noise when the truck was moving. I asked Debby to come outside to watch and listen as I drove slowly up and down my driveway a few times. She said that the noise seemed to be coming from the wheels, so I examined them more closely. It was then that I noticed one of the hubcaps wasn't fitted tightly on a wheel, and it didn't take me long to figure out why Paula had such a big smile on her face when I left her house. I took the hubcap off and discovered a handful of rocks and gravel inside. The other three wheels had received the same treatment, and when all the rocks were removed and the hubcaps replaced, the noise miraculously disappeared! That's when Paula Terry moved to the top of my hit list.

It wasn't long after that when Steve and Paula started noticing strange things being left at their house, mostly during the night. Some stinker left catfish heads on their front porch one night that all the neighborhood cats were enjoying when Paula went out to get the newspaper the next morning. Another morning, she looked out in the front yard and discovered that their house was for sale. Coincidentally, Paula's car developed the same noise problem that had plagued my truck a few weeks earlier. Someone, in an attempt to help with their landscaping, left ten old tires in their front yard one night. Steve actually appreciated that, and was planning to cut them in half, paint them white, and place them along the edge of their driveway. Paula vetoed that idea, fearing that such décor would cause too much jealousy among their neighbors. I told her that they would have probably been awarded Yard of the Month. Perhaps another candidate would emerge, though.

One of the relationships that I enjoyed most at Hartsville High School was with Dave and Juanita McFarland. Dave was an assistant principal and is as fine a man as I've ever met. He did his job exceptionally well, was a straight shooter, and I admired him greatly. Juanita was in the school counseling department when I became a counselor, and she did her work with great concern for her students and a high level of profes-sionalism. Our team chemistry in the department made each day a pleasure, and Juanita's kind nature was a big part of that. Sadly, she passed away in 2014, but she left that legacy of kindness with her children, Davita, Derrick, and David III. Juanita liked to laugh, too, and a sense of humor was another of her good qualities. One morning a practical joker put that to the test.

Dave and Juanita had become interested in making some landscaping improvements at their home on 14th Street. Part of that project was leveling their front yard, so they'd had some topsoil delivered. The dump truck left a huge load of it – probably ten feet high—right in front of their house. I lived on Edgewood Drive at the time, which is not far from the McFarland's house, so I'd noticed the work that Dave had ahead of him as the small mountain stayed untouched for several days. I figured that he might need some motivation to get started on the project, so I decided to help him out. I bor-rowed a piece of poster board and some magic markers from our school's art department, and created a beautifully deco-rated Yard of the Month sign. Our counseling department was scheduled to attend a meeting in Darlington later that week, and the four of us (Juanita, Paula Terry, Ray Petty, and myself) always rode together on those trips. Paula decided that would be a good time to pull the prank, so I left school early to put the sign up—right in front of that huge pile of dirt. When we all left the high school a few minutes later, Paula was driving, and we made sure that Juanita was sitting on the left side of the car in the back seat. That way, she'd have a good view of her house as we drove out 14th Street to the 151 Bypass. A minute later, as Paula came almost to a full stop in front of the McFarland's house, I exclaimed, "Look, Juanita! Y'all have won Yard of the Month!" She looked over, saw the sign and at first was totally baffled, saying, "Well, my goodness." We all started making a big deal about it and congratulating her, and she quickly caught on. Then, beginning with her trademark little chuckle, she got a nice laugh out of the scene, too. The first thing she did, though, when we got to Darlington was to call Dave. He must not have thought it was as funny as we did because when we drove back into Hartsville later in the day, the sign was gone. I guess he was thinking that their neighbors would be jealous, too.

49

A Little Bird Told Me

Another quality that is important for a top-level practical joker to possess is the ability to lie convincingly with an absolutely straight face. This ability often saves the day as the joke is playing out and the perpetrator's direct involvement is a necessary part of the sting. Also, once a scheme has reached its climax and the victim knows that he or she has been played, sometimes telling a bald-faced lie is the only escape route. Practicing a totally innocent look in front of a mirror for a few minutes each day is good preparation for this situation. I've never had to go to the extreme of swearing on a stack of Bibles, but that's been due to preemptive comments—sometimes just off-the-cuff—that have kept the conversation from escalating to such a point. Finally, one of the more subtle points of this sort of deception is being able to walk the fine line between denial and confession in order to further sow confusion. One tried and true way of using this technique to create doubt in the mind of the accuser when you're being pressed for information is simply to say, "A little bird told me."

Birds had a more direct involvement a number of years ago in a practical joke project that was actually sanctioned by Hartsville High School while I was principal. The Academic Booster Club (ABC) has been a tremendous supporter of the school for more than 30 years. In addition to many smaller projects helping and recognizing students and teachers during the school year, the ABC awards $500 college scholarships to around 30 seniors each year. The organization and its sponsors have presented over $250,000 in scholarships during its history. The scholarships and projects are funded by membership dues, sponsor donations, and fundraising projects. A golf ball drop has been popular and successful in recent years, but one of the most enjoyable projects involved flocking people's yards with plastic pink flamingos.

Pink flamingos have a wide-ranging degree of appeal for the American public. Some people love them, while others wouldn't be caught dead with one in their yard. This charm—using the term loosely—has resulted in plastic pink flamingos being widely employed in practical jokes and fund-raising projects. One such project involves a person's front yard being invaded by a large flock of pink flamingos during the night. The birds are accompanied by a sign informing the victim that he or she has been flocked. The only way to have the flock removed—assuming the victim is a good sport about it—is to make a monetary donation to the organization responsible for the birds' nightly migrations. Naturally, the first year that the Hartsville High School Academic Booster Club became the proud owners of 50 plastic pink flamingos, the principal's front yard was one of the first to get flocked. What the ABC officers didn't count on was my collecting the flamingos, taking a photo of four or five of them behind a chain link fence, and posting the picture on Facebook informing the ABC that their flamingos had been captured and were being held for ransom. After a brief period of negotiating in which the ABC officers signed an agreement acknowledging that they'd been out-flocked, the birds were released into the custody of their rightful owners. They obviously didn't know that they were messing with someone who already had plenty of experience with plastic pink flamingos.

Ray Petty retired from the Hartsville High School counseling department in 1990 after a long and distinguished career in public education. One of the ways that he was honored and his career celebrated was with a retirement party at the home of Steve and Paula Terry, who were then living on Richardson Circle. The party was a festive affair with good food and beverages, presents, a few gag gifts, cards, and many heartfelt tributes to the man who was one of the greatest influences of my life and the lives of many others. Mr. Petty's entire family was there to hear the fitting tributes to their patriarch and enjoy the fun. That also left their house unguarded, and about halfway through the party, Debby and I slipped out on an errand. We went to our house, which was only about two minutes from where the Petty family lived, to pick up six passengers before heading over to their house. We let our passengers out in the front yard where they took up their positions awaiting the arrival of Ray, Francis, Susan, Beth, Kerry, and Amy. Debby took a picture of the group, and we made it back to the party without anyone missing us. Later that afternoon when the Petty clan got home, they were greeted by six plastic pink flamingos right outside their front door. The five female flamingos had name tags for Frances and each of the girls, and Mr. Pink Petty had his name tag, too.

There's an old saying about life that "what goes around, comes around," and that's true in the world of practical jokes, too. Due to misconceptions surrounding my association with Jimmy White and Hal Baldwin, a lot of people were laying for me on the occasion of my 40th birthday. This time, though—instead of pink flamingos—they'd be accompanied by birds of a different feather. It started before I even got out of my driveway that morning when I noticed a sign in our front yard proclaiming, "Lordy, Lordy, Charlie's 40!" It continued in that fashion with similar signs posted all the way along my route to school. When I arrived at the campus and started down the road behind the gym to my parking place, the signs increased in frequency, Burma-Shave style. As I walked from the gym to my office in the counseling center, I was greeted by numerous birthday wishes, all of them referencing my age, the gibe "old man," or other remarks about being over the hill. I could tell that it was going to be quite a day.

By the time I got to the suite of counseling offices and the reception area, a crowd had gathered. I was on high alert already, and the smiles and smothered snickers of laughter let me know that something else was up. As I walked to my office door, everyone got quiet. Just as I started to put my key in the door, I could hear a scratching sound coming from inside my office. I stopped to listen further, and heard sounds of "cheep, cheep, cheep" in addition to the scratching. Slowly opening the door, I saw the floor of my office covered with yellow baby chicks scurrying around. And yes, there were 40 of them, all telling me "Happy Birthday!" Whoever had delivered them was thoughtful enough to put newspaper on the floor, and it was the scratching of 80 little biddy feet I'd heard. I eventually found out who was responsible for the birthday chicken caper, and when they asked me how I knew it was them, I just said, "A little bird told me."

The Petty Family

50

Somebody's Sleeping in Our Bed!

Dean Boyd and I began a long friendship in the summer of 1987 when he came to Hartsville High School to teach physical education and coach football. He had just graduated from Winthrop University but already had some valuable coaching experience while in college helping his brothers, J.R. and Steve, who were both successful head coaches at York High School and Indian Land High School during that time. Dean had played football and baseball at York High School for the legendary Bill Pate, and that experience helped prepare him for a coaching career as well. The 1987 season was my first year on the varsity football staff, too, and we developed a good relationship coaching our defensive secondary. On offense, Dean coached the wide receivers, and I coached the running backs. Our partnership was a good learning experience for both of us as we scouted video of our opponents together and devised our defensive coverages for each game. We also graded our players' game performances while watching video on Saturday mornings at each other's houses. We listened to country music while we did that, and we always finished up with David Allan Coe singing "You Never Even Called Me by My Name." We became big fans of the television police drama *NYPD Blue*, would discuss the previous night's episode at school the next day, and to this day often call each other Medavoy (Dean) and Sipowicz (me). At the end of Dean's first year in Hartsville, he married his high school sweetheart, Leigh Sherer.

Dr. Charlie Burry, Jr.

Debby and I called her "the little blonde-headed girl," and we all became close friends. Dean was an assistant coach at Hartsville for seven years and then moved to Williston-Elko High School to begin a highly successful career as a head coach. Four years later, he became the head coach at Marlboro County High School, and he is now back at his high school alma mater, York High School, as head football coach. While at Marlboro County, he managed to find time to earn a doctoral degree from the United States Sports Academy, so he is now Dr. Dean Boyd. During his time at Hartsville, Dean also had some tutoring from his fellow coaches in the field of practical joking.

At this point, we need to take a brief side-trip in order to establish some background information for this story. In a previous chapter, I mentioned stopping by my dad's bookstore to visit from time to time, and on some of those occasions assisting him with a small task that required a little more physical labor than he had on hand. I was visiting one Saturday morning, and he mentioned some display items that he had stored in a warehouse just a couple of hundred feet down the alley that ran in back of the bookstore. He needed some of the items moved to the bookstore, and he asked if I'd mind helping him. As we began our short walk down the alley, little did I know that I was about to be presented with both the means and the opportunity to pull what is undoubtedly one of the top five practical jokes of my career. We arrived at the warehouse, and my dad slid the wooden door open. It was dark inside, and I slowly followed my dad through the door. He knew right where he was going and in just a couple of seconds, he pulled the string hanging from a single bare 60-watt light bulb. As the light came on, my eyes adjusted, and I looked to my left. The first thing I saw in the dim light was the shape of a human figure, and then several more people became visible. Not expecting any company on our visit to the warehouse, the mannequins scared me half to death. I managed not to curse in front of my dad, and he just laughed at me. After a few moments, I was able to laugh at myself. And then, I once again fell victim to the temptation of the Baldwin-White thought process. I began to realize that my new friends could be of some assistance to me and said, "Hey, Pop, could I borrow a couple of these folks for a few days?"

During the time that the Boyds were in Hartsville, Dean was working on his master's degree from the United States Sports Academy in Daphne, Alabama. Much of the work was done through distance learning, either via email or regular snail mail. During one summer, however, students were required to spend a term—six or eight weeks—on campus. Not wanting to spend that much time apart, Dean and Leigh decided to go to Alabama together for the summer. In making arrangements to be away from home for that length of time, they realized that they'd need someone to look after their house for them. They didn't have any family close enough to do that regularly, so—because Debby and Leigh were such good friends—the Burrys became house sitters for the Boyds and were given a key. Proving that the stars just align sometimes, we were given that house key at about the same time I was becoming acquainted with my friends at the warehouse.

Patience is a virtue often required of practical jokers, since timing can be a key element in the success or failure of a prank. I was patient that summer while looking at a calendar and anticipating the date of the Boyds' return home from Alabama. The day before they were to arrive back in Hartsville, Debby and I went to check on their house. We were accompanied by Lila and Lily, two of my mannequin friends, and we invited them to come inside with us. Lila was a shapely full-length model, and Debby dressed her in one of Leigh's nightgowns. We then made Lila comfortable under the bedcovers in the master bedroom. Lily was only the top half of a model, so she ended up sitting naked in the bathtub, with the shower curtain pulled partially

Dr. Charlie Burry, Jr.

closed to protect her modesty. Debby and I then checked the rest of the house to be sure we'd fulfilled our trust as house sitters and bade Lila and Lily goodnight.

Another key to the success of a practical joke sometimes requires the discipline to be content with not being an eyewitness to its climax. Therefore, the remainder of this story is also a second-hand account related to us by Dean and Leigh in describing their return home. Dean was the first to enter the house, and as he carried luggage into the bedroom, he noticed Lila sound asleep in the bed. Completely startled (putting it nicely), he ran into the kitchen and exclaimed to Leigh, "Somebody's sleeping in our bed!" They both rushed into the bedroom to rouse the sleeping beauty and determine how she'd come to trespass in such a forward manner. After poking Lila several times and being unable to awaken her, they discovered the reason for her repose and that they wouldn't be getting any information out of her. It was then that Leigh—after a lengthy road trip and just moments after getting her heart rate under control—headed for the bathroom and rudely interrupted Lily in the middle of her bath. Lily, despite such embarrassment, remained much more composed than did Leigh and appeared to take no offense at the intrusion. Leigh, on the other hand, noisily requested Dean's presence in the bathroom to question their other houseguest.

As the Boyd household returned to normal, Lila and Lily were sent to the guest bedroom for the night. Even their presence there was disturbing on several occasions, as Dean and Leigh— temporarily forgetting that they had guests—would walk by that bedroom door, glance at the ladies, and be startled again. The next day, the Boyds made a trip to York to visit family, but we had not returned their house key. So, by the time they returned home again, the mannequins had disappeared. You might say that Lila—and especially Lily—had made a clean getaway.

Section 6—
People Who Made
Me Better

We are all products of our environments, at least to some degree, and have had people in our lives to help shape us in some manner. Hopefully, most of those experiences and relationships we've known have been positive, and we've gone on to personify those good influences in our own lives. In the following chapters I'm going to tell you about some folks in my life who made me better, simply by being the kind of good people they are. I've known them in a variety of settings, from a high school buddy and a teammate, to supervisors, to a college professor. A few inspired me by the manner in which they faced adversity. Another strengthens me daily with his faith. One gave me confidence to be more than I thought I could be. Still another tells stories so funny that I laugh until my face hurts. Some of them I seldom see or hear from, and a few might even be surprised to see their names in this section. One probably doesn't even remember me. A couple, sadly, have passed away. They've all been good friends to me in a number of ways, though, and they've lived lives to be admired and respected. I appreciate all of them, because just through their friendship and example, they've made me want to be a better person. I hope that in the following pages you'll get to know them some, maybe well enough so that they'll help you be a little bit better, too.

51

Coaching Cronies

Some of the best friends of my life are guys that I coached against, and I'd like to tell you about three of them in this chapter. While we schemed in practice and at other times about ways to beat each other, and the competition during games was intense, none of those issues ever became more important than the friendship that was always present in our relationships. The basketball coaching careers of Jimmy Harrell, Tommy Johnson, and Dave Neilson were far more successful than mine, but I was fortunate to learn from them and be able to apply those lessons later in my own career and life. I hope you'll enjoy learning a little about these friendships, why they continue to mean so much to me, and how they made me better.

Jimmy Harrell began his teaching and coaching career at Rosenwald High School in Society Hill in 1972 and came to St. John's High School in Darlington in 1983 when Rosenwald closed. He was Dave Neilson's assistant with the 1983 Blue Devil team that won the South Carolina AAA State Championship with a 27-0 record, and he became the head coach for St. John's in 1984. His basketball teams won 441 games, eight conference championships, and he was conference Coach of the Year four times. I coached against Jimmy many times and watched his teams play many more games, and there's no doubt that he knew the game from a technical standpoint. His greatest strength, however—at least in my opinion—was

Dr. Charlie Burry, Jr.

that his players believed in him and loved playing for him, and many times that's more important than the Xs and the Os. Jimmy was a master of both aspects of coaching the game—strategy and motivation. Our friendship deepened as we made two or three trips every summer to The Citadel in Charleston to work basketball camps where we roomed together, coached together, ate meals together, and attended mandatory late-night coaches meetings together. In recent years, if you've ever been eating lunch at Joe's Diner in Darlington and overheard someone exclaim, "Jiminy Crickets! I can't believe that!" you knew right away that Jimmy Harrell was in the place. His raspy, distinctive voice and his trademark phrase expressing surprise is unmistakable. I've known him for more than 40 years, and his friendship is just as authentic. He's a master storyteller, and his background from Pulaski, Virginia, graduating from Wake Forest University where he was on a baseball scholarship, his minor league pro baseball experience, and 30 years coaching basketball, baseball, and football gives him plenty of material. He can be hysterically funny one minute and speak with great sincerity the next, and every bit of it is genuine Jimmy Harrell. His sons, Artie and Todd, are fine men just like their father, and he is a championship grandfather, too. Jimmy Harrell is loved and respected by everyone who knows him, and I'm blessed to call him one of my best friends.

Tommy Johnson retired from coaching basketball in 2013 after more than 600 wins in a 38-year career at West Florence High School, Wilson High School, and Socastee High School. His 1986 West Florence team won the South Carolina AAAA State Championship, and he had four other teams advance to Lower State Championship games. He was one of the head coaches in the 2005 North-South All-Star Game and was the head coach for the South Carolina All-Star team in the 2010 Carolinas Classic. His last year on the hardwood was highlighted by induction into the Florence Hall of Fame and the South Carolina Basketball

Coaches Association Hall of Fame. He is a hall of fame friend, too, and you've read about our trip to the 1985 NCAA Final Four together. Tommy and I began our coaching rivalry and friendship when he became the head coach at West Florence High School. The 1982-83 region championship team that we had at Hartsville was one of the few teams to defeat the core group—Tony Black, Russell Green, Donald Nance, and Jay Nettles—of the 1986 state championship West Florence team twice in the same year. If you do the math, however, you'll see that those guys were in the ninth grade when that happened, and they never lost to us again. Tommy was described in one of the newspaper articles covering his retirement as being "colorful," and I don't think you'll find a coaching colleague or referee that will disagree. He used to accuse me of arranging to have my cousins referee the Hartsville-West Florence games, but he had to make those claims to take attention away from the way he worked officials for favorable calls. He's also falsely accused me of setting a world-distance record for throwing a sport coat during a ball game, but that toss was disqualified because the chalk, keys, pens, and peppermint candies in the pockets exceeded the event's weight limit for a coat. His sense of humor was on full display at a coaches clinic, though, when he made the following announcement over the public address system: "Attention, Coach Charlie Burry. Your wife called and said to bring home a gallon of milk." Jimmy Harrell laughed so hard that I thought he was going to fall out of the bleachers. You won't find many basketball coaches who are better or wittier than Tommy Johnson, and I don't have many better friends than him, either.

I coached against Dave Neilson in my first game as the boys' varsity basketball coach at Hartsville High School, and we won. Four years later, his St. John's team beat us three times on the way to 27 wins, an undefeated season, and the 1983

South Carolina AAA State Championship. He no doubt won hundreds of games during his career, but I was unable to find that information anywhere because he probably didn't think it was important to keep track of that. In addition to coaching, Dave was also a collector of art, a magician, summer camp entrepreneur, and could be found officiating any kind of ballgame anywhere, anytime—whether he knew anything about the sport or not. He was a bit of an eccentric, and Hal Baldwin—who played for him—has a thousand funny stories about things he did, especially about driving the team to ball games. For example, as a memory aid, he would take notes with a ballpoint pen on his arm instead of paper, and by the end of the day, his left arm would be completely tattooed with his scribbles. His curiosity and intellect always led him to look for a competitive edge or better way to do things and many times he found it. Whenever we played in Darlington, as soon as I walked into their gym, I was immediately greeted by two of Dave's managers—Woogie and Knick-Knock—assigned escorts who stuck with me like glue until the opening tip. They were good guys and I liked them, but they were much more of a distraction than a gesture of hospitality, and Dave knew that. He was highly respected as a coach, his students loved him, and going into his office in the back of his classroom was like walking into a museum. I never coached against a more competitive guy, and I came out of a few basketball summer camp pick-up games with the bruises to prove it. Dave had a soft side, though, and that was especially evident around children. On two occasions he showed up at our house in Hartsville in his jam-packed station wagon to do magic shows for my daughters on their sixth birthdays—at my request—and then he wouldn't let me pay him. He was a great coach and teacher, a man of high principles, and a wonderfully devoted husband to his lovely wife, Denny, until he passed away on October 4, 2018. You couldn't ask for a better friend.

Dave Neilson

Jimmy Harrell

Tommy Johnson

Dr. Charlie Burry, Jr.

52

That Darlington Crowd

I wrote of a rivalry between Hartsville and "that Darlington crowd" in an earlier chapter, and I hope that I conveyed that it is—at least in my opinion—a healthy rivalry. While the athletic teams from the two high schools competed with a high level of intensity, I always felt that the coaches respected each other professionally and had good personal relationships as well. Those feelings were generally reflected by the athletes, and in the times when there was trouble related to Hartsville-Darlington ball games, it was seldom students or athletes who were involved. The problems were usually caused by personal or social issues—almost always with young adults—that had nothing to do with either of the two schools or even the communities. I had great relationships with Keith Wilks, Pearl Jeffords, Greg Harrison, and Cortney Gehrke—who were the four principals of Darlington High School during my 14 years as principal of Hartsville High School. I've lived in Hartsville for most of my life since I was eight years old, and I don't know of anyone who dislikes someone from Darlington just because the person is from Darlington. I've been blessed to have many good friends from Darlington, and those who I'm going to tell you about in this chapter are some of the finest people I've ever known.

I got to know Harmon Baldwin through his son, Hal, who is one of the best friends of my life. One of the great benefits of that relationship was being able to spend time with Mr.

Baldwin occasionally, sometimes just dropping by his house on Spring Street with Hal to visit with him and his dear wife, Jane. Other times were on fishing trips, when the fellowship was the most enjoyable part of being on the river. I also developed a new relationship with Mr. Baldwin when I became principal of Hartsville High School, and he was a member of the Darlington County School District Board of Education. Mr. Baldwin spent most of his professional career in public service in the parks, recreation, and tourism industry, so there was never a shortage of common-interest topics for us to talk about. Actually, he did most of the talking—not because he was a big talker—but more because I was smart enough to ask questions and just listen to him share his thoughts. Mr. Baldwin's heart for public service and helping young people was evident during his time on the school board. He did most of the asking of questions then because he was interested in knowing what I thought and what the board could do to help me with my job. Mr. Baldwin was a key figure in developing interest in the International Baccalaureate Programme at Hartsville High School, and I will forever be grateful for his support of that initiative. Harmon Baldwin was always interested in making things better. His example (even after his death on March 22, 2007) continues to make me a better person, too.

Harvey Drawdy was the principal of Pate Elementary School in Darlington for many years. He told me one time that he came to Darlington to coach, but G. C. Mangum—then superintendent of the Darlington County School District—talked him into trying the Pate job for a year, and he just stayed there. Harvey became a beloved figure at his school and is an icon among his former colleagues in school administration, as well as in the Darlington community. He also has a special heart for children with disabilities, and he initiated programs that made significant differences in exceptional education services in Darlington County. Hal Baldwin is a good friend of Harvey's sons,

Dr. Charlie Burry, Jr.

Stan and Rick, and I think that's how I became acquainted with one of the best coon hunters, catfishing guides, and story tellers in the Pee Dee area. The Drawdys are also accomplished musicians in the genre of bluegrass and country music, and listening to them perform is a treat. Again, because of our common interests, and his wealth of experience and wisdom in those areas, there is always something that I can learn from Harvey by just listening to him talk. Stan has written a wonderful book about his dad, entitled *My Dad . . . My Father*, that tells great stories about being raised by such a good and spiritual man. Harvey Drawdy has made many people better in his lifetime, and he's managed to keep us all entertained along the way.

Renny Johnson is originally from Alabama, but there's no mistaking his loyalty in the world of college athletics because he's an Auburn Tiger/War Eagle through and through. All you have to do is ride by his house, and it's obvious that there's no Crimson Tide in sight. He came to Darlington in 1969 for a speaking engagement, got talked into taking a job teaching social studies at Mayo High School, and never left. He has a Master's of Divinity, as well as a Master's in history, so he also began doing some preaching in the area. If you ever need an officiant for a wedding or a funeral who will speak in a rich, baritone voice that sounds like it's straight from heaven, Renny Johnson is your man. You'll also find a man whose fervor for Darlington athletics is exceeded only by his fervor for the Lord, and he has used that combination to reach hundreds of young people throughout his career. It was my good fortune to get to know Renny through the world of athletics, too, and—having a heart for grace and forgiveness—he allowed a Hartsville coach into his realm of friends. He provided witness of that grace about nine years ago when Hartsville High School was going through an exceptionally difficult time with the death of a student/athlete. Renny showed up at my office with a heart full of kindness and a handful of books on coping with grief for me to share with our coaches and athletic staff, and his compassion touched my heart. God doesn't make people any better than Renny Johnson, and his Christian example makes many lives better, including mine.

As a Hartsville Red Fox who regularly traveled east on Highway 151 into foreign territory, the opportunity to spend time with "that Darlington crowd" and to know these men has helped me realize that mutually respectful relationships always transcend community, school, and athletic rivalries. My life is richer, and I am a better person for having known them.

Jimmy Harrell, Renny Johnson, Charlie Burry

Dr. Charlie Burry, Jr.

53

Bill Boyd

Dr. Willie E. (Bill) Boyd, Sr., worked in various capacities in the Darlington County School District (DCSD) for 50 years before retiring at the end of the 2017-18 school year. He came to Darlington County in 1968 as a teacher at Mayo High School after serving in the Vietnam War as an infantryman. He held principalships at both Rosenwald High School and Mayo High School before moving into several district-level administrative positions, culminating with his role as interim superintendent during his final year with DCSD. He was recognized with several civic and professional awards, including the Darlington Citizen of the Year in 2012 by the Greater Darlington Chamber of Commerce, and the Lifetime Achievement Award from the South Carolina Association of School Administrators in 2015. Dr. Boyd also served as a member or trustee on a number of boards, and once chaired the Florence-Darlington Technical College Board of Directors. I don't know of anyone who has had a longer, more distinguished, and more impactful career in education than Dr. Bill Boyd. I'd like to tell you about what he meant to me.

The first thing you notice about Dr. Boyd is his appearance. He cuts a trim figure, and I doubt that his weight has varied much at all over the years. He is always exceptionally well-dressed, usually in what looks to be a tailored suit. The pants are sharply creased and the perfect length, and the jacket is an ideal fit. His dress shirt—with cufflinks, not buttons—is crisply pressed, and his trademark bow tie is perfectly knotted. His dress shoes are always shined, the belt is stylish, and even when he shows up in more casual attire at a ball game, he is impressive. If you're looking for an example of a well-dressed gentleman, Bill Boyd is first-class from head to toe.

Clothes don't make the man, though, and there is much more to Bill Boyd than a sharp appearance. His genuine manner of greeting people always sends the message that he is glad to see you. He looks people in the eye, and his handshake is full and firm. When he puts his other hand on your shoulder while he's shaking your hand, that makes you feel special. He listens when people are talking in a way that makes them feel like what they're saying is worth his attention. When he responds, his words are measured and the result of a strong intellect, great insight, and some thoughtful consideration. Meetings with him are productive because he seeks the opinion of every member of the group, and he then helps people reach enough of a consensus to move forward. The mood of his audience is eased by his congenial demeanor, a ready smile, and a dry wit. While communicating in a low-key style, there is no doubt that he is the master of the room when he needs to be.

Dr. Boyd chaired the interview committee when I applied for the position of principal of Hartsville High School in the spring of 2004. As is the case with most interviews in such a setting, each member of the committee had predetermined questions to ask the candidate. When one of his turns came, Dr. Boyd asked me why I wanted to get into administration. I answered, "Dr. Boyd, I don't want to get into administration. I want to be principal of Hartsville High School." I then went on to explain what I felt was truly a spiritual calling to that particular job (not just administration in general) and my plan for a *Red Fox Renaissance* that would revitalize the school and make it the flagship school in

Darlington County. I believe that answer resonated with Dr. Boyd because of his experience as a principal at two Darlington County high schools and because he could identify with what I was saying. From that moment on, I never felt anything less than the strongest support from him in what we were trying to accomplish with our *Red Fox Renaissance* at Hartsville High School. Especially as a first-year principal, I needed the reassurance that we were headed in the right direction, particularly in terms of our school climate and discipline issues. Knowing that I was on the same page philosophically with a leader of Dr. Boyd's experience and caliber was certainly a boost to my confidence, especially during the difficult times.

I developed even more respect for Dr. Boyd during expulsion hearings at Hartsville High School when he served as the district hearing officer, and I represented the school administration. When a discipline situation reached that level—being sent to him either as a result of a school-level hearing or the severity of an issue initially—the student was already in deep trouble. As each hearing began, Dr. Boyd was clear in establishing the procedures and parameters for the meeting while courteously making everyone feel as comfortable as possible. He always gave students and parents ample opportunity to present their side of the story and plead their case. He was perceptive with his questioning and was usually successful in helping the students and parents understand the problem from the school's perspective. On the rare occasions when it was necessary to re-establish a respectful tone in a meeting, he did that in a calm, but forceful manner that left no doubt about who was in charge. In every hearing, our shared goal was to provide a consequential learning situation for the student and the parent while protecting the learning environment and school climate for the rest of our students.

I would not have become the principal that I was without Dr. Bill Boyd. His guidance and friendship were of immeasurable value to me, and I'll always be grateful for having the opportunity to work with him. The last time that I saw him—more than a year ago now because of the pandemic—we instinctively greeted each other with a brotherly hug that was symbolic of the mutual respect between two men with 95 years of experience in public education between them. Bill Boyd made me a better principal, and he made me a better person.

Dr. Bill Boyd

Dr. Charlie Burry, Jr.

54

B. Jane Hursey

Barbara Jane Hursey is as good and kind a soul as I have ever known in my life. I call her "B. Jane"—with equal amounts of respect and affection—because she signed all of her official correspondence as Assistant Superintendent for Human Resources for the Darlington County School District that way—B. Jane Hursey, Ph.D. She and I go way back to our high school days when she sat in the St. John's Blue Devil student section at basketball games and cheered against the Hartsville Red Foxes. I also fell in love with her cousin for a while, although I'm pretty certain that feeling was not mutual. B. Jane was a year behind me at Furman, and you may recall that she and I hitched rides home with Fulton "Big Cat" Elvington during her freshman year. She managed to overcome that experience and, after graduating from Furman, earned a Master's Degree from Vanderbilt University and completed her doctoral studies at the University of Virginia. You'd be hard pressed to find a more impressive resume' in educational circles than hers. She is the daughter of Ed and Christine Hursey, who were both iconic figures in Darlington County, with Mr. Hursey chairing the Darlington County School Board for many years. She also adored Tim and Joanne Watson, who were like a second set of parents to me, so that makes her my de facto sister. If you're thinking by now that Charlie Burry must love B. Jane Hursey, you're right, and you're about to find out why.

Jane was an elementary teacher and principal in Darlington County for a few years and then moved to Texas for a while where she was a school superintendent. I was pleasantly surprised early in my tenure as Hartsville High School principal to find out that she wanted to come back to Darlington County and that she'd applied for the position of Ninth Grade Academy Coordinator at our school. She came for an interview one afternoon, and all of those questions were quickly put aside as we spent more than an hour catching up as old friends. I'd have offered her the job in a heartbeat if I hadn't already decided to hire Paula Terry, and I'm pretty sure that Jane knew that. Darlington High School had the same position open, though, and Pearl Jeffords hired her there, so Jane and Paula became close colleagues and personal friends.

Jane was overqualified for that situation, however, and it wasn't long before she became Director of Human Resources for the school district. It was in that position that I developed a close working relationship with Jane and the others in her department—particularly Joy Goodson and Lisa Bruce—and grew to depend on her expertise, experience, and counsel. It is my strong belief that great teachers are the key resource in having a successful school. Jane shared that philosophy with me, as did our superintendent Dr. Rainey Knight, and Jane worked tirelessly to make that happen for me and every principal in the district. That was easier said than done, however, and I attended many teacher recruitment fairs, scoured teacher application databases almost daily, and still at the last minute, occasionally had to resort to the Visiting International Faculty program to hire teachers from outside the United States. Once I'd offered a position to a candidate, however, the district's Human Resources Department—under Jane's leadership—did everything possible to expedite the process, assure that everything was in order, and help us close the deal. That close working relationship—although she once described me (jokingly, I think) as being "salty"—was one of the big factors in Hartsville High School becoming a better school.

The field of human resources is much broader and more involved than the recruitment and hiring of teachers. Jane's experience and abilities in those other areas of personnel management—benefits, maintaining certification, performance evaluation, allocation of human resources, employee censure or termination, legal issues, etc.—were also crucial in supporting principals and schools. She wanted to be sure that we had the information about policy, procedure, and legal issues that we needed to make sound decisions, and she was always available to advise us on difficult issues. She also had a great deal of legal expertise, but knew when it was prudent to consult the attorneys who represented the school district. I was particularly appreciative of that assistance in 2013 when I scored a hat trick and was named in lawsuits three times during the same school year. Jane was straight-forward and by-the-book, particularly regarding the welfare and safety of students, and there was one particular issue that she mentioned as a word of warning at every principals' meeting. The potentially problematic situation had occurred at Hartsville High School, and while she never called me out by name, she always made her point. Jane also has a kind heart, and she made the tough decisions in as compassionate a manner as possible. I saw her a number of times with tears in her eyes, but firm resolve in her voice, when she told me what we had to do.

Jane is truly in her element when speaking before a group, and I saw her in that role most often at monthly principals' meetings. The Human Resources slot on the agenda was always last, I think probably because she was such a tough act to follow. She has a wonderful sense of humor and thoroughly enjoys telling a funny story as much as hearing one. Her information and instructions were always clear and well-organized but presented in an amicable manner—often with a little humor injected—that made her expectations easy to digest. She never failed to compliment us for our efforts to comply with policy and procedure, and always expressed her appreciation and respect for what we were doing for the students in our schools and the school district. The thing that I remember most, though, was her ability to connect with us in a deeply personal manner. She always had a selection from a book that she was reading, a poem she'd found, or an artifact with a story behind it that she'd share with us. Her comments were meaningful, thought-provoking, and often filled with emotion. It was the perfect way to conclude a meeting and send us back to our schools—not necessarily with something that got us all fired up, but rather an idea that quietly reinforced our resolve to keep doing the good work of our chosen profession. Jane Hursey was a remarkable educator and leader (recently retired after 47 years in the profession), and is an even more remarkable human being. B. Jane made a salty old principal better, and I'll always love her for that.

Dr. B. Jane Hursey

Dr. Charlie Burry, Jr.

55

Lewis Lineberger and Duke Hucks

I began my coaching career first and foremost as a basketball coach. In those days, though, also being a football coach came with the territory in just about every high school in South Carolina and probably a lot of other places, too. It was commonplace for head coaches in the other major varsity sports—basketball and baseball, for instance—to be assistant coaches at some level in the football program. Also, coaches who were primarily assistant football coaches had additional coaching duties in other sports such as wrestling, track and field, tennis, and golf. I certainly didn't object to those expectations, and in fact, I enjoyed coaching football. It was also helpful financially, because at that time, football coaches were the only ones who had additional paid contract days added to a standard teaching agreement. Even so, I'd been hired as the head boys' varsity basketball coach at Hartsville High School, and I was constantly stretched for the time that I needed to prepare for that season, which began as soon as football ended. In fact, because Hartsville's football team usually went deep into the playoffs, it was not unusual for three or four basketball games to be scheduled before we'd played our last football game. For this reason, after I'd been at Hartsville High three or four years, I agreed to assist Jimmy White with football at the junior high school, which allowed me more time for basketball.

Things don't always work out as planned, however, and after seven years as head boys' varsity basketball coach, I was fired from that position. I kept my teaching position at the high school, and I continued coaching junior high football with Jimmy and Hal Baldwin. While I put up a pretty good front most of the time and immediately busied myself pursuing certification as a school counselor, I was completely lost—professionally and personally. I'd been a basketball coach for 12 years, and when I wasn't that anymore, I didn't know what I was. My self-image took a beating, and my self-worth was running on empty. I've sometimes told people who are going through a tough time that you just have to tread water until things get better. I learned that lesson well through my own experience because that's exactly what I did—tread water—for two years. Finally, in the spring of 1987, Duke Hucks and Lewis Lineberger threw me a lifeline.

The first part of my redemption came in the form of a position in the school counseling department. I'm pretty sure that there was a fair amount of competition for the job, and when Dr. Hucks decided to hire me, it was a real boost to my confidence. After two years of floundering and doubting my self-worth, I felt like somebody wanted me again. After being lost professionally, I had found a new direction in my career. Although I had a lot to learn, I was immediately comfortable because I'd done my counseling internship in the department that spring. My colleagues on the faculty seemed happy for me, and I received a number of congratulatory comments and messages. Of course, a bonus was that I'd be working with great people—in particular, Ray Petty, who had been a role model for me since I was in the 11th grade. Looking back on that situation, I think Duke Hucks probably saved my career in education. In all honesty, if I hadn't gotten that job, I don't think I'd have handled the disappointment very well. I'm pretty sure that I'd have been looking for something else to do, and I don't

Dr. Charlie Burry, Jr.

know what that would have been because I'd already made a half-hearted try at my dad's bookstore. If you'll remember, though, I confessed earlier that I'd gotten into education in order to be a coach. That's where Lewis Lineberger came into the picture.

I'd been the head junior varsity football coach during the 1986 season, and I'm not sure whether Lewis felt like I'd proven myself there or whether he just didn't have any other options the following spring when he offered me a job on the varsity staff. In whatever manner it happened, just as with the counseling job, it began a reclamation of my coaching career. There were only five varsity football coaches at that time—Lewis, Keith Sanders, Lee Segars, Dean Boyd, and myself—and that put me in some pretty good company, which was another boost to my self-worth. Amazingly, that fresh start was punctuated by the Red Foxes winning back-to-back South Carolina AAAA-Division II State Championships in 1987 and 1988. That early success, at least in terms of winning state championships, was not matched again during my time on the football staff although we did play for state championships in 1992, 1993, and 1997. I was on the varsity staff for 17 years before I became principal, and for the first 11 years (1987-1997), the Hartsville football program was one of the most dominant in South Carolina. My struggles as a basketball coach were not forgotten—and won't ever be, at least by me—but the success that I was fortunate enough to be a part of in football certainly has helped me to view my coaching career in a much more positive light. I have Lewis Lineberger to thank for that, as well as a few other things.

Lewis Lineberger is one of the finest football coaches and one of the best men that I have ever known. He put more effort into a job than anyone I have ever been around, and his work ethic inspired everyone who knew him. I thank him for that example. His players knew that he was going to be tough on them, but they also knew that he would love them and return their loyalty many times over. I won't ever forget when Randy Wheeler had his accident in the summer of 1998, Lewis was determined to go see him. He couldn't find another way to Florida, so he got on a train and rode 700 miles to Miami to be with Speedy and took a bus back home a few days later. I thank him for that memory. Anyone who observed Lewis' relationship with Raymond Davis over the years knows of his kind regard for others. When my dad died on the morning of the Conway game in 1996, Lewis and Mike Young were the first two people to come see me. I thank him for that compassion. His character, honesty, and integrity are beyond reproach (although he does have a terrible weakness for hot dogs and banana pudding). I count him as one of the best friends of my life, and absolutely the deepest regret of my professional career is the collision course that my becoming Hartsville High School principal put us on in 2004. I thank him for his friendship, and I wish that I could have repaid it in a better way. Most of all, I thank him for pulling a failed, washed-up basketball coach off the scrap heap and giving him a chance to do better.

Lewis Lineberger and Charlie Burry

56

Maceo Haynesworth

People practice their religious faith in a variety of ways. I attended the funeral of a friend about a year ago, and the entire service was based on notes that he had made and passages that he had underlined in his Bible during his lifetime. I thought that was a wonderful testament to his time on earth, and that he had, in effect (while I knew him in life to be a very private person) preached his own memorial sermon. On the other hand, a number of years ago at the funeral of a man who never attended church at all, the preacher put an interesting spin on that issue by saying that "He didn't hinder the church none." While funerals and eulogies generally summarize people's lives, we offer plenty of testimony during our lifetimes about our religious faith by the way we live. Understand that I'm talking about more than just active church involvement and service that is usually pretty observable. Sometimes that can be a wonderful testament to a person's life, while at other times it can be, well . . . a bit misleading. I think that the true test of a person's faith comes when the circumstances of life become difficult with personal situations, the illness of a family member or friend, or the loss of a loved one. The more tragic, dire, or sudden the situation is, the tougher the challenge becomes. Some people question or blame God and abandon their faith. Other people rely on their faith to get them through a situation, and the difficulty actually strengthens their faith. I'm going to tell you about a friend of mine whose faith is as strong as anyone I know.

I've known Maceo Haynesworth for at least 50 years. Our friendship began with basketball, because Maceo is a Butler Tiger legend. He played for Coach T. B. Thomas, Jr., and other than Coach Thomas himself, the name Haynesworth is more synonymous with the great Butler basketball tradition than any other. Maceo's brother, Tim, came along later and was a tremendous player in his own right. Maceo, though, was a magician with a basketball whose ball handling skills would remind you of the great Curly Neal of the Harlem Globetrotters. His passing ability was amazing, and he could score, too. The excitement for basketball games in the Butler Gym was unmatched, as their high-scoring teams frequently routed opponents, and during Maceo's years as a point guard for the Tigers, he led the way. His playing career came to a successful conclusion at Morris College in Sumter, but his game remains unforgettable for those fans in his hometown who saw him play.

Maceo began his professional career in parks and recreation in 1982 when he went to work for the Hartsville Recreation Department. During the next 37 years until his retirement in 2019, he became an even more iconic figure on the courts and ball fields around town. He was a familiar smiling face to children and adults who participated in recreation department activities. He marked hundreds of batter's boxes and miles of baselines and foul lines on baseball and softball fields throughout the Hartsville area over the years, and he scheduled umpires and referees for thousands of ball games. I always enjoyed seeing him in his white recreation department pickup truck, and he never failed to give me a big wave. I also grew to rely on Maceo in my job as principal of Hartsville High School when hiring coaches for our basketball programs. Ever since my own coaching days, I'd always felt that he and I shared a lot of the same beliefs about basketball, especially regarding discipline, the fundamentals of the game, and teamwork. He'd learned that philosophy from the master, Coach Thomas, and anytime I had a chance to sit

Dr. Charlie Burry, Jr.

with Maceo at a ballgame and talk with him, I did that. He is very perceptive about people's character as well. I always kept our coaching searches quiet, preferring to limit involvement to Phyllis Griggs (our athletics director) and myself, but I also had confidential conversations with Maceo about who the candidates were and how the searches were going. I trusted his judgment and respected his advice, and his input was always valuable. I've not been able to publicly thank him for his help with those situations until writing this chapter, but upon his retirement from the Hartsville Recreation Department, he was recognized for his many years of outstanding service by the Darlington County Council. Ironically, it was Maceo's retirement that signaled the biggest challenge of his life, both physically and spiritually.

When Maceo began considering retirement, he discovered that he would need to have a complete physical examination done in order to meet health coverage requirements. His health had always been good, and he had no reason to suspect that an exam would do anything other than confirm that status. Unfortunately—or fortunately, if you consider the timing—the results showed evidence of prostate cancer. I don't know many of the details other than the condition required pretty extensive surgery and some aggressive follow-up treatments. I dropped by his mother's house (right across the street from the Butler Gym, where he was recuperating) one afternoon while returning from a principals' meeting in Darlington, and we had a good visit. He was still pretty much confined to his bed at the time and had lost a good bit of weight, but he was the same old Maceo—smiling, joking, and upbeat, although acknowledging the seriousness of what he'd been through as well as what he was still facing. It wasn't long after that visit when I began receiving daily text messages from Maceo. Apparently, he'd added me to a group of people to whom he sends those messages. The messages are always positive, uplifting, and a strong testament to his faith that everything is in

God's control and is going to be all right. Following is one that I received just a couple of days ago:

"We should forgive as Jesus forgives yah, luv as Jesus luvs yah, treat others as Jesus treats yah, do more for others than yahself as Jesus did, be like Jesus in luv! Believe the best and look for good in everyone and everything that happens to yah cause God luvs yah and works everything for yah good and his glory! God Gotcha! God Gotcha! GOD IS GOOD! GOD IS IN CONTROL! Every little thing will be all right! God bless! Luv God! Luv others! Luv yahself! Luv yah!"

These messages are a daily blessing to me, and his witness—even in the face of serious health challenges and hardship, as well as a pandemic—is an inspiration. I've texted him back a few times to thank him for that encouragement, and his quick response is always to give God the glory and credit for his strength. Maceo Haynesworth had hundreds of assists during his basketball career, and helped to provide recreational opportunities for hundreds more in the Hartsville community, but he's playing point guard now in a personal ministry that is making me and a lot of others better people. I thank God for his friendship and hope to have it for many years to come.

Maceo Haynesworth

57

Tommy Petty

I spent a lot of time with high school students during my 45-year career in public education, so I've got some pretty good perspective on that time of life from an adult point of view. I also have two daughters, so I know a teenager's side of the story from my experience as a parent as well. Although my former students—particularly from the time when I was their principal— might not believe it, I was once a high school student myself. My girls have looked at 1966-1969 Hartsville High School yearbooks, so they've seen evidence that my life didn't just begin when they were born. While the days of roaming the same hallways of Hartsville High School as a student that I patrolled as principal were quite a few years ago, I do remember that perspective, too. We all have memories of our high school experiences as students and, hopefully, most of them are good. I think high school reunions are enjoyable for most people as those good memories and friendships come flooding back. We can even laugh—or at least smile—about the tough times in high school, too, because time helps us heal. What seemed to be matters of life or death 50 years ago just aren't that important now. Whatever our stories from high school might be, it's important to have had friends—and maybe a best friend—with whom to share both the joys and the heartaches. In some cases, that friendship may have been important enough to change the course of a life. In other instances, that friendship could have served as a moral compass which kept us from going too far astray. My best friend in high school, and my moral compass, was a guy whose name is Tommy Petty.

I don't think that Tommy and I actually got to know each other until we were in junior high school. Before that, we didn't go to the same elementary school or play little league baseball against each other because he lived across the lake in North Hartsville. We became friends as we navigated our way through Mrs. Vada Gore's Latin class, Mrs. Thelma Hicks' Algebra I class, Coach Ed Foster's Physical Education class, and played on Coach James Gainey's junior high basketball team together. During those early formative years, we faced the same educational, social, personal, and moral issues that all teenage boys face. As those issues were sifted through our likes and dislikes, values, and consciences, we came out being pretty similar and began spending more time together. By that time, the three main sports that interested us were basketball, tennis, and girls. Tommy's family had built a house that was within a stone's throw of the high school, so I got to know his parents and his younger sister, Sonya, pretty well, too. His dad put up a nice basketball goal in their backyard, and we spent many hours out there playing HORSE and talking about life and the future. Tommy didn't play basketball on the high school team, but we were on the tennis team together, and we continued to play a lot of tennis recreationally as well. I won't say who usually won, but I did hit to his backhand a lot. In the romance department, we began dating girls who got along well, so we double-dated some. Our social lives were pretty tame, though, as neither one of us drank alcohol or did much partying. In fact, being a devout Mormon, Tommy didn't even drink caffeine, and he still doesn't. Our dates usually consisted of movies at the Center or Berry theaters, ball games, going to Florence to play putt-putt golf, climbing the fire tower, daring to ride by the witch's tree, or going over to the east side of town to shine the car's headlights on a tree which cast a shadow that looked like the profile of a

Dr. Charlie Burry, Jr.

woman on the side of a house. Yes, we were a wild and crazy bunch for sure.

Tommy is a really smart fellow, and he approached his school work with a good bit more diligence that I did. He studied hard, and that paid off when he earned a spot in Hartsville High School's Top Ten for the Class of 1969. I might have been in the top 30, give or take a few, and that was an accurate reflection of my study habits as well. When it came time for us to go to college, I headed upstate to Furman University, and Tommy went west to Brigham Young University. We corresponded regularly through the trials of the first semester of our freshman year and ragged each other about our school's athletic teams. Tommy also remained a Gamecock fan, so that put him in double jeopardy. His deep Mormon faith led him to a two-year mission in France after the first semester of his freshman year, but we continued to write and keep up with each other as best we could. That did hit a snag once when I put a regular six-cent postage stamp on a letter to France, and it took about three months—by boat—to get to him. Those two years were a difficult time for Tommy—I think they are for anyone who goes on a mission, especially overseas—but he fulfilled that calling, grew from it, and came back home a better man and servant of God. I was a bit surprised, however—and maybe he was, too—when he returned to BYU, met a California girl, and she immediately swept the boy off his feet. They got married on the same day that Debby and I did—August 24th—except two years earlier. Tommy and Patty have stayed in the western part of the country—Oregon, Idaho, California, Arizona, and currently Utah—and have a wonderful family. He's retired now, and he has become an expert at smoking all kinds of meats although he has yet to send me any proof of his talents. Obviously, we don't see each other very much, but he did visit South Carolina just recently (the previous time was five years ago, I think) for a couple of family reunions, and we were able to spend some time together.

I hope what I've told you about the history that Tommy Petty and I share will help you understand that our friendship is one of those rare ones in which distance and time apart don't matter. The next time we see each other, whenever that might be, things will pick right back up where we left them the last time. Nevertheless, I'll have to admit that after he read *Life Lessons . . . Principally Speaking*, his comment that "You've done some good things in your life" gave me pause when I realized that he'd learned so many things from the book about my life that he didn't know. I realized that we both have 50 years of life behind us that neither of us know a lot about. The foundation of that friendship remains solid and unchanged, however, because what was built into it was a common sense of values, support, and experiences—and for me, a moral compass—that has made us who we are today, no matter how much time has passed. I'm thankful that Tommy Petty was there for me so many years ago to keep me on a better path.

Tommy Petty and Charlie Burry

58

Nathaniel Rogers

I'm a Baby Boomer—born in 1951—and therefore came of age in the 1960s, which was a time of great social unrest in the United States primarily in reaction to the Vietnam War and the American Civil Rights Movement. I was not drafted into the military and never served although a number of guys my age and a little older were in various branches of the service. While some of them did go to Vietnam, the closest that I ever came to combat in those jungles and rice paddies, thankfully, was watching film reports of the action on the nightly television news. The Civil Rights Movement also brought horrific events showing the brutality of racism to our television screens and the front pages of our newspapers. Images of Bloody Sunday at the Edmund Pettus Bridge in Selma, Alabama, and footage of riots in Watts, Detroit, and many other major cities were viewed by millions of Americans. Our country saw four significant assassinations in the 1960s—Dr. Martin Luther King, Jr., Malcolm X, Robert F. Kennedy, and the 35th President of the United States, John F. Kennedy. The only civil rights demonstration that I recall seeing in Hartsville, however, was a peaceful march down Carolina Avenue by people of both races in response to Dr. King's assassination in 1968. The social unrest that we have seen across our country since the summer of 2020 has reminded many of us of the 1960s and has again raised our social consciousness about how far we still have to go in eliminating systemic racism and bringing about law enforcement reform where needed.

While the Civil Rights Act of 1964 legislated the opening of public facilities in the United States to all races, a most significant movement against racial segregation began in 1947 when Jackie Robinson became the first Black man to play in a Major League Baseball game. He played for the Brooklyn Dodgers, was Rookie of the Year in 1947, was a six-time All-Star, and won the 1949 National League Most Valuable Player Award. More notable than his baseball accomplishments, however, was his ability to deal with the racial abuse and hostility that he faced. Branch Rickey was the club president and general manager of the Dodgers, and he knew that for his plan to integrate professional baseball to be successful, he had to have a person who could handle the abuse and not retaliate with the hostility that would doom his social experiment. In a meeting prior to signing Robinson, Rickey shared those thoughts with him. Robinson's initial response was, "Are you looking for a Negro who is afraid to fight back?" Rickey's response was that he needed a Negro player "with guts enough not to fight back." The kind of courage that Jackie Robinson exhibited and the restraint that he showed in the face of hatred and abuse based only on the color of his skin was the dawning of a new age for Major League Baseball and America. While it would still be almost 20 years before President Lyndon Johnson signed the Civil Rights Act of 1964 into law and many more years before it even approached reality, Jackie Robinson led the way with his non-violent approach. As time passed, there would be others like Robinson such as Larry Doby—from Camden, South Carolina—who was the first Black player in the American League for the Cleveland Indians. Others like Roy Campanella, Satchel Paige, Minnie Minoso, and Don Newcombe followed in Major League Baseball. Twenty years later, Hartsville High School would have a young man with similar courage to break the color barrier there.

I was on duty at a Red Fox basketball game right before Christmas in 2012, and I'd gone out into the lobby to check on things in the concession stand area. As I was standing there, a gentleman who appeared to be about my age walked up to me and said, "I bet you don't remember me." I looked at him for at least five long seconds as years melted away, and finally said, "Nat! Nathaniel Rogers! How are you, man?" We shared big smiles, a handshake, and a brief embrace and began catching up with each other. After talking a while, I told Nat that I wanted to introduce him to Aric Samuel, our boys' varsity coach, and his staff. I wanted Aric and his coaches to meet and have an opportunity to speak with a man whose historical place in our community is unmatched in its significance. You see, Nathaniel Rogers was the first Black student ever to attend Hartsville High School, enrolling for the 1964-65 school year. He and I were teammates on the 1966-67 Red Fox basketball team when Nat was a senior, and I was in the tenth grade. He graduated from Hartsville High School in 1967, and we had not seen each other in 45 years. After his high school graduation, Nat attended South Carolina State University, played in the band there, witnessed the Orangeburg Massacre, and became an electrical engineer. His dad owned and operated Rogers Barber Shop, and his mom was a seamstress. As they were getting up in years, Nat had come back to Hartsville to help them. I couldn't have been happier to see him or more gratified that he sought me out to speak. We were still old teammates; more important, still friends.

As you might imagine, Nat was very quiet in high school. Most students didn't want him to be at Hartsville High School, so friendships—even just on the surface—were scarce. Any move in that direction by a classmate was either discouraged by peer pressure or parental influence. He was also shunned by some of his old teachers and friends at Butler High School and in the Black community. I have one mental image of Nat that I think typifies his daily existence, and that is of him walking—alone—in front of the three-story building with a stack of books under

his arm. He wore glasses, even when he was playing basketball, so he projected a studious image, and I think that was a
true representation of how hard he worked to achieve good
grades. I'm not aware that he was a victim of physical violence
at school, but the threats were certainly there. A shotgun blast
took out the front window of his house one night, and little effort
was made to find the perpetrators. He chose to ignore an ava-
lanche of racist comments, either spoken directly to him or at
least overheard in the hallways and classrooms. He knew—just
as Jackie Robinson did—that the only road he could take was
the high one and that to lower himself to engage in verbal conflict, or worse, would just make things harder. I don't know that
Nat thought of himself as a trail-blazer because that wasn't his
nature. He was just getting an education, preparing himself for
the future, and had just chosen to do it in a different place. Still,
our students today have no idea what he went through, and
they wouldn't be able to imagine the determination it took for
him to survive those three years. Bob Sloan, who was writing for
the *Hartsville Messenger* in 2012, published a tremendous four-
part series entitled "Forging A Path" that depicts the courage
and dignity of Nathaniel Rogers during his time at Hartsville High
School. Dignity—that's the word that comes to my mind when
I think of my friend, Nat. He faced everything with the resolve
of quiet dignity. I didn't realize it at the time, but that example
was making me a better person when we were teammates.
When he came back 45 years later—after all he went through
at Hartsville High School—and cared enough to speak to me,
that made me a better person, too. I hope that by getting to
know Nathaniel Rogers better, you'll grow to appreciate him
as much as I do.

Dr. Charlie Burry, Jr.

Nathaniel Rogers and Charlie Burry

59

Edward Thomas

Events happen in oddly coincidental ways sometimes, and timing is often the crucial factor in life's circumstances becoming important in one way or another, either as near misses or fortunate makes. At the end of a basketball game, was the potential game-winning shot in the air before or after the buzzer sounded and the red light on the backboard came on? When you're trying to get into a crowded parking garage, does the "Full" light come on just after you drive under the gate or right as you pull up to it? Have you ever been told by a prospective employer that the job for which you're applying was filled earlier that day? To make life even more interesting—as you may have read in *Life Lessons . . . Principally Speaking*—"time is a tree with many branches." In other words, one coincidental occurrence in life could well lead to a branch of circumstances that is completely different than others, and the next branch leads to still others. My recent visit to The Angel Oak on Johns Island, South Carolina, provided an amazing illustration of this metaphor. The shot coming too late could put a playoff team into another tournament bracket to compete against 15 different teams. Not making it into one airport parking garage and having to go to another one could put you on a completely different flight because yours was overbooked. Being too late applying for one job could lead you to another situation in which there's much greater opportunity for advancement. In another case-in-point, the coincidence could be something as simple as crossing the street.

Edward Thomas became a member of the Burry family in the summer of 1959, soon after he graduated from Butler High School. We had just moved to Hartsville from Biloxi, Mississippi, and my dad was in the process of opening his own dime store—the Hartsville 5 & 10—on North Fifth Street between the Peoples Bank and the Manhattan Steak House. That location is now the Wachovia Bank parking lot. Edward happened to be walking down the sidewalk one day on the west side of Fifth Street instead of the other side. He happened to be walking right in front of the new Hartsville 5 & 10 at the very same moment my dad was coming down a ladder instead of a minute or two earlier, or later. Edward may have even stopped for a few seconds to watch. The new sign that my dad was installing on the front of the store happened to be too large for one man to handle. My dad—on the spur of all those moments and circumstances—asked Edward if he was interested in a job. Edward said, "Yes, sir, I am," instead of "No, thanks." That chance meeting was the beginning of a kinship and deep friendship with the Burry family that has now reached 62 years. Edward became like another son to our parents, was a faithful employee, and later served 29 years in the United States Army, including three tours of duty in Vietnam. When our dad died in 1996, Edward was one of the pall bearers in his funeral. When our mom passed away two days after Christmas in 2014, he was at her hospital bedside holding her hand and praying in the days before her death. Edward is 81 years old now, and he still possesses those same qualities that our dad must have seen in him that summer day in 1959. Coincidentally, Edward Thomas became one of my most cherished friends.

Edward and I worked together in the dime store unpacking freight shipments of merchandise and pricing it; sweeping, mopping, and buffing floors; washing glass doors and windows; and helping my dad with any other odd jobs that might need doing. Edward is 11 years older than I am, so he was the lead man, and I looked up to him in every way. He was strong, quiet, mature, and didn't waste time, so there was no fooling around. He told me what to do, when to do it, and how to do it. I wasn't the boss man's son; instead, I was his little brother. I recall one time when we were unpacking glassware items and putting price stickers on them. He was holding a drinking glass about chest high while pricing it, and he dropped it. As the glass fell, Edward reached down—so quickly that I can still see him doing it now—and caught the glass about a foot above the floor. When I looked at him in amazement and asked him how he'd been quick enough to do that, he said, "Because when you break something, you got to pay for it." I remember another time when my dad ordered hundreds of Hartsville 5 & 10 newspapers—they were called circulars—advertising a sale that he was having. Edward and I put boxes of those circulars in the back seat of my dad's 1957 Metropolitan, and we drove all over town putting them on the porches and inside the front screen doors of houses. I guess my dad had figured out that Edward and I delivering them that way was less expensive than mailing them. By about the third afternoon of that job, I was getting pretty tired of it, and Edward—sensing my sagging spirits—looked at me and said, "Your dad paid for these things, and we got to get them out." As you can see, every lesson that my dad was trying to teach me about responsibility, honesty, and work ethic was being reinforced by my big brother.

I don't remember much at all about Edward's time in the military. I don't think he made it home very often, and I know our dad would ride out to his mother's house to check on her occasionally and be sure that she had everything she needed. Whenever I got news of Edward from my parents, I could tell they were proud of him—especially when he achieved the rank of Sergeant Major—and thankful that he was safe, and that just reinforced the respect that I had for him. I looked up to him, even while he was gone. The three tours of duty in Vietnam took a toll on Edward, and today he struggles with Post Traumatic Stress Disorder. His constant companion is his therapy dog, Ducky, a black toy poodle that is now 16 years old. Edward still walks regularly at Byerly Park and Kalmia Gardens, and everybody who knows Edward—even if they don't know him by name—knows Ducky, too. My brother, Brent, has stayed in close contact with Edward, and we've made sure that he and Ducky are honored guests at all of our family gatherings. A special treat for Edward is the sweet potato pie that Debby makes, and she always makes an extra one for him to take home afterwards. He calls her "the First Lady" (I think mainly to be sure those pies keep coming). We had to do drive-by greetings and pie deliveries for the holidays last year, but I still talk with Edward by phone every couple of weeks. He never fails to mention our dad and mom, and how much they meant to him, and that Brent, Emily, and I are like siblings to him. He always finishes a conversation by saying, "Anything I can do for you, just call." Relationships like the one between the Burry family (and that includes our own children now) and Edward Thomas illustrate what is really important in life—friendship, loyalty, kindness, and loving each other for a long time. Relationships like that, not just coincidentally, are the ones that make us all better.

Clark and Emily Phillips, Brent and Mary Burry,
Edward Thomas, Debby and Charlie Burry

Dr. Charlie Burry, Jr.

60

Craig Kridel

It is often said that the influence of a teacher ripples out forever. I tried to remind our teachers at Hartsville High School often—not just during American Education Week or National Teacher Appreciation Week—that their profession is unlike any other. Teachers shape minds and determine futures, and give some young people a chance in life that isn't available anywhere else. It takes a special kind of person to be a teacher, though, because—first of all—it's hard. The challenges that teachers face today probably couldn't have been imagined by the good people who taught them. Teachers also have to understand that the true results of an educator's work aren't immediately seen and usually aren't observed first-hand. Students earn passing grades, and get promoted and graduate, and maybe even earn scholarships. The true results come much later, however, as those former students enjoy rewarding careers, become successful spouses and parents, and live fulfilling lives themselves. Many years later, students might not retain much of the subject matter, but they will recall the caring, the guidance, and the character of a teacher. In my opinion, which is admittedly biased because of my 45-year career in public education, there is no higher calling. Teaching is an opportunity to have a truly meaningful career, but it is also an awesome responsibility. Teachers have to remember—each day, hour, and minute—that one comment they might make to a teenager could change that young person's life for the next 60 or 70 years. When I was taking a graduate course at the University of South Carolina, one of my professors made such a comment to me. I was 40 years old at the time, and it changed my life forever. Here's how it happened.

I began working on my doctoral program in the late 1980s when district-level administrators in the Darlington County School District arranged for professors from the University of South Carolina Education Department to come to Darlington to teach graduate courses. We met once or twice a week for three-hour class sessions during the semester. I made steady progress through my doctoral program for two or three years until I reached a point where I needed to take a course in Statistics. That area had not been a strength in my master's degree program, so I was a bit concerned about such a course before I even started. The Statistics course in my program was offered during the summer, and it was taught on campus in Columbia. I walked into the first meeting of the class and immediately became concerned because there were only four other students in the group, and I was terrified at the thought of receiving that much individual attention from my professor. The second red flag—and I'll admit that I was guilty of stereotyping—was the appearance of the professor. He looked to be a person whose total existence was crunching numbers in a lab 24 hours a day—slight-of-build gentleman, white, long-sleeve dress shirt, plastic pocket protector with several pens and a calculator, thin dark necktie, and black, horn-rimmed glasses with Coke bottle lenses. My third strike came when the professor asked each of us about our background in statistics and why we were in the course. When I finished speaking— which didn't take long—he looked at me and said, "Mr. Burry, you have no business taking this course." Having been called out looking, I said, "Thank you, sir," and excused myself. I was stuck at a roadblock in my entire doctoral program, though, because I thought I had to have the Statistics course. What was I going to do? Desperate for guidance, I made a phone call to my doctoral committee chairperson. His advice was "Well, you don't have to do your dissertation on quantitative research. You can do qualitative research. Why don't you take an Educational Biography course instead of Statistics?" That's how I met Dr. Craig Kridel.

A few days later at the first meeting of my newly scheduled Educational Biography course, the professor walked into the classroom of about 15 students and introduced himself as Craig Kridel. He was a big guy, maybe 6'2" or so. He was bearded, and his hair was pulled back in a short pony tail. He was wearing sneakers with no socks, shorts, and a t-shirt. My first thought was, "Well, this is certainly different from Statistics." His first order of business also was to have students introduce themselves and make a brief statement about why they were in the course. When it was my turn, I came clean and said, "I'm in here so I won't have to take Statistics." He suppressed a bemused smile and moved on to the next student. At the end of the term, Dr. Kridel and I were having a conversation about my successful completion of the course, and he said, "You know, at first, I wasn't sure this was your cup of tea." As it turned out, Educational Biography was exactly my cup of tea. My undergraduate major at Furman was in History, and I was sure better at qualitative research than I was at crunching numbers.

During his 35 years in the College of Education at the University of South Carolina, Dr. Kridel served as the curator of the Museum of Education. At the time I was taking the Educational Biography course, the USC Museum of Education was in possession of a large number of boxes containing the papers, correspondence, research notes, and other writings of Dr. Ross Mooney, who had been a professor at Ohio State University for 50 years until his death in 1988. My impression was that Dr. Kridel and Dr. Mooney had a close personal relationship and that Dr. Mooney had also been a mentor of sorts to Dr. Kridel in the field of education. Our major assignment in the Educational Biography course was to randomly select one of Dr. Mooney's boxes, go through the papers while taking notes on what we found to be interesting and meaningful, draw conclusions from our research, and write a paper on Dr. Mooney. We did that research during several class sessions over a period of weeks. I found the assignment to be not only interesting but also a kind of spiritual endeavor. While I was fairly pleased with my paper when I submitted it, I had no idea how close my interpretation of Dr. Mooney's life from my box of papers was to being accurate. When Dr. Kridel returned my paper to me, one of comments that he had written on it read "This is so wonderful. This is the first paper that has made me miss Ross." I still have that paper 30 years later, along with several others on which Dr. Kridel wrote more complimentary remarks about my writing.

My point is this. I liked Dr. Kridel and developed an enormous amount of regard for him as a professor and a scholar. The remarks that he wrote on my paper about Dr. Mooney and other comments that he made about my writing in the Educational Biography course became a watershed moment in my career as an educator. It was the first time in my life that I'd received compliments about my writing from someone for whom I had such immense respect. He gave me confidence in my writing that I had never before had, and that motivated me to move forward and write my doctoral dissertation as an educational biography. Dr. Kridel telling me that I could write something worthwhile shifted my approach to writing away from it being a chore to being a source of satisfaction and enjoyment. I haven't seen Dr. Kridel in at least 30 years, and while *Life Lessons . . . Principally Speaking* and this book certainly aren't scholarly works, I hope he'd get a sense of satisfaction from knowing that his influence is rippling out in this manner. I hope he'd be pleased that one of his former students has

Dr. Charlie Burry, Jr.

written a couple of books that could be described at least loosely as educational biographies—or educational autobiographies, to be more accurate. Craig Kridel, with one comment, made me better than I thought I could be, and I'll always be deeply grateful.

Dr. Craig Kridel

Section 7—
Some Better Advice

There have been times in all of our lives when we could have used some better advice. And—speaking for myself—a lot of those times were when I was too proud, or too stubborn, or too stupid to take it. You've just got to slow down sometimes, and admit that there are people who have been through the fire and who know more than you do. You've got to be respectful enough to keep your mouth shut and listen to what someone else has to say. You've got to recognize the fact that the really smart people never stop seeking advice and are always learning something new. Having said all that, these last chapters offer what I consider to be—through my own experiences in life—some pretty good advice. You'll find advice that was given to me by other people, and some that I managed to figure out on my own. Some of the advice is liberating, I think, and some of it is humbling. A couple of them are pretty idealistic, and one is a prayer. Without being so presumptuous as to offer these thoughts as absolute truisms, I do think they contain enough solid philosophy of life to be worthy of consideration. You might agree with some of them, and if you don't, then hopefully what's written will make you think enough to know why. In either case, I hope in the end, you'll have some better advice.

61

Is John Going to Be There?

A number of years ago, I was watching a Boston-Detroit professional basketball game on television. At halftime, an interview
with Bill Russell was shown, and I paid close attention because
he is one of my old Celtic heroes. In addition to being one of the
greatest players of all time, he is an intelligent man with a perspective on life gleaned from some remarkable experiences.
Russell talked about winning championships and success in life
for a few minutes, and then he suddenly changed course in
the conversation and said, "The greatest thing that any parent
can give a child is for them to know that they're loved." While
that's pretty simply stated, it's also one of the most profound
statements I've ever heard. It should hit home to every parent,
and anyone who is thinking of becoming a parent. Part of my
prayers every night for years has been that my girls will know
that they're loved. Like a lot of things in life, though, loving that
child is sometimes easier said than done. Love comes pack-
aged in a lot of different ways, and sometimes you need a little
help with the delivery.

Anyone who has ever been a mom or a dad knows loving
that little bundle of joy can become complicated. There is, of
course—beyond everything else—a parent's unconditional
love that knows no bounds, no matter what happens. Then
there's the nurturing and teaching love as you listen to them
learn to talk and watch them walk those first tottering steps.

Dr. Charlie Burry, Jr.

There's also the patient love as childhood adventures and misadventures occur. Sometimes there's the worried love when they're sick or hurting. Then there's the love for teenagers, a time about which Mark Twain said, "When a child turns 13, put him in a barrel and feed him through a knot hole, and when he turns 16, plug up the hole." While Mr. Twain's quote was obviously facetious, there are undoubtedly times when the adolescent years are challenging for both parties. That's when the concept of tough love sometimes becomes necessary in order to "prepare the child for the road, not the road for the child." Once those winding, mountainous teenage years are in the rearview mirror, the trip usually begins to smooth out a bit. There are still some rough patches to go, but adulthood begins to change a child's perspective on the issue of parenting. Mark Twain gave us further guidance on that issue when he said, "When I was a boy of 14, my father was so ignorant I could hardly stand to have the old man around. But when I got to be 21, I was astonished at how much the old man had learned in seven years." The bottom line is that no matter how smooth or rough a child's teenage years might go, a parent's love can always use some help. That's why I'm glad that I had John along on the trip.

I observed a lot of parent-child relationships during my career in public education. In 31 total years as a school counselor and principal, I saw just about everything imaginable and then some. There are two things in my experience that I found to be true about parenting. The first is that things are not always as they appear to be—meaning that, you never know what goes on behind closed doors in a home. The second, which hits upon the main topic of this chapter, is that parents can do absolutely everything right, and there's still one wild card that can make all the difference in the world. That wild card is a child's peer group, which is something that a parent has very little control over. When a young person becomes involved with a peer group and related pressures that are inconsistent with the parents' system of values and priorities, there is going to be conflict and heartache. There's going to be frustration, too, because the more parents try to control that factor, the more the young person (notice I've stopped saying child) is going to fight it. It's just a fact of life in parenting, that no matter how hard you try, sometimes you've just got to be lucky with the cards you're dealt. Debby and I were very fortunate in regard to the peer group issue with our daughters, Beth and Caye. I had an insurance policy with Beth, though, because early in her teenage years whenever she asked to go out somewhere with a group of friends, the only question I had to ask was "Is John going to be there?"

John Goudelock is the son of George and Kathy Goudelock and the grandson of Buck and Nelle Goudelock. He's a tennis player, just like his dad and grandfather. Those folks did a great job raising that young man: I knew his character to be beyond reproach, and his level of maturity to be exceptional. John was actually two years ahead of Beth in school, but their peer group was pretty much the same there and at church, and they were usually interested in doing the same things socially. I certainly wanted Beth to enjoy activities and time with her friends, but I also wanted her always to be in safe and wholesome situations. I had that kind of confidence in the rest of the group, too, but I was doubly assured that if John was going to be along, everything would be all right for Beth. She had a curfew, and I don't think I ever went to bed until she was home safely for the night, but knowing that she was in a group with John made it more likely for me to doze off in my recliner until I heard the back door open. I'll always be grateful for the assurance that I felt with that situation, and I wrote a couple of letters of recommendation for John in which I mentioned the degree of confidence that I had in his character and judgment. When you tell a college admissions officer or a prospective employer that you've trusted your daughter's welfare to a young man, there's not a much better reference than that.

John Goudelock followed in his dad's footsteps as a student/athlete at Erskine College, earned a Masters of Divinity degree from Southern Baptist Theological Seminary, and achieved a Doctorate of Ministry from Southeastern Baptist Seminary. He is currently an Associate Pastor at Living Water Baptist Church in Longs, South Carolina, which is about ten miles from North Myrtle Beach. John and his wife, Michelle, have a handsome son named James. I hope when he becomes a teenager, he'll have as good a peer group as Beth Burry did. I also hope when James Goudelock asks permission to go out with a group of friends, his dad's only question will be something similar to "Is John going to be there?"

Do Something Hard Every Day

One of my favorite comic strips is *Calvin and Hobbes* by Bill Watterson. The strip was syndicated for ten years, and although it hasn't been published daily since 1995, it remains popular enough to have sold millions of books. Calvin is a precocious and adventurous little boy who cavorts his way through family life and school days with Hobbes, a stuffed toy tiger who comes to life when he's with Calvin. One of the main themes of the comic strip is Calvin's relationship with his parents, who are constantly challenged by his imaginative and mischievous nature. In one episode, Calvin's dad has misplaced his eyeglasses. He finds Calvin wearing them, pretending to be a father, and marching around the house saying, "Calvin, go do something you hate! Being miserable builds character!" The last panel shows Calvin's mom laughing hysterically at her son's pantomime. I relate that story about Calvin as a humorous introduction and in order to offer some balance (more on that later) to a chapter in which I talk about the benefits of doing something hard every day. At least two highly successful high school football coaches whom I know implore players in their programs to "GBED—get better every day." Foundational to such a philosophy is that a person gets better by encountering resistance and by doing something that is challenging on a daily basis. I became a better tennis player during my senior year of high school because I was in the number one or two position in our lineup and had matches the whole season against opponents who were much better players than I was. I hated the misery of losing a lot of matches, but I improved my game (and as Calvin said, built some character) because of the tough competition. I think it helps people to do something hard every day.

Before going any further, I should offer this caveat, and we should acknowledge that the concept of something being hard to do is relative to one's life circumstances. If we're talking about doing something physically hard, then a lot depends on one's health. When I was working, I was able to get up every weekday morning at 4:30 and do an hour-long exercise routine or 30 minutes on an elliptical machine. Some of the exercises—push-ups and planks, for instance—I did to the point of failure, or near failure. That was hard, but it gave me a sense of accomplishment and the satisfaction of taking it to the limit. I was able to do that kind of workout because I've been blessed with good health and have been able to keep myself in pretty good physical condition for a guy my age. On the other hand, for someone who hasn't been as fortunate with his/her physical health, simply getting out of bed in the morning and starting to move around a bit is extremely challenging. For someone with fibromyalgia or another autoimmune disease, sometimes just making it through the day is a win. Also, as one gets older, some body parts and joints just don't work as well as they used to, and something that was pretty easy to do 25 years earlier is much more difficult than it used to be. Some hard things are more of a mental challenge. Sticking to a diet is a hard thing to do. Developing good study habits can demand a degree of mental discipline that seems almost impossible to summon. Mindlessly scrolling through social media websites can be a habit that is hard to break. Performing well in a work environment that is unpleasant requires an attitude toward the job—and maybe your boss—that tests one's restraint to the limit. Wrestling with an emotionally upsetting situation can be mentally exhausting. Battling an addiction of any kind day after day may well be the most difficult thing that a person ever faces in life. Obviously, there is no one-size-fits-all plan of self-improvement. Buying into the benefits of doing something hard every day requires establishing reasonably challenging, yet ambitious, goals that are tailored to one's physical and emotional capabilities and what one is trying to accomplish. In gauging one's capabilities, however, I think it helps to have the mindset that iron sharpens iron, and that if something is easy to do, everybody would be doing it. But everybody doesn't abandon all common sense and join the circus, either.

A number of years ago as I approached my 50th birthday, I apparently went through a midlife crisis that seriously impacted my judgment regarding the setting of personal goals. I decided that I was going to learn to ride a unicycle. My wife humored me, updated my health insurance policy, and about four months later Santa Claus delivered the instrument of torment to our house. Having only one wheel, it wasn't hard to assemble, and within minutes I had the seat adjusted and was ready to ride my new unicycle. I decided to start in our hallway in order to balance myself by putting my hands on the walls. I mounted the contraption and before I even knew what happened, I was flat on the floor and seeing stars. At that point I figured out that the most important thing about learning to ride a unicycle is learning how to fall off because you're going to do that about a million times. For about six weeks after Christmas, I was 71 inches of black, blue, and purple bruises, partly because I was too proud—or stupid—to wear any pads or a helmet. My daily 45-minute lessons (I was teaching myself, mainly to avoid embarrassment) took place early in the mornings at Hartsville High School before anyone else arrived. I started out in the back hallway of the main office, and as my skill level gradually increased and fall frequency decreased, I moved over to the Media Center. After a month or so, I graduated to the long—and then carpeted—hallway of Building 7 (which made for

Dr. Charlie Burry, Jr.

softer landings) where I continued to make good progress. A few weeks later, I'd moved over to Ulmer Gym, and I was riding in circles and figure eights on the basketball court. After about three months, my neighbors began to notice a crazy man riding a unicycle around Edgewood Drive. Miraculously, I avoided any broken bones or a traumatic brain injury during that time, but it was absolutely the hardest thing requiring physical skill and coordination that I have ever done in my life.

To paraphrase Calvin, learning to ride a unicycle builds character. It requires discipline, persistence, physical coordination, balance, and a high level of pain tolerance. If you don't already think I hit my head one too many times falling off, I'll also tell you that it's one of the most satisfying athletic (yes, I think that's an appropriate term) accomplishments of my life. While I wouldn't recommend unicycling for everyone, I do believe that people need a regular sense of satisfaction in their lives, and one way to achieve that is by doing something hard every day.

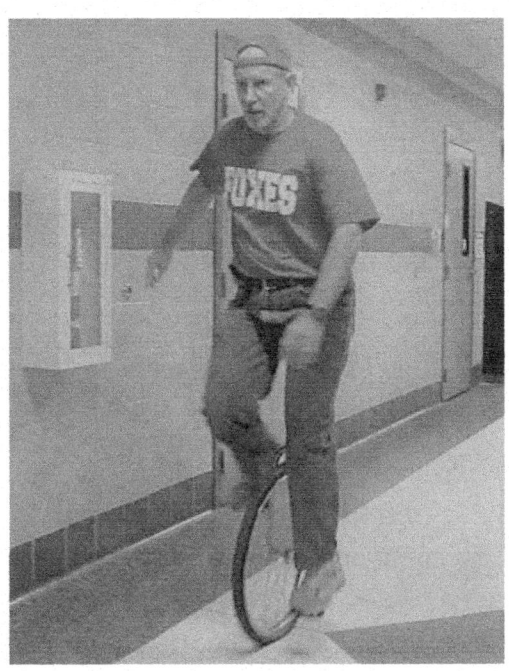

63

Some of the Best Lessons of My Life Were Screamed at Me

A little more than a year ago, I stopped by the office of Andrew Privette—who is an attorney in Hartsville—to speak with him about a chapter that I'd written in *Life Lessons . . . Principally Speaking*. Andrew is a Hartsville High School graduate, a former Red Fox football player and Red Fox wrestler. The chapter that I'd written was about his high school athletic career, and I'd asked him to read a draft copy in order to be sure that it met with his approval. He assured me that it did, and we continued to have an enjoyable conversation about his days as a Red Fox athlete and also his college experience at The Citadel. We talked about some of the hard things he'd had to do conditioning-wise in order to play football, and that he'd been coached hard, especially by his position coaches. We reminisced about the trials of football camp at Laurinburg. Andrew also spoke about his time on the wrestling mat and how that had been demanding as well, both in terms of the effort that he'd put into the sport and the tough manner in which he'd been coached. It was an easy transition from those memories to further discussion about his experience as a freshman Knob in The Citadel's Fourth-Class System, which is described on the school's website as being "deliberately and appropriately stressful." He assured me that it was. As I was leaving, our chat turned to how he strongly believed that those challenging experiences in his life had made him a better person. Andrew then said, "You know, some of the best lessons of my life were screamed at me."

The remainder of this chapter is going to expand on that line of thinking some, but I want to make it clear that I'm not condoning verbal abuse by coaches, teachers, parents, or anyone else. There's a big difference between what is truly verbal abuse and coaching players hard and aggressively by shouting at them from time to time. Anyone who is in a supervisory or more authoritative position using language—in content, tone, or volume—that is abusive, demeaning, or psychologically damaging is always unacceptable. So, having cleared that up, let's go ahead and acknowledge that athletics teaches valuable life lessons, and that much of athletic competition is aggressive in nature. A pitcher throws a fastball instead of an off-speed pitch to a batter. A golfer goes for the pin with his second shot on a par-five hole instead of laying up short of the green. A basketball player drives to the basket for a dunk instead of shooting a jump shot. A tennis player charges the net instead of settling for a long rally at the baseline. All of these situations are examples of playing aggressively, and I believe for athletes to play with that kind of intensity, they've got to be—at least in some manner—coached aggressively. Understand further, though, that "at least in some manner" covers a lot of territory. The most successful coaches know that individual players respond to coaching differently. Some athletes take aggressive coaching better than others, and some don't take hard coaching well at all. Good coaches know that a big part of helping players, and therefore teams, achieve maximum potential is understanding which buttons to push and when to push them. That's when knowing your players and their knowing you becomes important. Just as with all teaching—and coaching is teaching—relationships are key. I believe that Andrew Privette would tell you that he had good relationships with his coaches and commanding officers, or at the very least, understood and accepted that there was a method behind their madness.

In order to coach aggressively, and maybe do a little shouting occasionally, team members have to know that the coach cares about them as people and as players. With that kind of relationship in place, players know that criticism—no matter how it's delivered—isn't personal, it's meant to bring about improvement. A coach can tell players in no uncertain terms—and, if necessary, loudly—that the manner in which they just did something was horrible, but that doesn't make them terrible people. While constant berating in any manner is usually counterproductive, players learn to accept tough coaching if it's done in a respectful context. I used to tell my players that the only time they should be worried was if I ever stopped yelling at them. In addition to caring relationships, an additional factor that must be in place in order for tough coaching to work is the credibility of the coach regarding technical knowledge of the sport. A coach has to be able to teach how to do something, but also to explain why it's being done that way. Aggressive coaching falls flat on its face if players know—or even sense—that a coach is faking it and doesn't know what he's shouting about. I was able to yell at Kelvin Montague and Dennis Rogers, and hat-whip Michael Camak and Jacob Shumate because they knew that I cared about them and because they believed that I knew what I was talking about.

Raising one's voice, in order to be most effective, usually has to be intentional. What I mean by that is that the purpose of getting loud with a player or a team should be specifically for motivational reasons. It should be used judiciously to make a point, in a strong manner, about doing something better. It should be to explain something in such an emphatic way, that the cadet or the company clearly understands the importance of the issue at hand. Less than acceptable effort would be a prime reason for addressing an individual or group in an

Dr. Charlie Burry, Jr.

aggressive tone. Shouting—in a manner of speaking—can also be done quietly so that the tone of voice and the proximity to the player or players delivers the message more effectively than the volume. I also believe that a purely emotional outburst can be motivational; however, that sort of eruption loses its effectiveness if it happens too frequently. Finally, I don't believe that it hurts anything for a young person—especially an athlete—to be yelled at occasionally if it's for a good reason. It's been my experience that getting your feelings hurt a little bit sometimes drives a life lesson home more effectively.

You've noticed that I've been careful to explain my support for Andrew's statement mainly in terms of player-coach relationships, and I believe that his experience as a high school athlete and a Citadel Knob was his main frame of reference for that statement. I believe Andrew would agree with me that there's not much place—other than emergencies—for adults to be shouting at each other. I've observed that unwarranted behavior of that sort only escalates stressful situations, which then necessitates an apology. I learned that lesson from my wife a long time ago.

Charlie Burry

64

Don't Worry About What You Ain't Got

The Hartsville High School football staff always met on Sunday afternoons to develop a game plan for our opponent on the upcoming Friday night and to work out practice plans for the week. Those meetings, after watching a great deal of video-tape and analyzing scouting reports, entailed what we thought we could do successfully on offense and defense against our opponent. Evaluating our own personnel in terms of establishing a positional depth chart for the week was also important, and the injury report from the previous game was always a factor in those decisions. On one particular Sunday, the list of injured players not only was unusually long, but it also posed problems at some key positions. The tone of the discussion that afternoon was grim, as we all came to the realization that our personnel problems were going to make competing successfully against a formidable opponent even more challenging. It was then that Keith Sanders once again came straight to the point and said, "We can't worry about what we ain't got. We got to play with what we got." That admonition got us refocused on what we had to do, and we formulated our game plan accordingly.

That statement—that you got to play with what you got instead of worrying about what you ain't got—is a good piece of life philosophy. In the first place, I think it helps us clarify the difference between what we want and what we need. After watching ball games on television all Saturday afternoon along

Dr. Charlie Burry, Jr.

with the accompanying commercials, I might decide that I want a new truck. However, a meeting with the Burry family Chief Financial Officer helps me understand that while I might want a new truck, I don't really need one since the Chevy Colorado I've got still looks good and runs just fine. When our girls were in college, Debby and I wanted to go out to eat more often, but we didn't need to, so we got fish sticks out of the freezer and Hamburger Helper out of the pantry instead. I don't completely have a handle on the wants versus needs issue, however, as I've never been able to understand why the women in my family need 50 pairs of shoes in their closets. I'm sure that whichever one of them reads this first will explain that to me and further point out that I have about 50 hats in the house. In all seriousness, disciplining oneself to differentiate between wants and needs is a crucial financial issue, especially for young people. If you don't want to accumulate a mountain of debt, sometimes you've just got to live with what you've got.

Another life lesson which can be derived from Coach Sanders' words of wisdom is the importance of positive thinking. Being optimistic about what you have instead of being negative about what you don't have can make all the difference in the world in the outcome of a situation. It's the old "glass half full or half empty" question. While I was principal of Hartsville High School, every Friday I asked each member of our faculty, staff, and administration to send me a short email about something positive that had happened during the week. We called the initiative *Practicing the Power of Positive Thinking*, and the requested email was their PPPT report. The theory was that positive thinking is contagious, just as negative thoughts are, and we wanted positive thinking to spread throughout our school. There were a lot of things we didn't have at Hartsville High School during the time I was there, but I was asking our staff to think about the good things that we did have going on. I didn't require it, and everyone didn't do it—although I always sent them one of my own—but I think that it generally helped to foster attitudes that promoted a more positive school climate which was more conducive to success. We wanted that positivity to spread to our students as well, and we provided our teachers with signs for the doors to their classrooms with their names, room numbers, and the phrase "A Place of Hope and Possibility." As our students walked into their classrooms, we wanted them to think about the opportunities they had to learn and get better, not what they didn't have.

Hartsville High School improved academically over the years, and one reason that happened was because we didn't make excuses for what we didn't have. The demographics and socioeconomic characteristics of our school made it more difficult for us to compete with schools in other parts of the state. We told our teachers—like it or not—that's who we are, and that's what we've got. We promoted an attitude, however, that rationalizing for standardized test scores that were not where we wanted them to be was not productive. On the other hand, we wanted our data analysis to show us reasons for the scores we were getting so that we could identify instructional strategies that would help our students improve. Either way, we made it clear that we were going to play the cards that were dealt to us, we were going to bet the house, and we certainly weren't going to fold. Our philosophy was that every child could learn, and we were going to develop those abilities and prepare our students for the future in the best possible manner.

Another way to lessen worry about what you "ain't got" is to concentrate on what you can control. While I was principal, I always wanted everything at Hartsville High School to run smoothly, but the reality of the situation was that events were going to happen that I had no control over. I knew that teenagers were often unpredictable in their behavior and that by having 1,300 of them in the same place for eight hours every day, some craziness was going to be part of the drill. When something unexpected did occur—often simply controversy sparked by social media—all we could do was react in a manner that would get the school day back into a normal rhythm as quickly as possible. Before we began having our commencement exercises in the arena, the weather lent an element of unpredictability to that event as well. Every year, I began checking the weather reports a couple of weeks in advance of the date, and on the day of graduation I always had the WeatherBug tab open on my computer. Nevertheless, I knew I had no control over the weather and that I'd have been better off to just make our contingency plans and put Ed Piotrowski out of my mind. Learning to accept the fact that sometimes stuff happens and there's nothing you can do about it brought me a better sense of confidence and peace, at least to some degree.

People stress a lot these days about concerns in their lives which can't be controlled, especially when, as Queenie points out in *The Curious Case of Benjamin Button*, "You never know what's coming for you." Ambition and financial concerns consume people. Self-help books about how we can achieve inner peace in our lives are popular. People meditate, do yoga, exercise, listen to the sound of the ocean, and take all sorts of measures to achieve a state of tranquility. Perhaps part of a better game plan for our lives simply should be to understand that we shouldn't worry too much about "what we ain't got."

Keith Sanders and Charlie Burry

Dr. Charlie Burry, Jr.

65

If You Have an Idea What You're Doing, You Know the Difference

Okay, I'll go ahead and say it right up front. I spent too much time at Hartsville High School during my career, especially while I was principal. My wife tried to tell me that, but I didn't listen. My colleagues told me that when they saw my truck in front of the school late at night and on weekends, but I took it as a compliment. More often than not, I was there seven days a week, probably in excess of 70 hours, and that doesn't count attending ball games and other extracurricular activities. Being principal and making our school a better place was practically my entire existence, and the job and the place became who I was. When I retired, it was like a divorce, although it was ami-cable. I'm a quote collector, and use them to motivate others and myself and gain insight into life. Too late in my career, I ran across one by Ellis Johnson, a veteran and successful college football coach, who was the defensive coordinator at the University of South Carolina for Steve Spurrier when he said it. Coach Johnson was talking about time spent at work when he said, "I don't like leaving when you've got something to get done, and I don't like being here when you don't have any-thing to do. And if you have an idea what you're doing, you know the difference." That quote hit me right between the eyes.

Work ethic has always been extremely important to me. That character trait began to be instilled in me at an early age by my dad when I sold popcorn in his dime store on Saturdays when I was eight years old. He also set that example for me as I saw him work six days a week for at least ten hours a day for most of his career in the retail business. He was a perfectionist, too, and I'm sure those two attributes fed off each other to help create the successful businessman that he was. He had some hobbies on and off during his life—reading, gardening, fishing, golf, and woodworking—but all of those activities came in a distant second to providing a livelihood for his family. When our welfare and being able to afford to send his children to college depended on the success of the business, there wasn't any doubt about where he was going to be most of the time. So, being Charles E. Burry, Jr.—even though I chose a different career path from my dad—it was a given that I was going to work just as hard as he did. I think he had an idea what he was doing though.

When I began my career as a teacher and a coach, particularly in regard to my coaching, I was determined that nobody was going to outwork me. I would train myself to get by on four hours of sleep at night if that's what it took. If I never took a day off, that would be all right—vacations would just have to wait until later in life. I read books about coaching more often than I read my Bible. I was consumed with the idea of working harder than everybody else, and I told my teams that nobody was going to outwork us. When I became a principal—the head coach of a school—my thinking about work ethic hadn't changed that much. I never gave much thought to outworking other principals, but my mindset was that we were going to become a better school no matter how hard we had to work. I would be at school 20 hours a day if that's what it took. If I never took a day off, that would be all right—we were going to become a great school again. I went to church for an hour on Sunday mornings, and then I worked at school for six hours on Sunday afternoons. I was consumed with the concept of a Red Fox Renaissance. I didn't have an idea what I was doing, though.

What I hadn't figured out yet was that there is only so much time in the day, and all coaches and principals have that same amount of time. Even if I could work 24 hours a day, if another guy was crazy enough to do the same thing, I couldn't outwork him. Then I began to understand that the time element is not the only component of hard work. In fact, it's not even the most important one. Spending hours on the driving range won't automatically make you a better golfer. Even if you add the intensity of the work as another component, that doesn't come close to completing the big picture of hard work. There's a maximum level of intensity just as there is a limit on the amount of time. Swinging harder at a golf ball won't automatically translate into more distance off the tee. The most important component of hard work is how efficiently one is working. If one coach gets just as much out of a one-hour practice as another coach gets out of a two-hour practice, which team has worked harder? The team that practiced two hours may have worked harder, but that depends on the intensity of the other team's one-hour practice. A more important question to ask would be which team practiced more efficiently, and as a result, which team will be better in the long run? So, my focus at the beginning of my career as a coach, as well as when I became a principal, should not have been on working hard but on working better. When you figure out how to work better, that's when you have an idea what you're doing.

Ellis Johnson apparently doesn't like wasting time. Perhaps he learned that from being a survivor of Hodgkin's Disease, which he battled while he was coaching at Alabama and Clemson in 1993 and 1994. I remember seeing him at a Clemson coaches clinic when he'd lost all of his hair from chemotherapy and radiation treatments. He started a family after that, and his three children no doubt helped him understand the value of time with family. Maybe that's why he didn't like being around the football offices at Williams-Brice Stadium when there wasn't anything else to do. The coaching fraternity is special, but it's not family, and unless you're pretty old, it's not your children. I think the lesson we can learn from Ellis Johnson is about choosing what's important in life. Whether we do that by being forced into it by life's circumstances, or we decide to do it on our own, that's when we start learning how to work better instead of harder. It seems that Coach Johnson achieved a work-life balance that eludes people, especially early in their careers. He was close to 60 years old when I read that quote in *The State*, but I don't know how long he'd held that belief. I guess it takes some people longer to figure it out than others. When it hits you between the eyes, though—even if you're a high school principal about that same age—you can tape the quote on the credenza beside your desk to remind you that it's time to go home.

Dr. Charlie Burry, Jr.

66

Dr. Coach

I've always believed, especially since I became a school counselor in 1987, that academics and athletics could be—and should be—a good marriage. I've never thought that work ethic was something that should be necessarily exclusive to only one part of a person's life. If there was a great deal of inconsistency about someone in that regard, I would tend to wonder how genuine and embedded that character trait really was. My philosophy was that young people could apply great effort and dedication to excelling in their schoolwork, just as well as they could to being exceptionally good in a sport, if they would just see the value of that and make up their minds to do it. It was always rewarding to see a student-athlete who was talented enough to continue an athletic career in college have the grades to accept a scholarship offer. I admired an athletic program in which the coaches emphasized the importance of academics, and I had even greater respect for coaches who set that sort of example in their own lives.

That belief caused me to be intrigued in the 1980s when I would watch the Nebraska Cornhuskers football team play on television, and the announcers would occasionally refer to the Nebraska head coach as Dr. Tom Osborne. Tom Osborne was one of the most successful college football coaches ever, winning almost 84% of his games and capturing three national championships in his 25 years as a head coach. Coach Osborne also earned a doctoral degree in Educational Psychology from the University of Nebraska in 1965. There are a lot of really smart football coaches on every level, but you don't see many who have their doctorates. I was similarly interested during that same time period when I would watch the Iowa Hawkeyes basketball team play on television, and hear the announcers talk about Dr. Tom Davis, the University of Iowa head coach. Tom Davis was a highly respected college head basketball coach for 38 years and won nearly 700 games in his career. Coach Davis also earned a doctoral degree in History from the University of Maryland in 1969. I've known a lot of really smart basketball coaches, too, but I'd guess that those with terminal degrees are also pretty rare in that sport. I was fairly sure at that point in my career that coaching in college at any level was not in my future, but I started thinking that—if I had the work ethic to do it—I could be like Coach Osborne and Coach Davis in another manner and have a better academic credential to put on my resume'. I might even learn something along the way.

About that same time, I had the opportunity to take some graduate level courses sponsored by the Darlington County School District (DCSD) that would apply toward a doctoral program. Being perfectly honest about the situation, there were some financial considerations as well. Caye was just a toddler, Beth was seven or eight, and we wanted Debby to be a stay-at-home mom, at least for a while. Therefore, we were basically a single income family, and I wanted to make as much money as I could. I'd projected that taking the courses I'd need to complete a doctorate would cost around $20,000. I'd also looked at the DCSD salary schedule, and had seen that people who earned doctorates were compensated with an annual $7,000 bonus added to their salaries. While the initial investment would be costly, I'd make the money back in three years. So, armed with those dual ambitions—better academic standing and more money—I applied to the Ph.D. program in Educational

Administration at the University of South Carolina. A couple of months after going through the application process, I ran into my first obstacle. I wasn't admitted.

Apparently, USC only accepted a certain number of doctoral candidates in Educational Administration each year, and I didn't make the cut. I couldn't believe it, and I kept looking at the letter denying my admission and saying to myself, "This can't be true." I wasn't willing to wait another year, and I sought advice from one of my professors who suggested that I apply to the Ed.D. program in Curriculum and Instruction. I was accepted into that program, which actually turned out to be a blessing in disguise. The Ed.D. program is also a doctoral level course of study, but without the foreign language and residency requirements that the Ph.D. program had. So, my quest to become Dr. Burry was back on track. I just had to do the work (which was easier said than done), spend many, many hours in the Wardlaw College educational building on the USC campus, and eat a lot of hot dogs across the street at a Sandy's restaurant. Back at home, most weekday mornings for three years I would get up early and do my assigned course reading before going to work because I was too tired to do it at night. During one fall term, I had a class that met on Saturdays, and it was on November 23, 1991, that I really questioned my sanity. That afternoon during a class break, I walked outside and looked down the street to the south and saw Williams-Brice Stadium full of fans for the Carolina-Clemson game. I just shook my head and walked back inside Wardlaw for more lecture and discussion on curriculum theory. A couple of years later, on November 19, 1993, I had a much better day. That morning in Columbia I successfully defended my dissertation before my doctoral committee, and that night at Kelleytown Stadium the Red Foxes defeated North Augusta by a score of 34-0 for our 13th win of the season and a berth in the AAAA Lower State Championship game. It was certainly a full day, but one of the best professionally I've ever had. The icing on the cake was a few weeks later at graduation when my parents were doubly thrilled because the commencement speaker was John Jakes, a renowned author who had visited my dad's bookstore. I had finally become Dr. Burry, but who was that? I was still just a school counselor and assistant football coach.

People began asking me what I wanted to be called—Coach Burry or Dr. Burry—and I still get that question occasionally, even in retirement. I have joked about that issue some, saying that "I'm not really the kind of doctor who can help anybody," or when people have asked what to call me, I've said, "Call me anything except late to supper." I've honestly felt that using the title was a bit pretentious sometimes, but once I earned that degree, I absolutely added that "Ed.D." after my name on my official correspondence. I've never even imagined whatever prestige my doctorate holds to be in the same world as a medical degree or a juris doctor degree, nor to be worthy of the same respect. So, even though the Ed.D. is a terminal degree in my profession—to make things simpler—just call me Coach. In terms of relationships, which are much more important than degrees, I think that sounds a whole lot better.

67

Deserve's Got Nothing to Do with It

In an iconic scene from the 1992 Western *Unforgiven*, Little Bill—the unscrupulous sheriff of Big Whiskey, Kansas, played by Gene Hackman—pleads for his life by saying, "I don't deserve to die like this." William Munny—an aging outlaw and ruthless killer played by Clint Eastwood—replies, "Deserve's got nothing to do with it," and then with calm resolution shoots Little Bill with a rifle at close range. The theme of the movie, graphically portrayed in scene after scene, is that there is no justice for anyone. Munny's life has been a tragic testament to that idea, and his heartless belief—as expressed to Little Bill—is that few people get what they deserve from an unforgiving world. In real life, what people do and don't deserve is—thankfully—a bit more complicated than William Munny's line of thinking. It's a generally accepted belief that people who do good in their lives deserve to have good happen to them. On the other hand, most people like to think that what goes around comes around for folks who deserve a date with karma as repayment for the bad they've done. What sometimes makes life interesting and difficult to understand is that affairs don't always work out that way—for better or for worse—and too often it seems that there's some truth to the idea that "deserve's got nothing to do with it." I tried to teach my daughters about William Munny's philosophy of life in a more positive and forgiving manner. My suggestion to them was that treating people better than they deserve is a virtue. That's not easy to do, however.

I'm afraid that today we live in a world in which the virtue of turning the other cheek has become far less common than what is good for us. Many people are afraid, and rightly so, that such a forgiving nature leaves us vulnerable to those who would take unfair advantage of such compassion. Politics is the first thing that comes to mind when we consider—even with the Presidential election months behind us—the harsh disagreement that continues to find its way into what should be more bipartisan dialogue. On another front, our society has become more litigious than ever as many people seem to believe that legal action is the best recourse in any sort of disagreement, and one can find a lawyer in any television commercial or on any street corner who would be willing to file a lawsuit, even against a neighbor, friend, or relative. While we certainly have miles to go in terms of overcoming social injustice, eradicating racial inequality, and reforming some law enforcement practices, political correctness has become like walking on eggshells as people are prone to take offense at even the most unintentional slights. The cancel culture has raised some genuinely legitimate issues, but it has also become exceptionally difficult to determine the extent of its legitimacy. Even the traditional expression of compassion "Bless your heart," recently has taken on a meaning that is meant to be condescending or even insulting. And now, in the social context that I've just described, I'm suggesting that people should treat others better than they deserve? Just call me Pollyanna.

I'm going to go on down the track with this idealistic train of thought in advocating for compassion and kindness in such an underserving manner by further suggesting that we always have a choice about how we're going to react to what we see as insult or injury. First of all, understand that I'm not talking about ignoring injustice. I subscribe to the philosophy of the late Georgia Representative John Lewis when he said, "Never, ever be afraid to make some noise and get in good trouble,

Dr. Charlie Burry, Jr.

necessary trouble." What I am suggesting is that in the face of personal conflict, we can choose words and actions that will make the situation worse, or we can take a path that will deescalate the controversy. Maybe the person or the situation deserves to be criticized or chastised, but that doesn't mean we openly have to do it. Perhaps a better way to make people stop to consider the rudeness or inappropriateness of what they've done is to react in such a manner that disarms them because it is so totally unexpected. If they're looking for a fight, just don't give it to them. I think you can say, "Shame on you," without really verbalizing it, and it can be more effective than the embarrassment of a rebuke. Even if the desired response is not achieved, the satisfaction of remaining above the fray—at least in the long run—tastes better than the bitterness of controversy. The old saying that "Revenge is sweet" can be diluted with forgiveness, particularly when it's undeserved.

Abraham Lincoln said, "I destroy my enemies when I make them my friends." I don't mean to take issue with Lincoln's choice of words—especially given that he was a wartime President—but the word "destroy" doesn't quite fit my line of thinking in this chapter. I'm citing the quote because in the end it supports what I'm trying to say, but I would rather convert my enemies. Although destroying an enemy is no doubt a more final resolution than conversion, I still think that Mr. Lincoln and I could agree that one needs to have as few enemies as possible, and conciliation should be the desired, if not deserved, course of action. The bottom line is that if compromise can settle differences of opinion and resolve conflicts of interest, animosity begins to fade away, and what one deserves—or not—becomes less of an issue. Lest any of you think that this old principal has lost his edge, though, I'll also offer Oscar Wilde's advice to "Always forgive your enemies; nothing annoys them so much." That seems to be a particularly good strategy when the enemy doesn't deserve forgiveness. When you do that, even if you don't accomplish anything else, at least you're setting a good example by taking the high road—while leaving them on the low one.

Ironically, during the time I was writing this chapter, my daily Bible reading found me in the book of Job, and I thought it was interesting to compare Job's story with that of William Munny. Job was a good and prosperous man who had his wealth, children, and physical health taken from him by Satan—with God's permission. While we don't have as much background information on the outlaw Munny, we know that he'd apparently experienced similar undeserved heartache. We've seen how Munny reacted to his tragic circumstances with a lack of faith in anything, especially any sort of justice. The book of Job features dialogue between Job and three friends as they discuss the reasons for his misfortune. Job laments his condition, argues with his friends, but he ultimately affirms his faith by accepting his troubles as being God's will. In the end, Job's blessings in life are restored to an even greater degree than when the story began. The fundamental life-changing difference between William Munny and Job was their faith. Perhaps that at least partially answers the question as to how we can be virtuous enough to treat people better than they deserve.

Dr. Charlie Burry, Jr.

68

It's We, Not I

Leadership has been a concept and a personal quality that has interested me for a long time. Leaders whom I admired early in my life were men like J. T. Alford, Hubert Twitty, Cliff Malpass, and Tim Watson. Interestingly, you'll find in that list of names one Boy Scout leader, three coaches, and not a single school principal. There were certainly school administrators whom I respected, such as Mr. E. E. Truesdale, who was principal of Carolina Elementary School while I was a student there. Mr. Truesdale was ambidextrous and could write on a chalkboard with both hands at the same time. The amazing thing about his parlor trick was that he could start at the beginning of a sentence with his left hand and in the middle of a sentence with his right hand and finish both parts of the sentence at the same time. I saw him do it. Everyone I know was terrified of our junior high school principal, but later in life I got to know Mr. Charlie Smith as a trusted advisor and a good friend. I liked our high school principal, Mr. David Johnson, and thought he did a good job and was a nice man, but he didn't really inspire me to one day follow in his footsteps as principal of Hartsville High School. The men who impacted me most were leaders of teams of which I was a member. Teamwork and loyalty to the team were pillars of their leadership philosophies and were therefore ingrained in me and my concept of leadership. I read and studied books by well-known coaches—Woody Hayes, Bobby Knight, Bo Schembechler, Dean Smith, and John Wooden—and their beliefs reinforced what I'd learned from my own coaches. As a result, whenever I read or watch interviews with leaders—especially coaches—I always pay attention to their use of pronouns. I notice whether they say, "I, me, my, and mine" or "We, us, our, and ours." I wonder if that might be a clue, even subconsciously, about their concept of teamwork.

While I was one of 23 principals in the Darlington County School District, we had a superintendent who would say, "All of us are a lot smarter than one of us." As a leader, that's an important thing to acknowledge and to have guide decision-making processes. When a leader encourages team members to have input in a decision, two things happen. One is that a better, more well-thought-out result is almost guaranteed. An assistant superintendent or principal can have a shelf full of books on educational theory, principles, and practice, but determining the best fit for a particular school requires discussion among the folks who are where the rubber meets the road, and that is in the classroom. The experience and advice from the people who are actually going to implement the plan is invaluable, and a successful administrator will take advantage of that kind of expertise. The second thing that will happen is that the team members will be much more likely to buy into the plan, work to support it, and ensure its success. Ownership is a key component of teamwork, and when team members have that type of investment in a plan, the implementation is going to be easier, navigating the problems will be done in a more positive manner, and the success will be more enjoyably shared. Finally, when the work of the group is acknowledged and appreciation is expressed publicly—even if it's just in a faculty meeting—that does wonders for building team loyalty. Teaching is hard work, as is after-school committee work, and credit should be given where it's due.

I believe that language using plural pronouns can also promote unity when things get tough. Changing the culture of a school, or any organization, is not easy to do, and it doesn't happen quickly. There will be those who question change even if they have input. Others won't change just because it's too much trouble, and they're set in their ways. Some teachers will choose popularity with their students rather than holding them accountable to school policy. The rationale for every policy and rule that we had at Hartsville High School could be justified to anyone who might have a question, but what could never be adequately explained was faculty members intentionally choosing not to enforce those policies and rules in a fair and equitable manner. It was a situation in which anyone who was not with us was against us. We said, "We're going to become a great school again." We promised that "We're going to become an on-time school." We said, "Everyone is going to wear a school ID." We told our students that if they wanted to have a school in which fighting and bullying were rare occurrences, then they would be the ones to make that happen. Our students were told that in order for us to become a great school, that they'd be the ones to make the test scores, earn the grades, score the touchdowns and hit the home runs, be awarded the scholarships, and win the championships that would evidence that greatness. Our students eventually bought into the idea that our school climate would reflect their values and conduct, not the rules. We tried to help ninth graders understand that they had four years in front of them during which they could make a positive difference in our school. The Red Fox Renaissance didn't happen overnight, but we did it.

To be fair, I think it's also important to acknowledge that no matter how much a principal might use plural pronouns to reflect a philosophy, leadership can be a lonely job. Sometimes a school can't be a democracy, and the leader has to make a decision even if it's unpopular. University of Alabama football coach Nick Saban is noted for saying, "If you want to make everyone happy, don't be a leader; sell ice cream." Assistant coaches and assistant principals quickly learn when they're promoted to the big chair that there's a great deal of difference between offering suggestions and making decisions. The Harry Truman quote that "The buck stops here," might not actually be on one's desk, but that's the level of accountability which comes with the territory. Language using plural pronouns should never be used to mask accountability or deflect responsibility, and there would be no quicker way for a coach to lose the locker room or a principal to lose the support and loyalty of a faculty. No one likes to get thrown under the bus, especially when it's not deserved. There were times when, as important as the team concept was to me, the best option was for me to bite the bullet and just say to the superintendent, "It's my school, and what happened is my responsibility, and I will get it fixed." Sometimes, as uncomfortable—and maybe unfair—as that option was, it had to be me instead of we. Then, after the dust had settled, we—not I—would get back to work to make our school better.

69

You Don't Have to Be Wrong to Apologize

How important is it to win an argument or have someone apologize? Perhaps a less intrusive way to approach this subject would be to ask if you know someone who always—no matter what—has to get in the last word? If we find looking in the mirror too difficult to do when it comes to this issue, then go ahead and think of a family member, relative, friend, or work colleague who will—as my mom used to tell me—argue with a stop sign. Folks who are like that (never ourselves) abandon all facts, reason, and rationality in the interest of—at least in their view—coming out on top in a debate. The possibility that there might be another side to the story is never even a consideration. They'd never dream of offering an apology because, in their minds, they don't owe one to anybody. Knowing ahead of time that there's no way such people are going to change their minds on issues, the sane strategy for dealing with them is to go ahead and surrender and not lose any sleep over it. This tactic is in keeping with Ayn Rand's opinion that "Reason is not automatic. Those who deny it cannot be conquered by it. Do not count on them. Leave them alone." So, if necessary, just express your regret for getting in the way of their one-track train of thought and step out of the way. You don't have to be wrong to apologize.

The next step in working through this subject is to think about how we feel about being around people who are always right and won't take no for an answer. If issues don't flare up very often, we can just walk away without being too obvious about what we're doing. They probably won't even notice. In more extreme cases, though, relationships suffer because on one side there are those who value friendship, and on the other side there are those for whom friends come in a distant second to their opinions. Eventually, a demilitarized zone is established between the potential—or worse, former—friends, and they have their own little cold war going. The basis for a settlement has to be a mutually healthy regard for relationships and valuing friendship more than a won-lost record in the discussion of social issues, world affairs, politics, or the merits of Fords versus Chevys. The final, binding clause in the settlement should be an agreement by all parties which would call into play, instead of going into sudden death overtime to determine a winner, a willingness to compromise or simply agree to disagree, and—whenever necessary—apologize. Frank Howard, legendary former football coach of the Clemson Tigers, once said, "A tie is like kissing your sister." A tie game ending with mutual apologies, if it salvages a relationship, isn't that bad. Just remember . . . you don't have to be wrong to apologize.

If for some reason the cold war continues, a smart strategy is to pick your battles. Some just aren't worth the time and effort to fight, and an apology—even if you aren't wrong—can be a painless retreat from a minor skirmish. There's a chapter in *Life Lessons . . . Principally Speaking* about choosing to fight the elephants and letting the rabbits go, and that's exactly what I'm suggesting here. A long series of minor conflicts can be just as mentally and emotionally exhausting as one major battle, and if time and patience are in limited supply, those resources shouldn't be spent chasing rabbits when they might be needed at a more crucial time to do battle with an elephant. In another scenario, if the two sides are keeping score, a number of small concessions might be viewed as conciliatory in nature, and the resulting good will could be parlayed into advantageous currency in brokering a better deal on a bigger issue. Politicians do this all the time when they need votes in the legislature to get a bill which they're sponsoring passed. A principal might offer an apology to the parent of a student when one really isn't warranted, but it will keep the parent from going to the superintendent, school board, or local television station. You don't have to be wrong to apologize, and in cases like these, it's a smart move.

Sometimes the strategy behind an apology doesn't have to be all that smart, and instead, just needs to be straightforward and honest. Miscommunication can occur with hurriedly sent emails, and while no one was really in the wrong regarding the intended message, an apologetic follow-up is needed to clarify and create better understanding. Misunderstanding can result from the tone of a message; and again, while there was no ill intent, an apology is appropriate to calm emotions and sooth hurt feelings. I once delivered some news to a teacher by phone that should have been conveyed in person. While I certainly meant no harm, the teacher's reaction left no doubt that I needed to sincerely apologize for the manner in which I handled that situation, and I did that. Principals sometimes have to make hard decisions that, while being in the best interest of the school, are hurtful to those individuals impacted by the results. When that happens, an apology should express regret for the injury, and I did that. While I never asked teachers to do anything that I hadn't done myself at some point, sometimes tasks or reports were required of them that caused some consternation, and—for what it was worth—I often expressed my apologies for having to ask those things of them. You don't have to be wrong to apologize, but in cases like these, it's the right thing to do.

So, in regard to apologies in the grand scheme of life, what's the right thing to do? Here are some considerations. As with a lot of things, that route can be traveled too often and its effectiveness worn thin. Timing and circumstance can also be factors, and if an emotional situation is misread in that regard, an apology can do more harm than good. Sincerity can go a long way in having an apology received in the intended manner, while on the other hand, a perceived lack of empathy in the message will shatter any intent of good will. Apology is also a slippery slope to travel in regard to one's ethical standards, and sometimes that sort of compromise is simply too much to ask of a person's conscience. Having said all that, I think that in attempting to achieve the delicate balance inherent in the concept of apology, it's best to err on the side of kindness and compassion, even if you get burned occasionally. Relationships, when all is said and done, are the most important things in this old world. Valuing friendships above all else and being willing to apologize from time to time—even if you aren't wrong—in order to have a little more peace in the world is a better way to live.

70

Strength of Character and Good Judgment

Madge Windham Zemp and the Burry family go way back. When Madge was a reluctant kindergarten student at First Baptist Church and my mom was one of the teachers there, she used to help pry Madge loose from the car—kicking and crying—when her parents dropped her off in the mornings. As Madge reached adulthood, she and my mom began exchanging cards and messages on special occasions, and they did that for the rest of my mom's life. In 1987, when I became a school counselor, I ran into Madge in my dad's bookstore one afternoon and told her that there was a social studies vacancy at Hartsville High School. She got the job, and I gave her two notebooks full of overhead projector transparencies and all my tests from the US History and Sociology courses that I taught. During the time I was principal, there were a few times when I would have liked to kill her, but I guarantee that nobody loves Hartsville High School and the students there more than she does. At some point in time, maybe as long as 25 years ago, Madge and I had a conversation about parenthood and the special challenges of raising teenagers. As we were finishing our talk about our children, Madge said, "I just pray every night that mine will have strength of character and good judgment." That thought and those words stuck with me in a special way and became the subject of this final chapter.

I think that as a person grows older and settles into life, character and judgment become more solid personal traits than in one's formative years. Of course, an uncharacteristic decision or a mid-life crisis can alter the path of a person's future, but generally, values that are established by that time don't zig-zag much. That's why adolescence is such a difficult and critical stage in life. By their very nature, teenage years are an in-between time in one's development. In some ways, teens are still children, exhibiting the flashes of immaturity and selfishness that frustrate their parents and try the patience of their teachers. In other ways, physically and emotionally, they are entering adulthood and testing those waters for the first time. While parents might like for them to wear lifejackets for the rest of their lives, it's inevitable that at some point these young adults are going to have to swim into the deep water without one. I think that one big difference between the time that Baby Boomers (like myself) burst onto the scene and now when even the Millennials (like my daughters) are beginning to age a bit is that there are more dangers lurking in those deep waters. I honestly recall only a few temptations—like drinking and driving and unprotected sex—during my teenage years that could have truly life-changing consequences which might be challenging to overcome. Much later in life as a high school principal, I saw more and more challenges every day that could have absolutely devastating impacts on the lives of teenagers. One of the most frightening changes that I have seen is with the issue of fighting, which sometimes happens with teenagers and young adults. My recollection of fights when I was a high school student is that they were fistfights. Someone would end up with a black eye, a broken nose, or a missing tooth, and usually the next day the fighters would be friends again. On the other hand, my recollection of fights when I was principal is that I had to be careful when breaking one up because I

Dr. Charlie Burry, Jr.

didn't know what kind of weapons might be involved. While mass shootings make national headlines these days, gun violence on school campuses and in neighborhoods is much more common, and many teenagers just don't seem to understand the potential consequences of carrying a pistol in a bookbag or the waistband of their pants. All too often, we see anguished parents who have lost children because of immature, short-sighted approaches to deadly situations. My point so far in this chapter is that our young people need all the prayers they can get regarding their strength of character and good judgment.

When I was a teenager, I can remember my dad telling me that a man's reputation was his most valuable possession. I think my dad was right about that, but we also could have had some further discussion about how a man gets his reputation. A more nuanced take on this idea is that your reputation is what other people think of you—and that's certainly important—but character is a deeper and truer personal trait. While a person's reputation can be embellished by pretense or tarnished by social media, character is generally a better indication of one's values and morals when no one is looking. What I mean is that character is who you are—the decisions and choices you make—when nobody is there but you and God. The challenge in life is that character, like toughness, isn't something with which a person is born. It's developed and tested over a period of time, and while parents can certainly set good and necessary examples, there are many more variables involved in that process as young people venture out into deeper water. Prayers that there will be more good influences than poor ones while strength of character is being developed can provide some reassurance to parents that they've done all they can do.

Good judgment can be a more complicated issue than strength of character because judgment—while ideally being derived from strong character—is sometimes subject to circumstances that are more immediate challenges to one's values and morals. We sometimes make spur-of-the-moment decisions under pressure which, with the benefit of additional time and hindsight, look pretty questionable in the rearview mirror. The temptation to dive into deep water when there's no lifeguard around can sometimes cloud our judgment. Unexpected situations occasionally catch us by surprise, and our judgment gets carried away by a whirlwind of excitement. Sometimes our judgment is challenged when the circumstances regarding a decision are purposely misrepresented, and we need the insight and wisdom of experience to see through a fog of falsehoods. The value of relationships can be counterproductive when friends exert pressure to participate in ventures that we know to be against our better judgment. The roller coaster nature of life can put us in a state of mind in which judgment is lost in a storm of emotion. Prayers that good judgment will survive such challenges in the lives of our children might allow parents to sleep a little better at night.

Since that day long ago when Madge and I had that conversation, every night when I've said my prayers before going to bed, I've asked God to keep my daughters safe and well and to give them strength of character and good judgment. Even though they're both adults now, I will do that again tonight, just like always. I believe if He will answer that prayer, they'll be pretty well covered. Thanks, Madge, for helping me take better care of my girls.

Dr. Charlie Burry, Jr.

Madge Zemp

Epilogue

For a long time—since a light bulb moment in my life about 30 years ago—I've enjoyed writing and the thought process that is part of putting pen to paper and fingertips to keyboard. The satisfaction of finding just the right the words to convey my thoughts usually far outweighs the feelings of frustration and impatience that I experience when I hit the proverbial writer's block. Having said that, I must admit that I'm probably too much of a wordsmith, so much so that I've joked that to make any money writing, I'd have to be paid by the hour. The writing process for me is to get all of the ingredients into a first draft, and then put it on the stove to simmer, sometimes for weeks at a time. I return to it periodically while it's cooking for a taste and change a word or a phrase here or there until I'm satisfied enough to serve it to my readers. I still though, go back occasionally to read things I've written and find myself saying, "Dang, this word would have been better there," or wondering, "Why'd I say it that way?" It's like I'm never completely pleased with anything I write, and I'm always seeing room for improvement. Is that a good or a bad trait? I think in most cases it's healthy and productive as long as it doesn't consume a person. As with a lot of things in life, it depends on your perspective. Which brings us to this.

During the first five years that I was principal of Hartsville High School, Candy Holcombe was one of our assistant principals. She was highly capable, had a relentless work ethic, was intensely loyal, and was one of the key contributors to the Red Fox Renaissance in its early years. Her office was next door to mine in the administrative building, and that proximity lent itself not only to a close working relationship, but to a cherished

Dr. Charlie Burry, Jr.

personal friendship as well. We walked through the fire together many times. When Candy retired after those five years, she presented me with a framed calligraphy that reads "The people who share the journey of life with you are more important than the destination." A sound piece of life philosophy, indeed, and one that I've also tried to apply to my efforts as a writer and an author. I began to accept that—while I wanted my finished product to be as good as it could possibly be—what was more important was that I enjoyed the journey and the process of writing. And most importantly, if you enjoy the process, then the end result usually will take care of itself. Thank you again, Candy, for that perspective. I keep that calligraphy at my cabin in the mountains where I do a lot of writing, and where I see it often.

I'm pleased to tell you that the journey of writing *I Got a Better Idea* and seeing each chapter gradually take shape has been enjoyable. Have the new stories turned out to be better ideas or not? I hope you think so, and that maybe reading about some of my light bulb moments made your life a little richer and more pleasant, too. If those things happened for the better, then I'm glad this book found you, and I'm happy that it brightened some of your days.

Candy Holcombe

Index

I

J

K

References

Prologue

Meltzer, Milton. *Mark Twain Himself*. Bonanza Books, 1960.

Chapter 1

The Tams. *A Little More Soul*. ABC Records, 1968.

Chapter 5

Fate. *Merriam-Webster's Online Dictionary*. 2011. Retrieved from http://www.merriam-webster.com/dictionary/fate.

Fincher, David (Director) and Chaffin, Cean; Kennedy, Kathleen; Marshall, Frank (Producers). *The Curious Case of Benjamin Button* [Motion Picture]. Paramount Pictures, 2008.

Chapter 6

Hall, Tom T. *We All Got Together and . . . .* Mercury Records, 1972.

Chapter 9

de Cordova, Fred and Lassally, Peter (Producers). *The Tonight Show* [Television late-night talk/variety]. NBC, 1962-1991.

Chapter 16

Darabont, Frank (Director) and Marvin, Niki (Producer). *The Shawshank Redemption* [Motion Picture]. Columbia Pictures, 1994.

Chapter 24

Proverbs 27:17. *Life Application Study Bible*. Tyndale House Publishers, Inc. and Zondervan Publishing House, 1991.

Chapter 25

Petrie, George. *The Auburn Creed*. Auburn University, 1943.

Kipling, Rudyard. *If*. Doubleday, Page & Company, 1910.

Anonymous. *Dream Big*. Public domain. nd.

Rockne, Knute. *Win One for the Gipper*. University of Notre Dame, 1928.

Chesney, Kenny. *Hemingway's Whisky*. BNA, 2010.

Chapter 27

Bryant, Paul (Bear). *Bear Bryant Quotes*. https://247sports.com.

Chapter 28

Croce, Jim. *You Don't Mess Around with Jim*. ABC, 1971.

Chapter 29

Kellnor, Stan. *Taking It to the Limit with Basketball Cybernetics*. Durite Printing,1978.

Chapter 30

Royal Darrell. Public domain, nd.

Chapter 36

Reiner, Rob; Greisman, Alan; Zadan Craig; Meron, Neil (Producers) & Reiner, Rob (Director). *Bucket List* [Motion Picture]. Warner Bros. Pictures, 2007.

Diamond, Neil. *Sweet Caroline*. American Sound Studio, 1969.

De Haven, Carter and Pizzo, Angelo (Producers) & Anspaugh, David (Director). *Hoosiers* [Motion Picture]. Orion Pictures, 1986.

Chapter 40

Longfellow, Henry Wadsworth. *Paul Revere's Ride*. The Atlantic Monthly, 1861.

Lewis, Mario; Precht, Bob; Feldman, Chester; McGeehan, Jack (Producers). *The Ed Sullivan Show* [Television variety/sketch/comedy]. CBS, 1948-1971.

British Invasion. *British influence on US music*. 1964-1967.

Section 5

Bill, Tony; Phillips, Michael; Phillips, Julia (Producers) & Hill, George Roy (Director). *The Sting* [Motion Picture]. Universal Pictures, 1973.

Chapter 43

Horwitz, Moses; Horwitz, Jerome; Feinberg, Louis. *The Three Stooges* [Television/Vaudeville/film]. Columbia Pictures, 1934-1946.

Chapter 44

Barlow, Bill (Producer) & Di Bona, Vin (Director). *America's Funniest Home Videos* [Television/clip show/comedy]. ABC Productions, 1990-present.

Gray, William S. and Sharp, Zerna. *Elson-Gray Readers*. Scott, Foresman and Company, 1930.

Berenstain, Jan and Berenstain, Jan. *The Berenstain Bears*. Random House, 1962.

Chapter 45

Prine, John. *The Missing Years*. Oh Boy Records, 1991.

Dr. Charlie Burry, Jr.

Chapter 46

Kendall, Josh. *The Prank: How a Bold Gag in 1961 Mocked the Tigers*. The State, 2013.

Chapter 48

Oscar Wilde Quotes. Goodreads.com, GoodReads, Inc, 2021. 1 April 2021. https://www.goodreads.com/quotes/ oscar_wilde_imitation.

Chapter 49

Ecclesiastes 10:20. *Life Application Study Bible*. Tyndale House Publishers, Inc. and Zondervan Publishing House, 1991.

Crump, Paul. *Burn, Killer, Burn*. Johnson Publishing Co/ Chicago, 1962.

Chapter 50

Coe, David Allan; Goodman, Steve; Prine, John. *Once Upon a Rhyme*. Columbia Nashville, 1975.

Bochco, Steven (Producer). *NYPD Blue* [Television police procedural]. 20th Century Fox, 1993-2005.

Chapter 53

Drawdy, S. E. *My Dad, My Father*. Christian Faith Publishing, Inc., 2018.

Chapter 59

Branch Rickey and Jackie Robinson Quotes. Podcast. 28 August 2019. www.thisdayinbaseball.com.

Sloan, Bob. *Forging a Path*. Hartsville Messenger, 2013.

Chapter 61

Bill Russell Quote. Podcast. 29 June 2018. www.learningenglish. voanews.com.

Mark Twain Quotes. Goodreads.com, GoodReads, Inc, 2021. 1 April 2021 https://www.goodreads.com/quotes/mark_ twain_teenagers.

Chapter 62

Bill Watterson Quotes. Goodreads.com, GoodReads, Inc, 2019. 7 December 1990. https://www.goodreads.com/quotes/ bill_watterson_calvin-and-hobbes.

Proverbs 27:17. *Life Application Study Bible*. Tyndale House Publishers, Inc. and Zondervan Publishing House, 1991.

Chapter 63

Fourth Class System and Leader Development. www.citadel. edu.

Chapter 64

Fincher, David (Director) and Chaffin, Cean; Kennedy, Kathleen; Marshall, Frank (Producers). *The Curious Case of Benjamin Button* [Motion Picture]. Paramount Pictures, 2008.

Chapter 65

Johnson, Ellis. *The State*. nd.

Chapter 67

Eastwood, Clint (Producer and Director). *Unforgiven* [Motion Picture]. Warner Bros. Pictures, 1992.

John Lewis Quotes. BrainyQuote.com. BrainyMedia Inc., 2021. 1 April 2021. https://www.brainyquote.com/quotes/ john_lewis_810311.

Abraham Lincoln Quotes. BrainyQuote.com. BrainyMedia Inc., 2021. 1 April 2021. https://www.brainyquote.com/quotes/ abraham_lincoln_103475.

Oscar Wilde Quotes. BrainyQuote.com. Brainy Media, Inc, 2021. 1 April 2021. https://www.brainyquote.com/quotes/ oscar_wilde_105222.

Job 42:10. *Life Application Study Bible.* Tyndale House Publishers, Inc. and Zondervan Publishing House, 1991.

Chapter 68

Nick Saban Quote. amzn.to/29VuAc3 #leadership. nd.

Harry Truman Quotes. BrainyQuote.com. Brainy Media, Inc, 2021. 1 April 2021. https://www.brainyquote.com/quotes/ harry_truman_162071.

Chapter 69

Ayn Rand Quotes. BrainyQuote.com. Brainy Media, Inc, 2021. 1 April 2021. https://www.brainyquote.com/quotes/ ayn_rand_125048.

Frank Howard Quote. www.tigernet.com. nd.